Praise for *Performance Coaching*

"Angus has done excellent work, elegantly integrating and adapting the skills of Neuro-Linguistic Programming into the process of coaching. And it's an enjoyable read!"
Shelle Rose Charvet, author of *Words That Change Minds*

"This book gives any executive coach, as well as all managers for that matter, an extended frame of reference for finding new and creative tools for success in working with clients. This is stuff you can use. Examples are both inspiring and reassuringly practical. Angus McLeod has produced a book that deserves many users and a wide audience."
Julian Russell, Managing Director, PPD Consulting Ltd., executive coaching specialists, and co-author of *Alpha Leadership: Tools for Business Leaders Who Want More From Life*

"With this book Angus McLeod sets a high standard of teaching by story telling. His examples of coaching dialogues serve so well to illustrate how to skilfully handle many coaching situations. The layout and subheadings make them accessible to those who want to dip in and out of the book as required. I enjoyed it and learned from it."
John Whitmore, author of *Coaching for Performance*

"This book contains a wealth of knowledge on its subject. The author clearly has extensive experience of coaching and demonstrates this expertise effectively in the book.

"The major part of the book is a wide-ranging collection of cases to illustrate various coaching applications - an approach that really brings the subject to life. The cases are concise, yet clear and informative and each brings out one or more specific points about coaching processes and issues.

"I would recommend this book to people wanting to extend their coaching skills and to explore a wider range of approaches."
Carol Harris, author of *Consult Yourself: The NLP Guide to Being a Management Consultant*

"*Performance Coaching* is an in-depth overview of the whole field of coaching and mentoring. It describes a broad range of coaching models and draws on the best practice from each. The practical examples, useful tips

D0315685

and mini-transcripts will benefit those new to coaching, and profit seasoned old timers as well. We highly recommend this book."
James Lawley and Penny Tompkins, authors of *Metaphors in Mind: Transformation through Symbolic Modelling*

"The author has achieved the near-impossible - writing a book that demonstrates the potential of coaching as an effective and ethical instrument for change and gives a flavour of its depth, richness and subtlety, but is nevertheless accessible, comprehensible and usable for pro and novice alike. This title deserves to sit - hopefully well-thumbed - alongside the very limited number of internationally respected books on coaching."
David Hoad, Coach and HR Consultant, The Kingsmoor Consultancy

"Angus McLeod's *Performance Coaching* is an immensely practical aid to coaching and works at a level of detail - both in terms of language and process - that will allow HR professionals and managers alike, even with little formal coaching experience, to get to the heart of issues and resolve them elegantly and respectfully."
Anne Thompson, Group HR Director, Parity Plc

"Effective coaches can make the difference between good and great business leaders. This book is packed with practical examples, tools and tips to help the coach in this task - highly recommended."
Anne Deering, Director, AT Kearney

"As the field of coaching continues to discover the extensive skill-based models of NLP, *Performance Coaching* by McLeod will become one of the foundational books. This how-to manual provides an excellent use of NLP models and skills for coaching. I like it also because it is further enhanced by integrating much of Gallwey's Inner Game approach."
L. Michael Hall, PhD, Coaching Conversations and Meta-Coaching

Performance Coaching

The Handbook for Managers, H. R. Professionals and Coaches

Angus I McLeod, PhD

Crown House Publishing
www.crownhouse.co.uk

First published by

Crown House Publishing Ltd
Crown Buildings, Bancyfelin, Carmarthen, Wales, SA33 5ND, UK
www.crownhouse.co.uk

and

Crown House Publishing Ltd
P.O. Box 2223, Williston, VT 05495-2223, USA
www.CHPUS.com

First published 2003. Reprinted 2004.

Illustrations by Les Evans

British Library Cataloguing-in-Publication Data
A catalogue entry for this book is available
from the British Library.

ISBN 1904424058

LCCN 2003102582

Printed and bound in the UK by
*The Cromwell Press Ltd
Trowbridge
Wiltshire*

Dedication

Diane Fahy Browning (1948–2002)

This book is dedicated to the life of Diane Fahy and to her extended family and circle, who keep her memory in my mind as well as in my heart.

Sometimes one is privileged to meet and develop a friendship that persists through all changes and that is characterized by so much understanding, commitment, and unconditional love that one is regularly in awe of it. My friendship with Diane was like that for over twenty years. Many others enjoyed the same level of friendship and love that she effused. Diane influenced and affected a multitude of people in and around Delaware, where she settled. She captivated people with her acute attention and her laughter. She was a model for positive mindsets in the face of considerable adversity, both in life and in her dying.

Diane did not have the tools of the coach as described and illustrated in this book, but she had the instinctive qualities of a fine coach. She was a ready listener and she cared passionately about people, their targets and their aspirations. She dared to challenge and risk a relationship if she felt that a friend might be moving in harm's way, away from their targets and a healthy future. She saw people as holistic entities; she nurtured and underpinned hopes; she helped to sketch the dreams from which plans and targets would arise. She worked from a heart filled with love and with a mind passionate and hopeful about the human spirit.

A biography about the life of Diane Fahy would make a valuable and inspiring contribution to literature, but I offer this work to her memory instead. After she died, many people said, independently, that an angel had departed this world. I know her to be still with us. A spirit like hers does not die.

Contents

Acknowledgments

The idea to write this book came through the development of my practice and ideas about coaching. There are many friends and colleagues in and at the periphery of coaching who have influenced and helped develop that thinking and who have provided me with opportunities for growth and change. These include Denise Fryer, Sue Knight, Lynne Kerry, Carol Harris, James Lawley, Penny Tompkins, Judith Lowe, Shelle Rose Charvet, Julian Russell, Anne Deering, Robert Dilts, John Abulafia, and my colleagues in the Coaching Foundation, Steve Breibart and Sir John Whitmore. I am also grateful to Steve for his paper on the historical evolution of coaching and for many Web references given in the appendices.

A number of highly respected and productive people offered to read and offer comments on my drafts and they each have my gratitude and heartfelt thanks. They are Adrienne Carpenter, Angela O'Connell, Anne Deering, Carol Harris, James Lawley, Jean Kelly, Jill Dann, Paul Barber, Penny Tompkins, Shelle Rose Charvet, and Tim Nottidge. Of special note are the contributions of Anne Thompson and David Hoad, whose comments proved invaluable.

Helen Kinsey helped structure the book and gave me confidence in the final draft. It was wonderful to have her support for this first edition. I am grateful to Terry Fieland, the editor at the leading NLP journal, *Anchor Point*, who agreed to make this work the subject of their first-ever book serialization.

When it comes to writing a new book, the writer typically embarks on a solitary expedition in the certain knowledge that he can return to the comfort of those who support, love, and inspire. In writing this book, I wish particularly to acknowledge and thank Obie Jane Mitchell, who has total belief in my projects and who has helped me, in recent years, always to achieve what I set out to do. Her love and belief in me are exemplary.

Alison Adcock inspires the creative spirit and its expression (as so wonderfully demonstrated for the public, in her art) and she continues to quietly support me, steady and true to friendship. Other friends inspire even in their absence; knowing that their love persists is a great comfort. Those who knowingly, or otherwise, contributed to this book include Anne Robinson, Chris Stumpff, Frances Hall, Ian Brown, Janet and Laszlo Boksanyi, Jill Greenacre, John Sayle, Maureen Steele, Michelle Evans, and Stephen Carroll.

I continue to enjoy the encouragement and support of my long-term friend and co-director at Best Performance Ltd., Neil Davidson. Neil has the most infectious optimism I have ever witnessed and inspires success. Jean Kelly, my co-director at the Learning Exchange, is always encouraging and offered me good advice on the script.

I have been fortunate to have the love and friendship of Dr. Adrienne Carpenter, who offered me a perfect space to write this book. Adrienne provided a peaceful and beautiful environment; understanding and support for the habits of the author who is committed to writing (and exhibits the ebbs and flows of inspiration); and refreshments and diversions when the author left his inner world and returned to the world of people.

I thank my daughter, Alex, for her willingness to have an example of coaching described in this book. Her decisions sometimes make me fearful, but I am very proud of her self-determination, persistence, and myriad talents.

Last, but not least, I wish to give credit to all those who give me numerous opportunities to coach and to be coached. A coach would be severely limited with no experience, from the receiving end, of the processes and tools of coaching; I have been fortunate to experience the skilled interventions of numerous professional and trainee coaches, some of them working from entirely new orientations and experiences. To all of these people, I offer my thanks and love.

Angus McLeod, PhD
Philadelphia

Preface

The executive coach is a fabulously valuable facilitator of change. The coach is not the player, but an instrument, in service to the art of the coachee. The aim is to encourage the coachee to extend and explore their frame of reference, to help them find new and motivating tools for success in all they do and, with luck, inspire them to continue traits of self-learning that endure over time.

A frame of reference characterizes the nature and extent of the coachee's reality, and the coach intervenes to help the coachee discover new meaning and potential by stretching their frame of reference, extending their inner representation of the world. The coachee thus comes to new perspectives and a fresh frame of reference. These sometimes include a new perception of who they really are and their true purpose in being—hugely motivating perceptions.

Over a time, coachees open up to learning in new and inspiring ways, to self-coach, to self-challenge and redefine their own frame of reference. These new skills of mental agility assist them in the effectiveness of their thinking and their actions in other contexts.

The true coach observes miracles as incredible as the transformation that leads the tiny stirrings of the chrysalis into the bright magnificence of a butterfly. If one has not felt privileged and humbled in the act of coaching, one has probably not yet attained the mantle of the true coach.

Many of our trainees come to coaching bursting with questions for their coachees. They bombard them, hoping to find a weakness of either perception or thinking that they may attack and cure. The performances are breathtaking for all concerned! The transformation of trainee to coach is evidenced when the direction and pace of the session seems to be coachee-led. The coach spends more time listening rather than worrying about their next intervention.

Very few people exhibit the persona of the natural coach as evidenced by their inherent qualities and behaviors. Most of us have limitations. It is hoped that this book will help convince readers that we may still excel as coaches—by preparing our mindsets for coaching, by practice and experience.

Our initial motivations to coach may be myriad: a desire to make a difference, to lead, to be a rounded and professional manager and communicator, to look self-assured and worldly. However, if in reading this book I do not leave you with a shifted motivation for coaching, then I may have failed. This is because I believe that coaches need to learn that their desires to *do* something and make a difference need to be directed at themselves and not at their coachees. A coach with inner targets can make assumptions about the inner world of their coachee and distract that coachee from their most influencing path. Ultimately, I suggest, the best work is done by the coachee and not by the coach, even though the coach is more or less a catalyst for that.

It is easy to feel compelled by one's own motivation. When the coachee learns how to flex their mental resources, they develop competencies that are not limited to the issue at hand. By developing themselves, the coachees use their learning in many other contexts. True coaching unleashes the potential of the coachee for success and leadership in all contexts, both in work and outside.

Self-directed solutions lead to motivated targets. It's success in self-motivated targets that leads to sustained self-motivation. This is where coaching makes a value-added contribution to successful management.

Chapter One

Introduction

This book is accessible to managers wanting a resource where they may learn and access information easily. Human-resources (HR) professionals will find information helpful in deciding whether to establish a coaching or mentoring function, whether to insource, outsource, or use support strategies that could include e-mentoring (using an intranet or extranet). The book should appeal to both the novice coach trying to get a practical handle on coaching skills and to the more experienced coach wanting to widen their knowledge and to refresh the use of tools that have become rusty.

In trying to achieve an accessible book for all managers, I hope that I have provided an adequate structure, a functional contents list, and a detailed index to satisfy all but the most demanding and methodical expert. I apologize now for the word "coachee". Although I dislike this word, I have been unable to find something well regarded and more acceptable without introducing a new term. The word "client" will not do, since, in the corporate context, the client is always the party that pays.

Where a newly introduced tool or idea is mentioned in the text it is **shown in bold**, and this signifies that a box containing related information is nearby. This allows any reader who needs more information to access it while allowing other readers to continue reading, without having to break their concentration. I hope this also allows more expert readers with specific skill sets to skip sections (when they are already familiar with specific tools).

Other emboldened text, ***but italicized,*** is there to highlight linguistic tips that appear in the text. Linguistic tips are referred to in their own index for ease of reference.

Necessarily, many of the issues given as examples are incomplete: they are there merely to illustrate ways of approaching an issue and are not a complete transcript of all interventions. As a consequence, not all the issues raised in a given example are complete.

Many of the tools that are illustrated in the examples can be used in different contexts. It's hoped that, by reading through examples, you will become familiar with the tools and language of coaching and will build on your successes to use the tools fluidly. The choice of which tool to use in any given situation becomes more obvious with familiarity and practice.

Following these introductory sections, Chapters Two and Three are set out to be highly accessible to managers and novice coaches wanting easy access to practical coaching. Examples reflect typical issues seen in coaching practice. These offer a readable way of introducing the language and tools of coaching. Chapter Two looks at the most typical issues in coaching and Chapter Three follows this format to highlight typical drivers for change.

HR professionals with coaching experience may like to go directly to Chapter Four to gain insights into how coaching is applied in organizations.

In Chapter Five we look at a selection of methods taken from bigger developmental models that either are, or can be, applied to coaching. I have been highly selective in choosing those that I use or have seen to be highly effective. This is necessarily an individualistic offering. I also introduce my own **STEPPPA** coaching model ("STEPPPA" is an acronym whose meaning we will discuss later).

Chapter Six looks primarily at the development of the coach, drawing upon a number of philosophies and methods that underpin the practice of executive coaching.

Chapter Seven is unapologetically a place where I have put other background information that has not appeared elsewhere. This includes some additional information about questioning methods, and methods that are not invariably part of the coach's resource, such as storytelling, totems, and archetypes.

Chapter Eight considers some of the pitfalls of coaching and problems that may arise in coaching practice, including psychological projection and sexual attraction.

Chapter Nine is a brief resource about mentoring, and particularly e-mentoring, taken mainly from my experiences with Ask Max, our Internet-based mentoring service. I also mention telephone mentoring as an adjunct to coaching.

The appendices contain valuable information about the mechanics of setting up the coaching space, relationships between coach and coachee and between mentor and mentee, feedback sheet, code of ethics, and a brief history of coaching and mentoring, as well as a resource for additional reading and Web-based information, including some of the courses offered by institutions. Unless stated, I do not endorse any Web-based resource or any training course in this work.

Some of my readers will find issues that are close to something that they face themselves. The solutions to those issues were specific to the individuals concerned and not likely to be the best solution for anyone else. Coaching, as opposed to giving advice, encourages the development of coachee-specific solutions that are motivating *and appropriate* for them. This also highlights the separation between coaching and mentoring: coaching inspires internally motivated solutions; mentoring invariably offers externally derived solutions. In this book, I offer a variant on mentoring that I think offers the best of both worlds, and integrates them.

My books are designed to be picked up and read from any page, so the indexes are constructed to make the reader's life easier. If the structure of the book does not delight you, then do please look at the contents list and indexes! I hope you will enjoy reading this book.

Sources of inspiration

I was drawn into coaching from counseling. For years previously, I was a sound ear to many; on numerous occasions hearing the life-stories and traumas of people I had not previously spoken to.

3

This was long before I had a clue what to say to them. One time, someone I had never spoken with, not even by way of an introduction, provided me with a ten-minute medical history!

My approach then was to listen. Often I would then mentor them by offering solutions. It therefore came as a miracle to me that people can make improved progress if you let them find their own solutions. A workshop within our course called "Power of Silence in Coaching" produces miracles that are testaments to the cathartic potential of coachees, if only coaches will provide a space for that. I was naturally pulled further into person-centered intervention and undertook co-counseling training. NLP (neurolinguistic programming) has also contributed heavily. NLP provides great tools for change but tools do not make a good coach. The *principal instruments*, used elegantly, provide this. As the father of modern coaching methods, Tim Gallwey (1999) said, "Principles are more important than tools."

My linguistic background was enhanced by the work of David Grove ("clean language") and then of Penny Tompkins and James Lawley ("symbolic modeling"—Lawley and Tompkins, 2000). These three people have wonderfully presented us with simple and effective models for exploring the metaphoric world and finding compelling solutions.

Taken together, I provide a source of expertise in the principal instruments of coaching that will underpin any other skillset or toolbox you may wish to apply, whether illustrated here or not. When the principal instruments are coupled with coaching mindsets and the many tools illustrated, you will witness stunning change and performance that may make your heart swell.

Defining coaching

Many people have failed to define coaching because when they look at the market they find many varieties of "coach" and many techniques. Some of these techniques seem radically different in approach. People also discover that many coaches work from just one discipline in their work, while others, myself included, work from a range of disciplines. They may find provocative coaches, transactional-analysis coaches, life coaches, emotional-intelligence coaches, and so on. How can one make sense of all these approaches? I hope to help. We shall start by introducing the core elements that underpin best practice in all coaching methods. It is easy to imagine that a new set of tools sold by one or other brand will make you a coach. They will not. Without a foundation in principles, an appropriate mental attitude, and linguistic competencies, these tools are all highly limited.

Whatever their discipline, coaches are generally using two or three of the principal instruments to assist coachees to a defined target. Therefore, we will start there.

Principal instruments of the coach

The principal instruments of coaching are *silence*, *questions*, and *challenge* (McLeod, 2001). These are used to assist the coachee to meet their defined targets. Of the three instruments, silence is the most effective.

Silence

When a coachee makes a discovery, this psychological breakthrough in perception, or catharsis, is wholly internal. Even if the coach is speaking, the contribution of the coach to the actual event is insignificant. Silence is therefore the dominant of the triad of the principal instruments. Silence enables the coachee to think and feel (experience) without being sidetracked by a coach's agenda.

The real work of coaching is done in the coachee's episodes of thinking and feeling in which the coach plays no part other than silent witness (McLeod, 2002a). The coachee may be re-evaluating what they thought they knew, exploring a fresh perception on what they thought was real and fixed, developing new insight on a situation, understanding the depth and source of their motivation, and so on. The art of the coach is *not* to know when to be silent but when to break that silence.

I coached a sales trainer who is widely respected on the world stage. Bob had become stuck. Having decided on an important task he found himself demotivated to accomplish it, let alone start the job. He told me that he had become frustrated because the target was important to him but he kept putting it off. Over the course of the next ten minutes Bob explored his situation with me. He willingly entered his on-stage sales-trainer state by getting out of his chair and imagining/experiencing himself before one of his large audiences, ready to demonstrate his influencing skills to them. From that state of being, I asked Bob to offer his "stuck-self" (still metaphysically in the chair) some advice with his problem. He provided that advice immediately. Shortly afterwards, I asked Bob to return psychologically to his chair and then to listen to the best possible advice available from a leading trainer. I simply read back his exact words in the same tone and pace. There was a silence laden with spine-tingling suspense and "atmosphere". Bob was transformed. His concentration was internal and acute. His neck colored with blood, his eyes were defocused, and his whole being became energized. I let the silence run on. It was broken by Bob, who launched himself to his feet, saying, "I'm doing it right now! Sorry to cut the session short!" I couldn't reply because Bob was already out of the room and on his way to his office. You will find other examples in this book.

Jill Dann (2003) says, "In coaching, you have to allow prolonged silences, and intervene to push the coachee to reconnect with the moment, bringing them back to it and keeping anyone else silent. If they can revisit the moment they are often astounded by the range of emotions experienced." Emotion, once registered (and whether expressed or not), is a key driver for change. Silence and emotion are a facilitators of awesome power.

There is another lesson from the session with Bob. The most motivating behaviors come from self-determined processing. I could have offered Bob the same advice, but would he have leaped out of his chair and rushed out of the room to act upon it?

Questions

Questioning is another of the three principal instruments of coaching. We will return often to questioning techniques, because there is so much ground to cover. For now, it is worth defining why questions are used in coaching:

- to unlock more information for both coach and coachee
- to assist the coachee to explore available realities

Questioning can be approached in such a way that coachees can explore issues and reach motivated targets without the coach having to understand anything about the situation—such things as the people involved and the time or place to which the issue relates. This type of questioning is sometimes called *context-free* questioning/coaching. It is particularly useful where the coachee is dealing with highly sensitive issues, be they emotional, political, strategic, or interpersonal. For example, they may have a sensitive issue regarding the senior board member who hired them. By taking away the need for the coachee to express the details of their knowledge and experiences, they can roam freely through their solutions without concerning themselves with the appropriateness or otherwise of expressing factual information. If a coach is going to deal with such situations, context-free questioning can be considered—but more later! For now, we can see that questioning may support coaching in many ways. Here are just some examples:

- developing understanding of the issue and its context
- exploring historical situations with positive outcomes
- defining what is and is not in the control of the coachee
- redefining the target(s) and the timescales to success
- encouraging new perceptions
- helping the coachee to associate (experience) their situation/ state fully
- helping the coachee to disassociate from their situation and be more objective
- re-evaluating value judgments
- revisiting limiting beliefs
- recognition of patterns
- evaluating behaviors in the context of the coachee's identity and values

- defining the level of certainty the coachee has about their success (motivation)

Questions can help define the boundaries of the coachee's worldview. Questions can also assist them to re-evaluate those boundaries and extend what is possible.

Challenge

Challenges have similar outcomes to questions but often the approach is confrontational. For example, a challenge may require the reassessment of a firm belief. Challenges can be offered as statements or questions and can be especially helpful where a coachee is very stuck in a pattern of negative thought. Here are examples:

GILES: I'm useless at presentations!
COACH: So, you're the worst presenter on the planet?
GILES: I'm not that bad.
COACH: What are you "not that bad" at, in presentations?

Here, the aim of the challenge is to encourage the coachee to reframe their perception of their abilities so that they may have the confidence to do something about their skill level. The next intervention provides a base for that by exploring positives.

JOHN: The problem is insurmountable!
COACH: You're probably right. Let's ignore it and work on something else.
JOHN: I can't ignore this—I must do something!
COACH: If I had this problem, where would be the best place for me to start now?

Here, the challenge is "discounting" the enormity of the issue and is very likely to get a reaction. In this case, luckily perhaps, the effect is to accept action. The coach's question is designed to get the coachee to dissociate emotionally from the issue and appeals to their ability to "observe" the problem from outside and at the same time to "help" the coach. We will return to other examples of

challenge and of emotionally associated and emotionally dissociated states again.

Definitions of coaching

We are now in a position to define for the purpose of this book
both coaching and related services. Since our context is work-
based, the terms "executive coaching", "performance coaching",
and "coaching" are interchangeable.

Coaching: The use of silence, questions, and challenge to assist a
coachee toward a defined work-based target. These are often present issues or ones that relate to the future.

Performance coaching: It is sometimes considered that performance coaching centers only on mental techniques and targets without exploration of emotional material or the nitty-gritty of
communication and relationship. This is an absurd idea since a
huge bulk of issues affecting executive performance is about communication and relationships. Also, since emotion is the key element of motivation, any coaching method that missed emotional
investment in targets is flawed.

Mentoring: Mentoring ideally adopts all the skills of coaching.
The best mentoring helps the mentee to find their own solutions
using the three principal instruments. Most mentoring seems to be
on culture-specific advice and suggestions. It contains information
on organizational structures and procedures (e.g., politics, agendas and influencing strategies).

Life coaching: The use of silence, questioning, and challenge to
assist a coachee to a defined personal target.

Counseling: The use of questioning and silence to assist the individual to manage or redefine personal issues. Very often, these are
located in the past.

Note that nowhere have we said that coaching is founded upon a
particular set of tools. To requote Gallwey (1999), "Principles are
more important than tools."

Chapter Two

Coaching Issues—New Skills

We will explore numerous examples that deal with typical issues brought to us during coaching intervention. The first and most overarching of these is communication.

Communication

In my work as a coach and team facilitator, I guess that 80 percent of the issues are dominated by communication factors. By "communication" I mean both the quality and appropriateness of spoken and written words as well as their interpretation by the hearer/reader. For example, I remember being welcomed to a business meeting in Pennsylvania with the words, "It's good that you could be with us today." The simple interpretation is clear: my host was expressing his pleasure at my being there. However, some months earlier, I had postponed this meeting because my US travels had been overbooked and my itinerary had to be changed. Therefore, my immediate reinterpretation of his welcome was, "So, you finally deigned to grace us with your presence. Now you're here, let's press on quickly before you get bored and have to leave us." After I got over that possible meaning I came up with a third interpretation for "It's good that you could be with us today." Maybe he was acknowledging my busy schedule and expressing gratitude that, in spite of limited time and the location of their plant, I had agreed to travel out of the way specifically to meet with them.

If a simple, unambiguous phrase containing only positive messages can be interpreted so differently, it is small wonder that communication is at the heart of so many executive issues. Throughout the issues examples in this book, you will find that communication is often at their heart. The key to moving past such communication shortfalls is invariably **conscious perception**.

Conscious perception re-evaluates the communication and looks at negative, neutral, and positive possibilities in the message. More than that, conscious perception looks beyond the message to the possible states of mind of the originator. Thus, a voicemail message from my boss's boss picked up one Friday evening stated simply, "Angus, this is John. I've checked your program for next week and see a gap Monday morning and want to see you in my office ten o'clock."

What do you suppose my interpretation was? He is unhappy with my performance? My immediate boss has died and I am up for that job? Conscious perception forced me to look beyond the interpretations to explore Mark's state of mind. I noted that the communication was briefer than usual. This could mean that he was angry with me and did not want to say too much in case he blew up over the phone. It could also mean that he was under pressure. Suddenly I heard bells clanging in my head. The full board on which Mark sat was due to meet the following Tuesday in Birmingham. Mark could be feeling a little short on business performance. Maybe he was seeking support from me to embellish his results with some healthy news on prospective business that might boost the following quarter. That interpretation proved correct. I had increased my conscious perception by self-questioning.

Increasing conscious perception offers more choice and strategies for dealing with issues, for moving ahead effectively. More than that, the process starts a whole new habit of self-inquiry that improves all decision making and performance. All executives can do this and perform at a higher level. That is just one area where coaching can make a huge difference to executive performance.

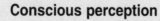

Conscious perception

Conscious perception is stimulated by questioning and challenge around established realities. The art of the coach is to recognize inhibiting and unnatural perceptions and to encourage the coachee to new perceptions. Questions include the following:

- Who says?
- How do you know?

- Can you say more, can you convince me?
- Always? Can you think of an exception?
- Why must you? What other choices are there?

Additionally, there are numerous coaching tools that encourage conscious perception, many illustrated in this book.

Let's look at some examples of coaching where communication is the major element of the coachee's issue.

Territory invasion—getting in their shoes

Helena ran a department of almost a thousand people within the IT industry. She had come into the sector from chemicals six years before. Her record in project management and her interpersonal ability had got her the first role. The same skills had propelled her up the ladder to run a department operating as a business center netting over $130 million a year. Her department contained technical, technical sales, quality, and administrative functions.

Helena had very good reason to believe that her quality division was about to be poached and merged under another manager, Paul. Helena felt that, if he were successful, it could impact badly on her business area, since, she said, quality underpinned the salability of her product lines. Helena's anxiety festered for some weeks. She considered contacting her original mentor in the corporation to seek her support. Perhaps wisely, Helena held back from asking for intervention. She realized that at this stage in her career she should be able to fight her own battles using available resources. Her issues centered on the loss of the quality division, her protagonist, Paul (a slightly more senior manager with strong corporate connections built up over several years), and the financial controller, Alan (who in her eyes had no loyalty to her and would be more influenced by Paul and by any argument showing cost reduction).

We explored her perceptions of these three relationships: with Paul the protagonist, with the financial controller, Alan, and with her mentor, Georgina. When Helena came to me, she had already decided to contact Georgina only as a last resort for guidance, not proactive support. While talking about Alan, we had the following development:

ANGUS: Helena, do you recall a significant meeting with Alan that represents your typical engagement with him?

HELENA: Yes, I do.

ANGUS: I'd like you to have an *experience* of being in that meeting now. Put whatever you need to make this experience as real as you can. How light is it? Where is that light coming from? How warm or cold is it? Where is Alan? How does your body feel? Has Alan spoken? If he has spoken, how does he sound?

Linguistic tip
Experience

Use the word "experience" rather than restrict your question to "see", "feel" or "think." Asking the question, "How do you feel about it?" will be misleading to the coachee who is exploring a visual and/or auditory experience. The coachee will have a conscious experience but it may not be represented internally as an image, emotion, or thought. Without evidence from the coachee, it is better to use the word "experience," and they will then tell you how they represent their experience internally. The coach must get out of the way of the coachee's mental processing to get the best possible result.

Helena was encouraged to re-experience the meeting with all her senses active. She entered a state of recall, an "induced state". I did not know what she was experiencing and did not need to know. However, I did want a check on how perfectly she was experiencing the situation.

ANGUS: On a scale of *zero through ten*, how real is this experience?

HELENA: Eight.

ANGUS: Eight is good. Do whatever you need to do to make this experience even more real.

Helena sat up a little straighter and her face and head looked more toned and poised. I asked some questions about the specific dialogue and more about how Helena was feeling before inviting her to return to our dynamic, in the present. I now wanted Helena to break her (induced) state and come down from eight to zero. I wanted her to be able to think objectively about that experience. I asked a series of questions that would be least likely to involve emotional recall of the induced state.

Linguistic tip
Zero through ten

This device is a useful measuring stick and is favored by John Whitmore; I use it frequently. It is a good way of getting information about the experience of the coachee without making presumptions. It can be applied just as readily to describing the level of perfection of their experience as to the extent of their commitment: "So, how certain are you to complete that action on time, zero through ten?"

ANGUS: Helena, how many chairs are there in this room and how are they different?

ANGUS: Can you shake out any tensions in your body?

ANGUS: How many colors can you see in my tie?

The first question was designed to move Helena's concentration and focus on internal processing followed by external observation, the second to break her apparently fixed physical state, and the third to bring her attention back to her coach. These rapid changes of focus activate different parts of the brain and help **break the induced state**. I wanted to check that my observation was correct.

Breaking induced state

The coach wants the coachee to have exquisite learning experiences from the states that they visit. When it is time to think logically in the present about those experiences, it is best if the coachee is not in a hinterland, a blurred state that is neither here nor there. Breaking induced states requires tasking to be done by the coachee in the present. Physical activity, logical processing (counting, observing, and calculating) all help to bring the coachee back into the coaching dynamic and ready to work. By being explicit, as in the example of Helena, the coach then checks to make sure that this breaking of state has been successful:

"Helena, on a scale of one through ten, how perfectly are you back in this room?"

Helena returned a "ten", so we were ready to work again. I always want a top score before reviewing the experience and learning.

Questioning revealed to Helena that she always felt slightly tense in Alan's presence. She was certain that, "Alan resents my youth and my lack of dedicated career within IT. He does not like me one bit." Now the good coach is bursting to question and challenge these perceptions, so I made a note of these for later in the session. I then invited her to explore the meeting with Alan in a different way: "Helena, if we were in that room with Alan now, where in this room is he, and where is Helena?"

Linguistic tip
Tense change

If we were in that room with Alan now, where in this room *is* he?

Note the change of tense to the present. I wanted Helena to have an experience of that situation in the present and to connect as holistically as possible with that earlier experience, in that moment.

Helena pointed to a place in the room where Alan was seated, in her imagination. She also offered the information that she would be in her own seat. I moved a spare chair to where Helena said Alan would be sitting and checked with her the *exact* positioning and orientation of that chair. Since she pointed very specifically and was able to coach me to move the chair by precise amounts, it was obvious that the location of the chair was critical to her experience. To fulfill that job perfectly, I asked for feedback. My interventions continued.

"In a moment," I said, "I am going to ask you to return to that meeting with Alan. This time I am going to ask you to move over to Alan's chair to adopt his bearing and personality, to be Alan. As you move across I want you to become his age, to have arrived by his car or train, to have walked to that chair from his office, to carry his responsibilities, and to move in his circles."

Helena thought about this for a while and accepted the invitation. She was ready to experience being in Alan's shoes. This is sometimes called *taking the second perceptual position*.

I then said to her, "In your own time I want you to come into this meeting of Alan and Helena, who is sitting in that chair." I pointed to Helen's chair. "As you move across, you are entering the state of Alan and will be Alan as you sit down in his chair."

Helena rose and walked slowly to "Alan's chair". As she did so, she became slower, more deliberate and "gray".

I spoke to Helena again but this time addressed her appropriately, as "Alan".

ANGUS: Alan, what's going on here?

HELENA (Alan): Helena wants something but she is holding back. She always holds back. She has an agenda but I will not bother to engage fully until she gets direct with me. She is a little nervous as usual because her experience and understanding of the financials is not anywhere as comprehensive as my own. She understands the fundamentals that we use to highlight and monitor performance but not the underlying strengths and weaknesses that carry those indicators. If she took the trouble to get alongside, I could help her.

ANGUS: Alan, what do you feel about Helena?

HELENA (Alan): I don't. I'm here to do a job and feelings don't come into it. I'm influenced by the business and by sound arguments that support the business objectives at the best possible value for money. At this stage in my career I am lucky to be able to plan my own exit as a matter of choice. That will be in a couple of years. Tim, Paul, and the others have limited impact on me. I do my job well and am respected and supported by the key players both inside and outside our business area.

Note my mistake in using the word "feel". I might better have asked, "What's going on with Helena?" I invited Helena to return to our dynamic in the present.

ANGUS: In your own time, I am going to ask you to return to Helena's chair. It's Tuesday the 27th at 11:23 and you will be back in the present with Angus.

Helena rose again, walked briskly the short distance to her chair, sat bright-eyed and upright and checked out the room and me deliberately. She was already becoming expert at state management. I let the silence run.

HELENA: OK, I'm back. That was really useful! I'm going to look at a financial case for restructuring my quality division. I will think about splitting it and putting some of my people out in the field alongside technical support. I think I can find both sales and business arguments for this approach and maybe some overhead savings if I work on it. I'm going to discuss the draft plan with Alan and seek his advice and involvement before I prepare a full paper.

Helena may not have learned anything about the truth of her relationship with Alan or about his mindset. She had found a new perception and entered a new and motivated reality characterized by a new frame of reference. It was certain that her relationship with

Alan would not be the same. Clearly she was motivated to take action. I had two things on my mind, though. The first was my note about Helena's original view of Alan's negativity toward her. The second was the dynamic (interaction or relationship) with Paul, the protagonist in the current equation.

ANGUS: You said earlier that Alan resented your youth and your lack of dedicated IT career, and that he does not like you. Is your view the same or different?

HELENA: I don't think Alan likes or dislikes me. He's ambivalent to both me and to others. He is consistent. It's not about me at all.

ANGUS: Are you also saying that it's possible for you to assume negativity toward you and then later to realize that you were wrong?

(Helena nods.)

ANGUS: Is it also possible that you might have similar negative projection about Alan or others in the future and change you perception again?

HELENA: Yes, it is.

I wanted Helena to acknowledge fully what she had learned and to "own" that learning. I also wanted to make it more likely that she could carry this learning into possible future scenarios, not just through a new skill set but because she accepted that she was now someone who could reverse negative projection and see things in a positive light. Once a person believes that they have the identity of someone with certain characteristics, they are automatically more likely to demonstrate those same behaviors again. It was not the time to do more work on this. We scheduled an appointment to look at her communication with Paul for two days' time.

Helena came back to that session having worked on her restructuring ideas and having explored the second perceptual position for a previous meeting she had with Paul. She came back more certain than ever that Paul was poised to capture her quality division and had circumstantial evidence to support her argument. It sounded pretty convincing and I wondered whether she had acted too late. I also wondered whether Paul's restructuring plan might be a good thing for both Helena and the business. I let those thoughts pass to engage fully with my coachee.

At this point many options could be explored in the session. Was there scope for Helena to work and communicate better with Paul? How would Helena feel if she lost her quality division? How could she minimize any negative impact that could have on her performance? Could she capitalize on any positive features? If Helena's reorganization looked like a good policy, how could she best sell that to the key people and maintain morale and efficiency among the staff affected? What might the price of success or failure be?

Before we met again, I had thought of the wider implications for the business. The client was Helena's company and I had a duty both to her and to the corporation. My overall aims were twofold: to support the objectives of the business and to help Helena be the best manager that she could be. Helena lost most of her quality-division people but within a year was managing a much bigger part of the business. Her skills in second positioning contributed to that success.

Let us look at another communication issue involving the second perceptual position.

Who's the boss?

Communication is about understanding as well as about messages. In this example, I was coaching through a medium-sized company from middle managers to CEO. Two of my coachees worked together and each had issues concerning the other. Coaching in the team context is especially interesting and saturated with information—sometimes too much! It takes concentration to stay with the coachee and not be mentally sabotaged by the bigger plot.

The wider corporate/team picture often does influence the course of an individual coaching session, especially when coaching an entire team. I rely on my homework and intuition during the actual sessions to offer possible directions that bring alignment to team and corporate targets. I also have a model for that.

Janice was sales manager and had been in that role for less than four months, following promotion. Mark reported to Janice and he led the telesales team. Janice was out of the office at least four and a half days per week. Mark rarely left the office or got in front of customers. Mark said that his boss was dogmatic, inflexible, and territorial but effective at maintaining good customer rapport and winning new business. Her communication skills were not great by all accounts and this caused problems for Mark and for senior management. I knew already that Janice did not consistently inform the board about new and significant contracts in the pipeline. The directors were not happy about this, since large new pieces of business affected the supply chain and other supporting functions in process control and purchasing. These needed to be project-managed.

Janice complained that Mark was not respectful toward her and would often deprioritize her instructions, particularly concerning sales reports.

Mark complained that his boss was surly, offhand, threw mundane tasks at him, and did not offer any credit, ever, for the success of his department or the groundwork that he did with customers that made Janice's job easier. Mark regularly won business because his turnaround on quotes was always lightning fast. A big proportion of total revenues came from those quotes. Mark's priority was to put these out first and fast before reporting to Janice.

My first session with Mark was warming. With almost no previous exposure to development or training initiatives, he was able to work with the second perceptual position and maintain state at will. Mark provided the following insights from his second positioning of Janice:

MARK (Janice): I am Janice. I work hard because my home life is terrible. My husband has a chronic disease and will die. My private life is a series of doctor and hospital appointments. Mark is disrespectful toward me. He does not realize that the sales reports give me the confidence I need in order to achieve what I do with customers. It may seem trivial but I want to know *all* the history so I am not exposed through ignorance in front of my customers. I am out of touch with the office because I am out of town almost full-time. Mark does not help me enough and has the ear of my key colleagues. He is often giving new sales information to them before I have the courtesy of being told. That makes me very angry although I am careful not to lose my rag with Mark. I feel undermined and am sometimes verbally short with him as a consequence.

From these perceptions Mark was able to see how he might improve the situation with his boss. The issue of sales reports was an awkward one. The MD and other senior staff had grown the business from nothing. They still had the habit of running to Mark to get fresh updates on sales activity from the hive of the business. Because he was at the center, Mark was the obvious place to get information. He undertook to call Janice or leave her voicemail whenever this happened and to provide reports routinely by email. These were not quite as detailed as Janice wanted but could be produced automatically by the software system as a delegated action. If Mark were busy with quotes, the reports would still get through. Their relationship improved dramatically. Second positioning had again been fruitful.

Ultimately, I recommended that Mark's department be floated away from Janice, under Mark's leadership. After Janice's coaching, it became clear that this would be best for all concerned even if her first feelings were of disappointment. Management agreed and within three months the relationship between Janice and Mark improved by a further major step. Janice now invited Mark to visit customers with her from time to time and their ability to share information and capitalize on the market has transformed. This illustrates the benefit of helping staff to work on the same team rather than against one another.

My boss is not involving me

Roberto works for the European division of an international firm. He was based in a different city and country from his immediate boss, whom he saw perhaps twice a month. He rarely had one-to-one time with Alain, his director of HR. Communication was usually by email. Meetings were rarely private but Alain would sometimes call Roberto to get an immediate update if a staff/union situation demanded his attention.

Roberto liked the freedom of his role but was dismayed that he had so little impact within Europe. Roberto brought up a specific issue with me at our coaching session. Alain was planning a Europe-wide rollout of 360-degree feedback. Roberto had pioneered the 360-degree initiative in England. If it was successful in Europe as well, there was little doubt that the scheme would be continued worldwide. Roberto was not involved at all in the policy, strategy or project management. He was feeling left out. Roberto had recently written to Alain as follows:

> To: Alain
> From: Roberto
> Subject: 360-degree feedback—rollout for Europe
>
> Alain,
>
> I am pleased to be included in the mail to Euro-managers. As you know, I believe that the skill level of our managers in Europe is generally higher than necessary for successful implementation and that this next-level communication strategy will reap benefits. If I can assist in any way, do please let me know,
>
> Roberto

Roberto explained to me that Alain had responded three days later by telephone message and had said something to the effect, "Roberto, Alain here. Thanks for the email about the three-sixty. I am happy with the responses from the Euro-team so far. On the whole, it's taking shape. I don't need to steal time from your UK activity. I'll see you at the next management meeting in Brussels."

Roberto felt that this message continued to keep him uninvolved and believed that no path was left open for him to continue dialogue on the subject. As I knew Alain very well, I could have had a word with him, but this is not what coaching is about. My aim was to encourage Roberto to be more effective in his thinking and actions. To do this, my questioning would encourage conscious perception of the communication, an exploration of new meaning.

ANGUS: Roberto, when Alain said something like, "I don't need to steal time from your UK activity", what interpretations can you find?

ROBERTO: He probably means, "Leave it to me. It's my baby now."

ANGUS: And?

ROBERTO: I should stick to my patch and not get above myself.

ANGUS: Possibly. And?

ROBERTO: OK. My UK work is my main responsibility. He wants my eyes on the ball and anyway wants the credit for my work on the three-sixty initiative!

Roberto had a new perception that seemed to contain some impression of value about his own work in the UK, but not convincingly. Clearly, the issue of stealing credit remained foremost in his mind. I tried a new tack to encourage Roberto's conscious perception.

ANGUS: Roberto, if Alain had some hidden agenda with a *positive intention* to you, what might that positive intention toward you be?

ROBERTO: My UK work is vital and he wants to see me succeed and not get immersed in European politics.

ANGUS: And if there was another positive intention toward you in his statement, "I don't need to steal time from your UK activity", what would it be?

ROBERTO: He could be protecting me from the backlash if the European managers dislike the program.

Linguistic tip
Positive intention

Where a coachee has fixed negativity about the motivation of another individual, it can be helpful to challenge them to a new perspective by offering the concept of "positive intent". In the example of Roberto, we see that the question, "Roberto, if Alain had some hidden agenda with a positive intention to you, what might that positive intention toward you be?" raises a new perception of what Alain may be motivated by. As soon as there is a possibility for other motivation, there is doubt about the original belief. The new perception does not have to be right. The point is to get the coachee to new conscious perception. With new insight, whether right or wrong, the coachee has new options for interacting with the third party and invariably this will help resolve a negative experience.

I asked Roberto the same question again to see whether he had any other new perception, but he did not. However, Roberto's evident relaxation seemed to show that he believed that Alain did have a positive intention to protect him from any backlash. The evidence in his world was exactly as it was before our interventions; his map of the world—his perception—was different. In this case, it was questioning to increase conscious perception, including the concept of positive intention that helped Roberto to a new mindset. This took the emotional heat out of the issue for him and his relationship with Alain continued to improve. This is a typical example of the benefit of the coaching process. The coachee learns how to find new perceptions on issues over which they have no control. They learn to focus their energy on finding new realities for those issues and to maintain energy and direction in doing so.

In coaching, we are not just helping people to deal with their issues and we are not just helping them learn strategies for self-coaching. We are also trying to enhance the dynamics of the teams in which our coachees do work. Communicating, understanding and perception are at the heart of effective team dynamics. Necessarily, this means that the team needs a range of such skills. Coaching supports that.

Feedback

The giving and receiving of feedback are often coaching issues. Although communication is invariably the principal feature, I am separating it out because of the frequency with which these issues crop up. This is particularly so where feedback is part of appraisal schemes and personal-development plans. Companies are often too quick to bring in such schemes before recognizing the limitations of their managers. It is important to raise the general level of communications, including feedback skills, before instituting such manager-run schemes. The fact that feedback issues come up so often may indicate the significant weakness that persists in many organizations.

My personal-development review is unfair

Joanne had waited two months for her personal-development review (PDR). Her line director, Philip, had rescheduled twice and when the PDR did occur it was interrupted several times. It was still finished within twenty minutes. The corporate system indicated that PDRs should take at least an hour and a half. Philip expected Joanne to sign her acceptance of the PDR but she refused. He told her to take it away and come back with it the following week. She understood that she could seek HR involvement. The issue for Joanne was his commentary, "Joanne has a need to develop improved team skills and should undertake the Team Journey Course for Managers."

Joanne was very angry, because she considered herself a key player in the department. When she showed me the PDR, it appeared that Philip had a good impression of Joanne and it seemed reasonable and supportive. Was her issue about the process, her assuming the feedback as an insult to her competencies, being "judged" by others, or specific to Philip? In any case, she was fixed in her understanding about it and any further dialogue might be likely to be prejudiced by that perception. If she could be open to other perceptions, she might handle her relationship with Philip better.

ANGUS: What is it about Philip's commentary that you are unhappy with?

JOANNE: He gives me no credit for contribution in the team.

ANGUS: *Could you contradict that* by looking at the PDR?

(She thinks for a moment.)

JOANNE: Yes, he has scored me nine for participation.

ANGUS: So, what is it about the commentary that you're unhappy with?

JOANNE: It's not fair, and he's singled me out for training as an example when there are others in the team who are much weaker than me.

Linguistic tip
Could you contradict that?

The question is offered when a statement is given of absolute fact, when other more useful possibilities occur to the coach. When the coachee looks for contradictions to their own argument, they necessarily have to change their focus on their situation and enter a state closer to that of a dispassionate observer. In so doing, they gain conscious perception and new scope for useful action.

ANGUS: And could he have singled you out for training because of your team strengths?

JOANNE: No, he wrote, "Joanne has a need to develop improved team skills and should undertake the Team Journey Course for Managers."

I thought it useful to get Joanne to explore the issue from a more objective distance. I suggested a new form of second position, one that is outside of the present scenario. This can help reduce emotional impact on logical thought and increase conscious perception.

ANGUS: Think of someone you know who works in a team. Do you have someone in mind? [She nods.] Their manager has written a commentary about that person that says they should undertake a team development course for managers to develop their skills. How can you help that person feel better about that commentary?

JOANNE: My friend is an able person and the manager wants him to hone his skills for a bigger role in their department?

ANGUS: It could be that. What is your advice to them?

JOANNE: Stay open-minded and ask for clarification.

ANGUS: Joanne, you have this commentary in your own PDR and the best possible advice available is this: "Stay open-minded and ask for clarification." What is it like to receive that advice?

JOANNE: I wish I had it before. I was bound to explode and do something I might regret. There is no obvious bigger role for me unless we split the department. That's also possible.

Again, we see that the facts are the same. It is the coachee's reality that has changed. Coaching is not the Holy Grail of truth. Truth has nothing to do with coaching. We are dealing only with coachees' realities about their issues. Joanne managed and maintained her relationship with her boss and now sits with the senior team.

Giving feedback with sensitivity

Toby ran two departments with no logical relationship. He struggled to broker time between the two, especially during the PDR season. One of his staff members had taken 48 days off owing to ongoing family health problems and gone way over the corporate limit. Toby had discussed the issue with the appropriate HR manager and was limited in what he could offer; pay would have to be docked if absenteeism continued at the same level. The staff member, Lauren, was emotional and prone to tears, something with which Toby was uncomfortable.

TOBY: *It's bound to be difficult for her.*

ANGUS: Could it be that she might be relieved?

TOBY: Why? She is going to lose money.

ANGUS: Could she be relieved because of the uncertainty over this issue?

TOBY: I doubt it. The money will be important.

ANGUS: We know that she doesn't know where she stands. She could be worrying about losing her job. She may want to go part-time and have greater flexibility of working. Could discussing it be a relief?

TOBY: I doubt it.

 Linguistic tip
It's bound to be difficult for her

In the example, Toby said, "It's bound to be difficult for her." When coachees (and coaches) have such beliefs, they restrict the potential for conscious perception and the likelihood of a positive outcome. These are what are termed limiting beliefs (see the box called "Limiting beliefs"). Coaches need to be aware of such statements and, where appropriate, question, challenge, and encourage new perception to open up new possibilities for their coachees.

ANGUS: Let's imagine that you're sitting here for your PDR in this office now. You have had forty-eight days off because of medical procedures. *Instinctively, how do you experience that now?*

TOBY: I will expect a formal written warning and letter.

Linguistic tip
Instinctively, how do you experience that now?

This question and "What is that like for you?" give no specific sensory hint and the result may be sensory information that is specific to the coachee or a metaphoric representation that they have about that situation.

ANGUS: You have had forty-eight days sick but I can tell you, with good authority, that you will not receive a written warning. What is that like?"

TOBY: It's *very good news*.

ANGUS: So, soon you will be with Lauren. You will tell her that she will not receive a written warning. Is it possible she may regard this as *very good news*?

TOBY: Yes.

Linguistic tip
Very good news

Repeating the coachee's map: I had used an expression of my own, "relieved," to describe how Toby's staff member might feel and he disagreed with me. Ultimately, he reframed his perception to include the possibility that she might feel the meeting "very good news." In my reference to this, I dropped my own description and stayed with his. The coachee is always right. I do not wish to damage my rapport by insisting on my own language. In any case, my understanding of the words and phrases is certainly different from Philip's. It is the coachee's map (of the world) that needs the coach's attention during the session, not their own map.

ANGUS: And how might she experience *"very good news"*?

TOBY: She could feel good about it.

ANGUS: So, now that you feel that Lauren may feel good about very good news, what will be different about your experience of the PDR?

TOBY: Maybe if I can get this out in the open at the beginning, the meeting will go better than I expected.

Toby had altered his mindset about the meeting and for sure this would alter the progress of the PDR, I hoped positively. This was only the first part of the work with him and his ability to deal with staff issues improved dramatically.

 Limiting beliefs

Limiting beliefs arise from a mental filtering of information that Noam Chomsky (1957) called generalizations, deletions, and distortions. The need to reduce the mass of information reaching the brain is obvious. If we had to rethink the process of getting ourselves out of bed, standing, dressing and driving a car, it would be bedtime before anything useful happened! As it is, much of what we observe fits into a neat category of "experienced data" or "patterns" and, for much of what we do, we operate on autopilot. Without self-challenge, we can get very mixed up about our world.

When we have repeated experiences, like getting out of bed, we subconsciously generalize those experiences when faced with a similar situation. In a hotel room, this may cause us to walk into a wardrobe. In the same way, someone who has had one or two bad experiences with drinking red wine, for example, may reject any offer of red wine permanently. While these traits are essential to efficient working, they can create powerful limiting beliefs that are not useful or appropriate.

We delete, generalize, and distort massive amounts of information. These internal processes function automatically in the subconscious. In road accidents, investigators find that, where witnesses are highly stressed, they produce wildly different accounts of the same event. In the criminal process, this causes many problems for justice, particularly where people have been traumatized by robbery or other violent crime. Police generally dread identity parades in these circumstances, as the witness will tend to pick out the individual who most closely resembles their inner expectation of what a bad person looks like.

In the work context, it is quite common for people to believe that an individual is deliberately trying to undermine them when this is not the case. The coach will look for statements of limiting belief and wish to challenge them (McLeod, 2002b) so that the coachee may have new conscious perception of the world around them.

Presenting

Presentation issues often come up during coaching, even among skilled and experienced managers. Additional stresses can arise because a new post is desired, because senior or external people will be present, because it is the first in a new role, or because people from different cultures will be involved. The most common problems for less experienced presenters are of self-confidence and technique. Coaches typically direct their coachees to learning resources for technique but do sometimes get involved in offering a number of alternative ideas for preparation. Self-confidence is often an issue and is typically a longer job, but the coachee can still be helped with an upcoming presentation where they are stressed and lacking confidence.

Shareholders' meeting

Jane works for a big consultancy firm that holds a large annual shareholders' event that includes exhibits and short presentations from members of staff at all levels. Although she is a relatively junior manager, her enthusiasm and bubbly personality make her popular at all levels, and the executive chairman had arranged for her to be on the list of those presenting. She was nervous.

JANE: I'm useless at giving presentations.

ANGUS: *Can you contradict that?*

JANE: What do you mean?

ANGUS: Can you contradict that you are useless at giving presentations?

JANE: I've given brief presentations to small groups of colleagues and prospective customers, which have been friendly and easy and well received but—

ANGUS (interrupting): *So, Jane has given brief presentations "that have been friendly and easy and well received"?*

JANE: Yes but—

ANGUS (interrupting): So, again, Jane "*has* given brief presentations that have been friendly and well received"?

JANE: Yes she has. I mean, I have. [Smiling.] You are annoying!

Linguistic tip
So, Jane has given brief presentations "that have been friendly and easy and well received"?

Repeating positive statements and interruption: Where individuals are generally being negative about themselves but offer something positive, as Jane has in this example, the positive statement is often overlooked, or undersold (internally) by that individual. The coach can check and help the coachee by repeating exactly what they have just heard until full acknowledgment of the statement is understood at both logical and at emotional levels. In this case, I kept breaking in at the word "but" because Jane was rushing to communicate the negative without attending, I thought, to the positive element of her statement.

ANGUS: Is there a chance that this shareholder meeting will also have many people who will be friendly toward you?

JANE: I suppose so. I just thought it would be formal and like a big crowd.

Jane's language suggested that she was already moving her belief about the way the big meetings might be.

ANGUS: ***And is there a difference between*** thinking about a big crowd and thinking about individuals, some of whom may be friendly toward you?

JANE: Yes, there is. People tend to like me. I guess if I could go in without nerves and be myself, like at other presentations, that it would be OK.

I thought it essential that Jane rethink the issue of nerves. The reality might be that she could have nerves on the day.

ANGUS: People "tend to like" you. Could you be nervous and also be yourself?

JANE: Yes, but I might need some help.

ANGUS: If you agree, we will work with that.

Jane's foreboding had been getting in the way of her objectivity. The question about contradicting herself was formulated to encourage a different and more useful perception from which to work.

Linguistic tip
And is there a difference between ...?

This challenge is to get new conscious perception where there has been contradiction. Contradictions often arise through emotional reluctance about an issue. By engaging in logical (rather than emotional) process, we can hope to bring new perceptions to the absurdity of the coachee's emotional world, and maybe even our own!

In the course of further coaching, Jane learned some new mental skills that enabled her to perform brilliantly on the day, even though she began nervous. Within a few seconds she was very much herself, presenting as if to only a small group within the whole meeting. She self-selected that group and spoke to them. It was clear that learning how to self-contradict limiting beliefs, noticing negative statements about herself, and emphasizing the positives were key elements in raising her effectiveness.

European management meeting

Jules was nervous because he might be called upon to present at a meeting. He had already prepared a presentation, just in case. In fact, it might not even be required, and he would not know until the day was under way. His nervousness arose because it was his first presentation at this level. His elevation to European manager was a big one in this US-owned company. He perceived his new colleagues as worldly, multilingual, talented, and cosmopolitan. He was right, but compared with them he felt very much the junior. On top of this, he had difficulty understanding some of his new colleagues owing to their accents, and he was aware that some of them had problems with his accent, too. His stress was manifest as he spoke about it: he chewed at his cuticles. Until we spoke about that later, it was a useful indicator of his state.

JULES: I'm finding this presentation very difficult, even though it's only to be ten minutes.

ANGUS: What is this "very difficult" experience like?

Jules thought for a moment, his concentration seemed to go deeply inside, his eyes defocused.

JULES: It's like being in a wet barrel. There's water in the bottom and I'm crawling up the slippery sides. I can see the bright light above but all around the top are my colleagues' heads. Their

35

eyes are looking down at me, staring without blinking. The sides are very slimy and I can't make my way up without slipping back.

Jules was chewing his finger and looked most uncomfortable. The story or **metaphor** was clearly powerful for him—unfortunately in a negative way at that moment. It had been triggered by repeating his language and asking the question, "What is this [coachee's language] experience like?"

ANGUS: And this being in the wet barrel with water at the bottom and the faces looking down at you, how is this similar to or different from when you have presented successfully at other meetings?

JULES: The walls of the barrel are overlapping. They are sliding down and the light is getting bigger and wider. I can see the faces now. It's my old team and I can see one of my slides projected against the light. They are smiling and clapping.

ANGUS: And what happens just before the walls slide down and the light gets bigger and wider?

JULES: It's my math teacher at school. He was the one and only person who truly believed in me, no matter what. I was third from bottom of my grade at age ten. Due to him I went on to be top of the grade and to get a first-class degree in pure mathematics at university. He was smiling down at me and I then felt his hands on my shoulders, telling me I could do it.

Jules's metaphor was very powerful for him, as are most such metaphors. Additionally, he had found a trigger for transforming his experience and state. The "trigger" was the sensation of his math teacher and he was able to reuse this repeatedly, and at will, as an "anchor" to transform his state.

Metaphor

The question, "What is this experience like?" is "clean" in that it does not stimulate the coachee to have logical thoughts about what they feel, see, or hear. In this case, Jules offered a metaphor, an internal representation of the situation that was impactful and specific to him. These metaphors are powerful representations that can keep a coachee perpetually stuck or, by careful and skilled help, free them permanently. In working with metaphor, it is important to maintain the language of the coachee and to maintain the correct tense. Other highlighted text—"how is this similar to or different from" and "what happens just before"—is designed to help the coachee develop their symbolic awareness. We will return to metaphor and symbols.

I am often surprised by both the graphic nature and precise detail of people's inner world as expressed through their metaphors. Usually, the metaphor has been hidden or dormant for many years, waiting for expression. Just as Jules's first metaphor of the wet barrel was powerful, so were the transforming metaphor and positive influence of the images that developed.

Invariably, the coachee finds a solution based upon a new or transformed metaphor and these are as powerfully positive as the initial ones are negative. The result is often self-motivated action and successful outcomes.

As in most cases where there is a specific future target or event, it is helpful to ask the coachee to imagine being there with the new-found skill. This is sometimes called **future pacing**. I was careful to repeat Jules's language.

ANGUS: Jules, let's go forward to the management meeting, only this time, when you choose, you have your math teacher from school who believes in you. He is smiling down at you and you feel his hands on your shoulders, telling you that you can do it.

Jules did this several times and feedback from him gave us both confidence that Jules would link the two experiences together on the day. Metaphor is a powerful change medium but it is still necessary for the coach to check that action is realistic and fully committed too. Future pacing helps to do just that.

Future pacing

When a coachee has found strategy for action, it is important to check their confidence level and commitment to undertaking that strategy in the future. Future pacing is one way of achieving that and involves asking the coachee to imagine the next event where the strategy may prove useful. In the example of Jules, I invited him to future-pace by saying, "let's go forward to ..." By helping the coachee to a very real experience of that, the coach obtains more information to assess the realistic chance that the strategy will work and be undertaken. I invariably follow this with a question, "Zero through ten, how confident are you that ...?"

First national sales conference

Emily works in a predominantly male company selling photocopiers. She had a superb sales record, often in the top league month on month. Emily was promoted to an entirely new role, managing half the geographic country and over 60 per cent of revenue. She was very effective in that role in spite of the stress of managing an all-male sales force. She made it evident that she was kind and supportive of people who were behind targets and managed by establishing absolute boundaries. She said that she was literally loved, respected, and feared, sometimes all at once.

Emily's first national sales conference in her new role was coming up after eight months in the job. From attending previous conferences, she knew the score. There was no forgiveness for losers. Negative judgments were usual. It was a tough environment for anyone. There would be several hundred people at the conference and she would be one of only two women there, the only manager. She expressed nervousness.

EMILY: Only ten days to go and I'm already finding sleep difficult. My concentration is poor and I nearly crashed my car twice this week.

ANGUS: *What would you call this state when* your concentration is poor and you find sleep difficult?

EMILY: I guess it's stress.

Linguistic tip
What would you call this state when ...?

Naming the emotion: Emotions tend to keep coming back if we do not acknowledge them. Sometimes, the mere act of giving the emotion a name can be enough for it to disappear completely! I had been very much affected by three unpleasant things happening on one morning. Try as I might to be positive and to get back to productive thought, the feelings kept niggling at me and I kept recalling the individual events and playing them over and over. Suddenly, I stopped and said to myself, "These were not nice things to happen—I have a right to feel bad about that." Within a few seconds I surprised myself in noticing that my step was light and that I felt positive and happy again.

ANGUS: Have you thought of any relaxation techniques that you might use to counteract this stress, poor concentration, and difficulty sleeping?

EMILY: No. I fiddle with the radio in the car when not on the phone but don't hear the radio when it's on. I can't concentrate on it.

ANGUS: What could you do?

EMILY: Hot baths and alcohol used to help.

ANGUS: Would alcohol help you to deal with this stress issue or with the presentation itself?

EMILY: No.

ANGUS: So, other than hot baths, what else could you do?

EMILY: Maybe music. Something favorite, peaceful.

ANGUS: Something favorite and peaceful would be what, specifically?

EMILY: Chopin. Number-one piano concerto.

ANGUS: And is there one phrase from the concerto that conjures up a good peaceful feeling?

EMILY: Yes there is.

Emily then hummed the phrase. I worked with her to see if we could establish a relaxed state linked (anchored) to that Chopin phrase.

ANGUS: Here we are in this room discussing how you can deal with the stress that the presentation has been catalyzing. Shall we use this phrase to anchor good, peaceful feelings that can help you to relax before, during, and after the event?

Emily agreed. Several times she willingly went from a "present" state in the room to one associated with the last time she had listened to the Chopin. It happens that the occasion has been while she was in the tub.

ANGUS: In a moment, and *in your own time*, I am going to ask you to take yourself back into that warm, comfortable tub listening to Chopin. As you experience that relaxed state I want you to play that phrase in your head and hold that state as long as you wish. If you feel less relaxed, then let the phrase go. Wait again for the relaxed state and, when it comes, play your phrase again. Try to deepen that experience.

After five or six times it was clear that Emily could revisit her relaxed state skillfully. Her tension evaporated like steam; she radiated and looked content. After another three times we checked out the perfection level of her experience, zero to ten. She scored nine. I invited Emily to return once more to our room.

ANGUS: Emily, what day is it and what is the exact time?

Emily brought her attention to this question and then to the room. I invited her to check whether the anchor was fully operational.

ANGUS: When you are ready and *in your own time*, I would like you to play your anchor and see what happens.

Emily reran the phrase and it triggered the same state as before. On this occasion the music triggered the mental state rather than the other way around. She scored herself eight out of ten. The "anchor" was set. She tried a few more times cycling between our room and the state that the phrase induced in her. Soon she was consistently achieving eight or nine and the phrase was working faster.

I still speak to Emily from time to time and she has been using the phrase often and to this day. Positive anchors are used by multitudes of managers to great effect.

Linguistic tip
In your own time

This phrase is used to confirm to the coachee that the pace and direction of the coaching session is in their control. Maintenance of this in the coaching dynamic helps the coachee to feel good about their own self-determination and proactivity. These are vital spin-offs of true coaching but are often ignored by many who call themselves coaches.

Keynote presentation of technical information

Brian had little experience of presentation in spite of a technical education and career. His area of work was not academic but the technical content of his work was detailed and highly professional. The success of his company's products hung on the innovative developments he initiated. As a member of a professional body, he was given the honor of making a keynote presentation at a biennial conference. His thoughts were entirely negative.

I asked Brian if he could imagine a scenario that had a good out-come and what that might be like.

BRIAN: *People <u>would be</u> nodding and clapping* at the end.

ANGUS: *People <u>are</u> nodding and clapping*. What else do you notice?

BRIAN: I feel a weight off my shoulders. I can now be a participant again.

Note that Brian used the future conditional tense and I responded with the present tense. He then replied in the present, perhaps showing that he was more closely "associated" in his state.

Linguistic tip
People <u>would be</u> nodding and clapping/People <u>are</u> nodding and clapping

Changing tense to present: It can be useful to encourage the coachee to have a more emotionally associated state. This can be helped by reflecting the same language but in the present tense. This helps the coachee to experience that event now and that typically engenders a more emotional experience of the event. The other words are kept the same to help the coachee stay with their material. As we see in the example, Brian then follows the tense by making his next statement in the present tense also. This does not prove any-thing but is an indication that he may be more deeply involved in his experience and hence may learn more from it. We will return to issues of emotion later and in more detail.

We explored more about Brian's experience to get an idea of how well he could imagine a new experience that was positive. This is sometimes called a **future desired state**.

Future desired state

A coachee may spend an inordinate amount of time talking about how stuck they are. The coach lets them express, and then will want them to have a positive experience of what a successful outcome might be like. This is the future desired state, an NLP term. We hope that this state will be so compelling that the coachee will find a strategy of motivated action to achieve it. There are a number of ways to help the coachee establish what that future desired state may be like and, in the case of Brian, we explored the use of a timeline.

Timeline

I wanted Brian to consider future-pacing the event and so invited him to explore a timeline. This would have a start point within our session and run into the future as far as his experience of hearing clapping and seeing people nod approvingly. I asked Brian to establish for himself where the "present" would be and where the finishing point or "future desired state" would be. He indicated two points in the room about eighteen feet apart. I use colored hula hoops to mark the spots and he chose the colors and position of the starting and finishing points.

The timeline offers a simple method of helping a coachee develop an experience of a future desired state. The great benefit of the timeline is that it helps the coachee move at their own pace through a number of critical steps and to obtain new perceptions and understanding of what is needed to achieve their targets. Timelines also underpin the need for a strategy, or procedure, and this is vital if the target is to be realized.

Physical movement associated with the process of moving toward a desired outcome can be very helpful in enhancing a state, particularly where the individual is highly (emotionally) associated with the developing scenario. It is noteworthy that there appear to be two distinct categories of people:

- "In-time" people are focused on the present and their experience of that.
- "Through-time" people are psychologically removed from the "now" and appreciate the timeline more holistically than as a set of individual and developing scenarios and states.

"Through-time" people tend to be better able to manage their time whereas "in-time" people tend to let events determine the course of their existence.

The timeline can be carried out as a mental process without "walking the line." In small spaces this can be useful. Remember, too, that timelines need not be straight or horizontal. The coachee will know where their present, past, and future are if they are asked appropriately.

ANGUS: Brian, in a moment I am going to ask you to walk your **timeline**. When you step onto the starting point, I would like you to fully experience the world around you and your state. What do you feel and where? What can you see? How is it to look at your finishing point where people will be clapping and nodding at you? As you walk your timeline, I would like you to be very aware of how you experience each moment along the way. You may want to stop and assess what needs to be done, how you respond to that information. You can stop as long as you wish at any point. Eventually you will reach the end point where you will experience the clapping and nodding.

(Brian steps inside the first hoop facing his objective. He centers himself.)

ANGUS: From this point, does the finishing point look the right distance away from you?

Brian made no adjustment and, having checked his awareness of both himself and his direction, he moved forward. I walked with him. He stopped very frequently. My questions were something like:

- What is it truly like to be here now? Experience how far you have come. What, if anything, can you hear? What, if any, activities are taking place?
- Zero to ten, how complete is this experience of being here?
- What else is going on?

At one point Brian did not appear at all happy. I asked him if he wanted to get off the timeline and get far enough away from it to get an objective impression of what was going on. He did so. From this "**observer perspective**" it transpired that there was an argument going on about some know-how that, although patented, was not yet in the public domain. Brian wanted to include it; his CEO did not. He made a mental note to speak to his CEO about it and returned to the timeline. He re-established his state at that point on the line.

ANGUS: You are here on the journey. There is an issue about know-how. You have some good advice that says that you need to talk to your CEO about this issue. How is this experience? Share it with me if you wish.

Brian chose to tell me very little. Evidently, he found expression got in the way of his state. I was happy for him to make progress without any context being revealed to me.

ANGUS: Make sure that you are as perfectly in this moment as you can be. Only then, and in your own time, move forward to the next step.

At the finishing point almost an hour later, Brian was very happy indeed, basking in relief. Once again, I suggested that he might like to get off the line and take an objective look some way away from the line and its associated experiences. He decided to get off the line. I asked him if he could give Brian some advice from the remote **observer perspective**.

BRIAN (observer): You have the resources. Don't organize the talk on technology advance but on the drivers for the advance. Tell them why advance would be a benefit. Describe possible progress plans and why some were discounted, others failed, and why the successful ones worked. Show the benefits in terms of what they offer the customer. Sell the products as well as the underlying technology that makes our products what they are.

Observer perspective

The *perceptual positions* offer a new view of a situation and hence increase the likelihood of conscious perception and new action. The "observer"—or third-party—position is one that gives rational thought to experiences that might be poisoned by emotional overlay. It is important that the coachee be far enough away from the perceived situation to have a cool and reflective look at the situation. The coach can ensure this is done by asking the coachee to move physically away from the scenario they hold, or by having the coachee move ahead in time and looking back from days, months, and years ahead.

ANGUS: *So, if I hear you correctly*, you advise Brian that he has the resources and you suggest a new way to structure the talk to the customer, based upon drivers for advancement and the benefits those bring?

BRIAN: That's about right.

ANGUS: *In a nutshell*, how would you offer this advice more exquisitely?

BRIAN: You have the resources and should base the talk on drivers for advance.

I asked Brian to go back to the finishing point and, as he did so, to re-establish that state again. I checked with him, zero-to-ten, how excellently he was experiencing that. After his reply (8), I asked him to accept the advice. He did so and smiled broadly. I invited him to go back along the timeline, stopping where he liked to re-evaluate the steps he had taken before, this time in the light of his experience and the advice he had received. This took some time as Brian stopped at what seemed to be every single point. When he returned to the starting hoop we checked that he was fully back in the room and I asked him to re-evaluate the timeline in terms of its length.

BRIAN: Maybe it should be shorter but I'm happy the way it is. I would like to make some notes now if that's OK.

Brian sat down and proceeded to make detailed notes based upon, he said, all the steps he had taken, each with one or more actions and reminders. I have never encountered such precision and it was clear that his logical processes were very highly developed. It was interesting that this high logical ability was accompanied by both creative skills and the flexibility to go along with new experiences and ideas.

Linguistic tip
So, if I hear you correctly ...

This phrase shows the coachee that you are listening and that your question is only to clarify your own limitations and understanding. When supported by accurate reflection of the coachee's language, it shows effectively that the coach has been listening attentively and that there is no judgment implied about the coachee's ability to communicate clearly.

Linguistic tip
In a nutshell

This phrase is useful, particularly when the coachee tends to draw out dialogue. The objective is to help the coachee crystallize the issue in their own mind.

Interpersonal conflict

Interpersonal conflict in organizations is an enormous waste of energy that should usefully be directed at both improved personal and team performance. Conflict crops up often wherever groups of people work together and organizations are fortunate if coaches are on hand to help. Sometimes executives are reticent to exploit coaching. Perceptions in the situation are important and the ability to coach the coachee to both second and third perceptual positions can help transform frustration into deliberate and constructive action. New perceptions lead, as we have seen, to renewed motivation to act.

One of the most useful tools in conflict or potential conflict is the **"fifty-one percent rule"**, which I first published in 2000 (McLeod, 2000). It has been used widely in many organizations. The rule is stated thus:

> **In any given interaction I am 51 percent responsible**
> **for that interaction.**

If I were less than 50 percent responsible then I would probably do nothing. If I were 100 percent responsible then I would probably exhibit neurotic behaviors and keep interfering in matters that did not directly concern me. By establishing my responsibility at 51 percent, I put the onus on myself to act and not let the issue stew. The rule reduces the possibility of "stalemate", since action invariably follows. This rule is simply a device, or tool, to encourage new perception. In coaching it is quite acceptable to offer a device for extending thought and encouraging new perception. In all cases, the coachee should determine whether the device is suitable for them. For example:

ANGUS: Wendy, I have an idea, a device, that may be useful. [Awaits reaction.] It's called the fifty-one percent rule. Have you heard of it and would you like to know about it?

WENDY: OK.

ANGUS: It says that in any given interaction with another person, you are fifty-one percent responsible for that interaction. In the situation you have been describing with Adrian, does the idea offer any ideas that may be useful?

WENDY: I will not wait for Adrian to take action: I will do so myself. I will make it clear that the relationship with him is more important than the issue itself and ask for his participation in finding a compromise that we can both live with. If he will not engage then at least I have tried to resolve the situation and will let my line manager know what I have done, in writing, for the record.

The fifty-one percent rule

Offering coachees the fifty-one percent rule provides them with a simple and memorable fix for situations where there is stalemate: "In any given interaction with another person, I am fifty-one percent responsible for that interaction."

Once they take on board the idea that they are 51 percent responsible for any given interaction, then stalemate is impossible; action invariably follows. The actions themselves may not give the expected outcome but will usually move the dynamic to a different dimension.

In conflicts among colleagues, perceptual positions are often helpful too. To summarize, these are:

- first position (holistic experiencing of self, looking out)
- getting in their shoes (second position)
- thinking of someone else in a similar situation (contrived second position)
- the observer (third position).

The first position may allow for the greatest emotional experience of a situation and the third, the most dispassionate. We will consider emotion and the selection of these tools later.

My chairman is stifling me

Mary was the president of a successful electronics business. The company had been driven by the executive chairman, who took technology hunches and saw them through. He had a keen sense of business and won big deals while keeping his proprietary rights. Now in his sixties, he had appointed Mary to run the day-to-day business and to groom to take over from him within two years. When discussing ideas with Mary, the chairman would often discount a prospective idea (for a new initiative) with a wave of his hand. Fifteen months into her contract, Mary was prepared to leave the company because of frustrations in trying to get her policies adopted.

Mary told me that the final straw had been a meeting at which the chairman had been pushing Mary for ideas and initiatives and knocking them flat, one after the other. I offered Mary the possibility of revisiting this unproductive meeting with her chairman. As luck would have it, we were sitting in the boardroom where that meeting had taken place and it was easy to establish which chairs in the room they had both sat in. Mary was quite exceptional in her ability to transform her state and her chairman almost seemed to be in the room with me when she sat in his chair. In adopting the second position, Mary came to some new perceptions about her chairman:

MARY (as her chairman): I can't let go. This company has always been mine. I want Mary to succeed but I can smell the paths to success and avoid the pitfalls. Mary has great experience but does not know our markets as well as I do. I can see that she is frustrated. She has some good ideas but some of them are not right for us.

Mary was not overexcited by the new perception. She could see that there were things she could do to improve matters but this was not enough to change her underlying desire to get out. Her initial frustration was increasingly obvious as she spoke about the situation. Mary identified more thorough market research and business planning as being important to getting her ideas accepted. In her enthusiasm for exploiting obvious gaps in the market, she had taken shortcuts rather than develop more professional arguments for her policies.

I asked Mary if she could explore the situation again but this time in third perceptual position, as observer; this to gain detachment and some logical processing around the issues.

ANGUS: Mary, in a moment I am going to ask you to imagine yourself remotely observing the meeting with the chairman who will be sitting there. [Points.] The meeting will be taking place as you observe what is going on.

The boardroom was big and we could get the distance she needed, up against a window at the far end. Mary was still very unhappy about the situation and needed to be a considerable distance away before she could let her feelings about it subside.

ANGUS: What's happening with Mary?

MARY (as observer): She is unhappy and increasingly reticent to talk about plans. She looks fed up. Several ideas have been blown away during the last twenty minutes. She thinks her chairman has not noticed. She is not involving the chairman, just trying to illustrate how bright she is.

ANGUS: And what about the chairman, what's going on with him?

MARY: He's unhappy too but quietly excited by some of the ideas. It's his habit to be the Devil's Advocate with everyone. He expects better arguments. Wait. All the developments in the company have his stamp on them. Mary is too possessive with her initiatives and not offering them with sufficient grace. As the major shareholder, he wants to hang onto his ownership a little longer, until Mary proves herself.

ANGUS: *If the chairman had advice for Mary, what would it be?*

MARY: Hang in. Play it my way. I want you to succeed.

ANGUS: And you, the observer, *if you have advice for Mary, what is that advice?*

MARY: Do more research, exhibit more grace, acknowledge the master, give him some of your ideas as if you had rejected them and allow him to repossess them as his own.

Linguistic tip
If you (or the chairman) had advice for Mary,
what is that advice?

We have already seen an example of this intervention on Brian's timeline. These questions are useful devices for finding positive advice and solutions from logical thought. The perceptual positions enable such emotional distance. Having determined what the positive advice or solution is, the coachee is typically invited to accept that view when back in the first position.

Mary then came back to the room and our session. I asked her to go back to the meeting as herself. She returned once again to that appropriate chair. I asked her to accept the advice from both her chairman and a very wise observer who had a gift for her. Using her own words, exactly as she had spoken them, I gave her the advice and asked for her reaction.

MARY: It's good advice. I'm going to give it four more months and adopt new strategies of approach. I shall make better business plans as if I was producing for all the shareholders. I have two project ideas that I have not dared bring forward. I am going to discount their value and ask the chairman to look at them as if I had pretty much rejected them and see if he will take the bait. I don't care if he pushes the boat out as long as they get a good airing and the projects can be floated.

The use of receiving advice and solutions from the second and third perceptual positions is a good illustration how a coachee can find sustained, motivated actions from within. This is true coaching at its best, and the coach merely facilitates the innate ability of individuals to solve and learn from their own challenges.

Mary got through the four months but not without further set-backs. The chairman was susceptible to her subterfuge and picked up several ideas that Mary had "rejected". Two major initiatives were started, one later dropped, and the other made early gains. It took another eighteen months before the chairman suddenly took a back seat and retired overseas. By then, Mary's relationship with him was better. Although this was far from ideal, Mary was able to get on with her job without daily interference.

My boss is embarrassing me

Rosie came to see me privately. She worked in HR consultancy, successfully selling a personality-profiling instrument. She had been in her present company for just three months and already was turning over large amounts of business. She was on a revenue percentage and earning more than the established partners. She came to our session straight from work, carefully groomed and with pages of hastily written notes detailing incidents and dialogue that had upset her. Rosie appeared to be dressed for the evening rather than for work, sheer stockings, high-heels, and an unusually short skirt.

She complained of not being able to sleep, of feeling stressed, and being very anxious. She hated going into work but felt compelled to keep striving in spite of the environment. Most of the problems involved her main boss, Robert. He was negatively judgmental about some of her language and phrases when she was speaking to customers on the telephone. He would even complain about her in front of other staff to make an example of how not to relate with customers, in his view. In fact, Rosie was already ahead of anyone else that month in signing new business. Additionally, most of her signing was made without seeing clients; her ability to inspire confidence and establish friendly rapport on the phone was obviously exceptional.

Coaches are mortal and a thought came into my mind that Rosie might have been hired because of her sales history but might not fit the culture. I put those thoughts away and gave her my full attention. During the course of our first session Rosie started to deal with her insomnia. She committed to establishing a pattern of behaviors before going to bed. Evidently, she had no pattern before that and had a history of sleeplessness. Owing to the stress and anxiety, this was worse and she was waking in the early hours. The idea was that her new pattern would settle her down to a relaxed and familiar state before going to bed. This included things that she used to bother with when younger but had given up on: warm bath, hot drink, reading something easy for ten minutes. We also looked for a resourceful state that she could anchor and use when feeling anxious or stressed. This simply means having a mental state, an **anchored state**, that is positive and can be accessed at will.

Anchored state

It is useful to access resourceful states at will. In order to do this the coachee is asked to think of a resourceful experience, or an invented one, that is positive, easily entered into, and easily repeated. To anchor this resourceful state the experience of having that state is linked to a trigger, sometimes a physical touch, imagined image or sound, as illustrated earlier with the Chopin phrase. By carefully anchoring the state with this trigger and repeating this several times, one links the two events. When this is properly done, the trigger will automatically initiate the state. Jill Dann (2003) suggests that, when introducing positive anchored states for the first time, it is useful first to explore negative anchored states that are already part of the coachee's response to events around them. These might include highly negative behaviors triggered by certain people or their views. Having realized that they already have anchors, the coachee has improved willingness to explore anchoring as a positive tool for changing negative patterns of response.

ANGUS: Rosie, can you recall a really good feeling when you have been with work colleagues?

Rosie could. If she had not been able to, then I would have asked for a situation outside the work context.

ROSIE: I have been given a citation at work. It's two years ago. I sold more business in one month than anyone has done in the history of the company. My boss and the MD are there. I am standing and all the team are standing and clapping. My boss is showing the citation and is shaking—holding, really—my hand. I do not think we have ever had physical contact before. I have a wave of heat across my chest and it is coming here.

(She points and touches just below her ribcage.)

ANGUS: Hold onto that experience of heat *if you will*. Try to repeat that touch of your finger at the point where that wave of heat has come. Maintain that touch as long as the heat is there.

Linguistic tip
If you will

Coaches should think of their interventions as gifts to be offered. It is not the job of the coach to drag the coachee by the hand and lead them to those gifts. Phrases like "if you will" and "in your own time" reinforce the coachee's experience that the coaching session and its direction is in their control. This is important. When the coachee has success, those successes will add to their self-confidence (if they truly feel that they did the work).

Rosie continued in her resourceful state for some time. I invited her to remove her finger pressure as the state diminished. Her attention came back into the room and she started to talk about it and ask about the finger contact. I gave her a brief explanation of anchoring and invited her to return to that resourceful state, then replace her finger at the same spot, keeping it there and at the same pressure until the state diminished or until she chose to come out of that state. Our session had to end before we could fully establish the anchor, but she felt able to practice at home.

By the time she returned three days later she was easily able to get into her resourceful state, and out of it again. I had explained that there would be further steps and she was keen to start. Having run through the same procedure of inducing the resourceful state and making the finger contact, we moved on. "When you're ready," I said, "place your finger in the same place as before and see what happens."

Rosie immediately went back into her resourceful state as a result. The anchor was set. The resourceful state was triggered by the finger contact instead of vice versa. I explained that she could get rid of the anchor by touching in the same way when holding onto a different state. Rosie practiced some more times to induce her resourceful state by finger contact. I then asked her to consider making the finger contact mentally rather than physically. She sought some more information before she was ready. I told her that I wanted her "to imagine" that she was moving her finger to that same spot and with the same pressure but without actually doing it physically. When Rosie tried this, she found that she could do it but the effect was not quite as profound. With practice, she was soon able to get back to nine out of ten scores she had been getting when she had actual finger contact. Rosie now had a resourceful state that she could even use in public without needing to make any physical movement.

Anchors are, I think, best established in ways that reflect the actual experience of the coachee. Sometimes, when there is a physical act, the coachee finds it harder, as Rosie did, to transpose the anchor to one that is merely imagined. In other cases the anchor may not be a physical sensation at all. We saw that Emily's anchor was a phrase from a Chopin piano concerto. Some coachees have visual anchors that they use to trigger resourceful states. In coaching I have had the privilege to hear many and these have included faces, a hot-air balloon, an album cover, a key, a wooded area, a dolphin, and many more.

It is possible, where an anchor is required at work, to set it with contact between two opposing fingers so that it can be done surreptitiously. Practitioners of qi gong have used this Oriental technique for thousands of years before it was reinvented as a tool of NLP.

I am being bullied to stay on after work

Kathie came to me privately. In her view, her boss, Alan, was poorly organized but was not amenable to help or change. Her main issue was that Alan would give her work late in the day and want it prepared for him that evening. She came to realize that he was happy to be *seen* working late but, once other managers had gone, he would be anxious to leave and would press her to work faster. It was getting her down. We established that her job could not be compromised by her refusing to work overtime: she had no overtime arrangement in her contract of employment.

She gave me an example of a typical scenario as she remembered it:

ALAN: I need this for a presentation tomorrow.

KATHIE: I'm just leaving for a dinner party, Alan. I should have left already.

ALAN: Everybody is late for dinner parties. It's only a simple thing, and if you're quick won't take long.

KATHIE: I'm being picked up from my house and have to change. I don't have enough time.

ALAN: I'm sure they'll understand the importance of your work. The longer we spend talking about it the longer it will take you to finish.

(He walks away.)

I did not want to give Kathie helpful scripts of my own and so asked her if she could come up with some herself, having given some examples. We took the above dialogue as a model for finding some new scripts for Kathie. Here is one wording she came up with:

KATHIE: I have an important appointment and can't be late. I'm sorry but I have to go.

ANGUS: Imagine that you're in a shop having been back once before with faulty goods. You've been kept waiting and it's now almost closing time. The floor manager is saying to you, "I have an important appointment and can't be late. I am sorry but I have to go." What do you experience now?

KATHIE: I would be irritated. I am irritated. They have not heard my problem.

ANGUS: So how would you improve the manager's script to make it more satisfactory but without giving you what you want?

KATHIE: "I'm sorry I would like to help you now but I can't. I simply have to go. However, if you're happy to leave the goods with the receipt and your name and address, I'll deal with it tomorrow. Oh, let me have your telephone number and I'll call you tomorrow if I need anything else."

ANGUS: How can you apply that same strategy to your response to Alan when he is saying to you, "I need this for a presentation tomorrow"?

KATHIE: "I'm sorry. I'd like to do this for you now but I can't. I have to go to a dinner party now. I'll try to come in early and do it then for you."

ANGUS: And can you take out information and still make the message clear?

KATHIE: He doesn't need to know it's a dinner party.

ANGUS: Here's what you said written down. [Hands her his notes.] Can you take the dinner party out and anything else but convey the same message? The aim is to keep the script simple so that he can't attack parts of your argument.

KATHIE: "I'm sorry. I would like to do this for you now but can't. I'll do it first thing in the morning."

ANGUS: How many individual messages are there in those two short sentences?

KATHIE: Messages?

ANGUS: Yes. For example, "I'm sorry" stands by itself. How many other parts of the sentences stand on their own as individual messages?

KATHIE: "I'm sorry" is one. "I would like to do this now" is another. "I can't" is a third. "I'll do it in the morning" is a fourth.

ANGUS: Good. Three messages are ideal, as it gives us about twelve different message combinations by using the messages as individual or combined phrases. You have four messages and that is OK if they are simple enough to recall.

I then introduced Kathie to the "broken-record technique." This is simply a means of repeating the same scripts without embellishment. This prevents a bully from finding new angles and countering arguments. I provided examples:

(1): I want it now.

(2): I'd like to give it to you now but can't. Call tomorrow and my manager will be here to see you.

(1): That's not good enough. Why can't you do it?

(2): I wish I could but I can't. My manager will be here to see you tomorrow.

(1): Give it to me now and tell the manager tomorrow if you must.

(2): I'd like to give it to you but can't. Call tomorrow and my manager will be here to see you.

Kathie agreed to rehearse her script so that she might feel better able to deal with a likely future situation. I would adopt the position of Alan and she would respond accordingly. Kathie provided me with some sentences that were typical of Alan and she coached me to say the words and phrases in the right tone. Kathie also chose another chair that would represent where she was at work and told me where I would stand to harass her (as her boss). As we know, the physical movement of a coachee can help stimulate (mental) state change. Kathie would be walking to her "work chair" to resist evening work in a contrived future scenario. She would be being herself in that state and I would role-play.

ANGUS (Alan): I need this for a presentation tomorrow.

KATHIE: I'm sorry. I'd like to do this for you now but I can't. I'll do it first thing in the morning.

ANGUS (Alan): I need it in draft tonight so I can make revisions in the morning. Here.

(Holds out hand with papers in it.)

KATHIE (restraining to not take papers): I'm sorry. I'd like to do this for you now but I can't. I'll do it first thing in the morning.

ANGUS (Alan): How does that help?

KATHIE: I'm sorry. I'll do it first thing in the morning.

ANGUS: What's so important that you can't place this work first?

KATHIE: I'd like to do this for you now but can't. [Picks up her handbag.] I'll do it first thing in the morning. Goodnight, Alan. I'm sorry.

Kathie had instinctively used one or more of the four individual message phrases in different orders so that she did not sound like a recorded message. She refrained from saying, "It's not your business where I'm going" or anything else that might further anger Alan.

Often in this situation, the change in the dynamic (of bullying) can create a difference in the scenario. It was quite possible that Alan would become more physically agitated if frustrated in his pattern of control. We discussed this and Kathie thought it most unlikely. However, she decided that she would leave earlier from that point onward and try out her new skills when people were still in the building. The strategy was successful.

Another approach that Kathie might have used, and one supported by Jean Kelly (2002), would have been for Kathie to "**model**" other people in her organization who were not bullied. **Modeling** would have involved my asking her to think about successful strategies that colleagues used and then try to emulate those strategies herself, perhaps doing some role work with me in preparation. It might also have been useful for her to "anchor" a resourceful state, using an element of some past experience of being powerful and in control as a trigger for that.

If they cannot think of someone like that, I would ask them to think of a time when they have been strong themselves (maybe in a very different situation or even with the problem person) and invite them to anchor how this was.

Bullies, like those who sexually harass, operate from emotional/psychological weakness, not strength. They like to think of themselves as tough but they are invariably covering up for inherent weakness in their characters. These behavioral characteristics are often targeted on one person whom they perceive as more vulnerable than they are. If one can safely change that dynamic, then the bully or pervert may be frustrated. In an ideal situation, organizations have policies and procedures for these eventualities. They will also have training programs and other supporting interventions for staff who are subjected to possible abuse and for those people who exhibit these inappropriate behaviors.

Modeling
Emulating successful mental states (mindsets) and strategies

The tools of modeling are from NLP. The most influencing component of success is mental attitude, or "state". Modeling attempts to understand the mindset of a successful person (or people) and then "take it on" oneself. Thus, one might find that, by "borrowing" a set of empowering beliefs—a value, a sense of self, and so on—from a successful person, one can create a resourceful state for dealing with one's own issue. Furthermore, this state can then be anchored to provide a resource state instantly, as required.

> Modeling does not involve physical skills and practical expertise. If you need to jump a ravine, then some suitable sports coaching is also advised!

The senior partner will not appoint me to the main board

Judith is a city dweller, single, agitated, work-focused and dedicated. She is slick and hard, and colleagues find her difficult to gauge. In her legal work, Judith sets her own standards and does not suffer fools gladly. Apparently, she was clinical in her relationships with colleagues and clients. She spoke in sharp bursts. Her work within the firm was respected in terms of its sheer weight and quality. She had been with the firm for eighteen years and in spite of her seniority and contribution had not been invited to join the main board. Judith had tried to argue her case for full partner status with the senior partner, Giles, but he said that board appointments were not made because of revenue earned or time with the firm, rather because of the contribution that members brought to the management of the firm. Judith believed this to be an excuse for not elevating her or rewarding her financially at the next level. Having first established why she wanted coaching and some working level of rapport, I asked some questions to try to encourage a wider perspective of her issue. Her answer was typical and included this example:

ANGUS: What do you imagine that other colleagues think of you and your situation?

JUDITH: Naturally, they see me as effective and clearly that I am overdue for promotion.

I tried a different approach.

ANGUS: Judith, do you recall the exact words that Giles used when he turned you down?

JUDITH: Yes, he said I'm good at what I do but the appointments are not based on revenue or service.

ANGUS: So, his exact words were …?

JUDITH: It was last Tuesday at three in the afternoon. I remember what he said exactly: "You do good work for the firm and have a heavy case load but neither of these are relevant to appointments to the board. Neither is length of service. Appointments are only made when additional management and strategic skills could strengthen the board."

ANGUS: Judith, in a moment, I would like to ask you to place yourself back into that room with Giles. I want you to try to experience what it was like exactly and imagine that I am Giles. Can you do that? And, if you will, do we need to reorganize the room to help reconstruct that meeting?

JUDITH: I am not sure I see the point but will try. You should be behind that table.

ANGUS: OK [moving], let me know when you are ready.

When she was ready, I paused while waiting to see if her state would become more obviously emotionally associated with her recall of that meeting. I had written down the words that Giles had said and, emulating the pace and intonation as she had related them, I read them back to her. Judith shrank down about an inch but showed no obvious emotion in her face. I moved out of Giles's chair.

ANGUS (emulating): You seem to have shrunk like this. *Can you exaggerate that?*

Judith looked at me as if I were entirely mad, just for a fleeting moment, and then copied my movement, shrinking down into the chair. As she did so, tears rolled down her face and the energy seemed to wash away from her. The movement she had initiated contained "**associated emotion**" that she, as a pattern of behavior, was ignoring. Because I asked her to exaggerate the movement, the emotion became more intense and she associated into the situation she was recalling. Conscious of me, I suppose, she scrabbled to find her purse. I encouraged her to remain where she was. I remained neutral but attentive. Her tears continued while she

63

stared into the middle distance. After some minutes, I said, "Sometimes it's hard to be turned down, especially when you feel you deserve something."

Linguistic tip
Can you exaggerate that?

This intervention comes from the discipline of co-counseling (see for example Evison, Horobin, 1990) and is used when a nonverbal expression in the physical body (or sound) is made and appears significant. The coachee is invariably unaware of the expression and an encouragement to exaggerate it can help them get a more powerful sense of what the expression means to them.

These tics or mannerisms can hold powerful metaphoric significance. Lawley and Tompkins (2000) describe a client's response to noticing that her hand was patting the arm of her chair as, "It's how I keep my emotions down." While I do not intend to develop this further here, readers are invited to see my reading list if interested in their approaches.

Associated and dissociated emotional states

Judith appeared to have a physical manifestation attached to her emotional state. Emotion is critical to motivation and demotivation and the coach needs to be alert to the coachee's level of emotional "connectedness" to their material. This connectedness is sometimes called *emotional association*; the contrary state of "detachment," which is termed *emotional dissociation*. The coach will find clues in body language and in the coachee's speech. Is the coachee speaking dispassionately and logically about their issues or are they deeply involved?

To help the coachee to get as much useful information as possible from their coaching experiences we may often choose an exaggerated position. If they are to have high emotional involvement, then the language and support of the coach will be encouraging emotional association. Where there is already excessive or destructive emotional association with an issue, it can be helpful to encourage the coachee to have a more objective, dissociated state in order to appeal to their reasoning powers. We can use physical distance and time to help the coachee achieve that dispassionate perspective, thus:

"Now, Judith, we have moved forward some years in time: from here you can see Judith there in that situation with Giles. What advice could you give Judith that would have made a difference back then?"

The associated state is helped by using reflective language in the present tense: "And when it's hard to be turned down, especially when you feel you deserve something, what is that 'turned down' like?"

There was another run of tears before Judith looked at me for the first time in many minutes, sat up, and wiped them from her eyes. Her voice was cracking.

JUDITH: I've worked my butt off all my life to keep ahead of people's expectations. My father worked overseas and I never had his approval. I think that's why I work so hard. Giles has made me feel like I did as a girl.

The last sentence is normally a cue for the coach to challenge the origin or etiology of the emotion. Giles could not *make* Judith feel anything. Ultimately, she might be able to exercise choice about how she reacts to comments from Giles and others, but this might be a longer problem and one best supported by more person-centered intervention. I decided to leave the issue and help her look for resources within her competence at the time.

ANGUS: If you're right and Giles sees you as a girl, is it likely that he would welcome you to the board?

JUDITH: No. You're right. I need to think again.

ANGUS: I don't know about being right or not. If you were to think again now about how to establish a relationship with Giles in which you are not the girl, what are you thinking of doing?

This question stays with Judith's frame of reference, working with thought and looking for action. It also brings the tense into the present to help her hold state, as we saw with Brian with his issue of the keynote speech.

JUDITH: I've been needing this promotion. I deserve it. My inclination now is to be frank with Giles and tell him that I want the recognition and reward that comes with promotion, whether appointed to the board or not. I want to meet with him and ask him what skills I have, or can research, or enhance to be of value to the board. I wish to know if, when I acquire those skills, whether he will support me at some time in the future.

ANGUS: And when can you have that conversation?

JUDITH: I have a regular meeting every Friday at eight thirty a.m., and we raise any issues we wish to at that time after discussing actual cases. I will take this up with him this Friday morning.

My question was designed to encourage Judith to define her target. In NLP, this is part of the "**well-formed outcome**", although establishing a realistic target and a calendar of actions to get to that target are standard project-management skills.

Well-formed outcome

The well-formed outcome is one of the four pillars of NLP along with sensory acuity, flexibility, and rapport. The coach may use any number of outcome models to help the coachee test their strategies and these may include SMART and GROW (*goal* setting, *reality* checking, *options* and *what/when/whom*). In any case, the essential clues to realistic and achievable targets have to do with the following:

- personal control
- specific

- simply and positively stated
- an understanding of the benefits of achieving and not achieving
- personal cost of achieving the target
- an understanding of the cost to those closest to them
- strategic planning
- an understanding of all resources
- specific time-frames
- internal commitment
- having a motivating (emotionally rewarding) outcome that fits with the coachee's values and purpose
- a real experience of having already achieved the target

Note that a number of these issues include the wider context, or ecology, of the outcome, including relationships that may be affected. The coach will help the coachee make sure that these aspects are all well considered and check directly with the coachee for their level of commitment (in space and time) to that strategy.

Stuck in a corner

Many issues among managers are generated by a lack of perceived choice. This is particularly true among cultures that promote people to management without providing training and development in order to encourage solutions thinking. Coaching and mentoring offer rapid means to broaden the horizons of an executive both for the specific issue and in a broader context. If properly coached, they learn one or more new tools that they can apply in other situations and contexts.

Where coachees experience being stuck, they lack choice; the coach's job includes opening up of their perspective by encouraging conscious perception and thereby, new choices. Questioning and challenge are at the heart of that encouragement.

Project-management problem

Julian was recently promoted to project manager but had received no formal training and no PM software to support his new role. He said that he was undertrained and underresourced. Further, his immediate boss, having given him his first sizable project, had gone overseas for four weeks. Julian was clearly stressed and very much associated with his issue. I asked him to define the project, for his benefit, but its complexity meant that, in his current state, he was unsure about prioritization. I thought that some emotional detachment might help, so I asked a question that could take him into the contrived second position.

ANGUS: Julian, imagine for a moment that you are me. Sitting over there [pointing] is a skilled engineer who has been given a new project to manage. It's pretty big. On paper at least, he is under-trained and underresourced. What advice can you give him?

JULIAN (Angus): The issues are largely about prioritization and those are only difficult to define because of his inexperience. He has colleagues who do project management, although not by that job title, in other parts of the company. With their knowl-edge of how things get done, they should be able to help him prioritize the plan and then discuss the outline with the key partners.

ANGUS: And how is he best advised to seek help from these col-leagues?

JULIAN (Angus): If people ask me for advice I'm always ready to give it. If he were to appeal to his colleagues' willingness to help, he will have a good chance of getting the help he needs.

I engaged Julian to get him back into our dynamic and then reflected his own advice.

ANGUS: OK, Julian. We have some expert advice from someone who understands your problem very well. In essence, the advice for you is this: you have colleagues who do project man-agement, effectively, in other parts of the company. With their knowledge of how things get done, they should be able to help you prioritize the plan and then you can discuss your outline with the key partners in the process.

It never ceases to amaze me how simply people solve their own problems if the problem is externalized. Julian had been "internal" with his problem; by asking him to help a fictional person with the same issue, and making that situation as real as possible, he was able to advise himself. The result was swift and effective action that also helped him to establish co-working relationships across the company. So much of the work that coaches do would be unnecessary if schools trained children how to learn and how to have conscious perception about their issues. Once learned, these tools can be applied effectively again, and again in any context.

An unpopular new protocol

Philip was stuck. A new audit system had been introduced for all purchasing over a certain value. The new approval form had been thrust upon the whole company from their international head office and was unpopular because it was complicated, inflexible, and time-consuming. Approval forms had to be sent via their intranet for passing at two levels, national and international, before an order could be raised. Philip loved his job but took exception to both the process and the vernacular of the new forms. He also did not like some of the parts that had to be completed if the approval was to be given. They included future-pricing pre-dictions that in many cases had to be invented, because his suppliers were unwilling to enter into commercial discussions about future price without a contract. In practice, Philip was holding orders back because he found the forms onerous; he had a signifi-cant backlog, which, if not cleared quickly, would compromise his position. He said that, if he completed the forms, he felt angry and resentful and these feelings influenced his motivation and work effort. If he did not fill in the forms, work was held back and he felt frustrated and demotivated.

ANGUS: Philip, in your work, what are the two or three most important things you **value** about what you do and achieve?

PHILIP: I get value for money without crippling my suppliers and have good working relationships with them all. I'm always ahead of expectations. I contribute to the business.

 Values and motivation

Values are very important in influencing beliefs and behaviors. As Philip appeared to have a dilemma at the level of identity or value, my question was pitched at this high level in order to help him restructure what was important in deciding what to do. For more on the motivational impact of values and identity, see 'Hierarchy of logical levels' in Chapter Three.

ANGUS: As someone who clearly contributes and is always ahead of expectations, how is your experience now of having a backlog of orders?

PHILIP: I feel frustrated with myself.

ANGUS: And what is this "frustrated with myself" experience like?

This question invites the possibility of a metaphor. It does not always work but Philip had a metaphor and shared it with me.

PHILIP: It's like trying to get through a dark doorway with a big, shadowy faceless figure in the way, like filling in the whole doorway.

ANGUS: A big, shadowy faceless figure is in the way of the dark gateway. *What else?*

PHILIP: He is the stupid policy geek buried somewhere at headquarters; his pockets are full of useless statistics; he's a lightweight but is filling up that gateway and I want to get past him, push him over, but he's wedged in.

ANGUS: This wedged-in geek is filling up the gateway and you want to get past him, push him over. How can you change this situation to make that possible?

I was inviting Philip to find a solution that might make the doorway bigger or float away, that might make the policy geek shrink.

PHILIP: I have a pin-stick on my desk. Completed orders go on that. I'm pushing it into the geek's stomach and he's just a bag of wind; he's shriveling, going translucent pink, and the papers are drifting away in the wind. There's just a pink mat with the words "You're welcome" written on it.

ANGUS: And you pushed the pin-stick into his stomach and he's shriveled down to a pink mat with the words "You're welcome" written on it. *What happens next?*

PHILIP: I skip over and through. The gateway is polystyrene, breaking up and is flying away. All my orders are on the stick. The phone's ringing.

 Linguistic tip
What happens next? How is this different?
What else?

These questions are designed to encourage the development of the symbolic world of the coachee and to explore it more widely. A fuller description of these interventions is described in the sections "Clean language" and "Symbolic modeling" in Chapter Five.

ANGUS: And this experience of the pin-stick and shriveling geek, the pink mat and the gateway flying away, then you find your orders all on the pin-stick. *How is this different* from, where you were before, a shadowy faceless figure in the doorway?

PHILIP: I was stuck but I had the solution all along. It's my pin-stick. I stab that geek every time I bang an order down on it!

ANGUS: So what is the likelihood of your completing the orders on your desk within the time frame you mentioned earlier, zero through ten?

PHILIP: Total, ten plus!

Philip had explored his metaphor and found a new solution, literally right in front of him on his desk. No external factor had changed, just his perception of it. This is another example of the benefits of conscious perception, this time by involving his metaphors. The example is different from others so far in that one of the questions was to encourage him to adapt and change his negative image of the gateway by using color, light, texture, and so on to change the way he experienced the situation. These parameters of sensory information are termed **submodalities** and are widely encouraged in coaching and NLP therapy. In this case, Philip changed the big, shadowy figure to a pink bag of wind and then to a doormat with words on it; he changed the dark gateway to something made of polystyrene. This just broke up and blew away. With submodalities we can encourage changing perception of any experience or metaphor whether visual or not. The submodalities of a boss's voice might include a squeaky voice of Donald Duck. Smell can be changed. Visual material can be altered to reduce the size of an obstacle (as Philip did with the geek) but also to expand and lighten it until it is invisible. An obstacle can be framed and then moved so far away that it is insignificant.

Submodalities

Submodalities are simply variants in experience. In coaching, it is possible to extend the coachee's experience of the world by inviting them to focus on, and play with, those experiences. Needless to say, these ideas sprang from California in the 1960s but are no less important for that. Exploring the submodalities of experience may involve changing a visual representation, an auditory representation, or any kinesthetic (feeling) representation.

Clues to how people store information are available in their language. Phrases like "I see what you mean" and "I think I grasp that idea" suggest that the representations of these ideas are tied in with preferred mental (including emotional) representations. Inviting a coachee to experiment with the submodalities of their experiences can enable them to find more constructive ways of managing future situations and can be anchored to provide automatic support for difficult scenarios, including phobias. For a more comprehensive look at submodalities, see Bandler and MacDonald (1988).

Inner conflicts

Many issues boil down to conflicting ideas and contradictions in the mind of the coachee. Where these arise, the coach has numerous options. As always, any intervention that will encourage a wider perception will assist. The key word to listen for is *"but"*.

"I could get the report done on time but ..." If the word "but" appears and the limiting element is within the control of the coachee (whether they are aware of their control or not), then the issue is almost certainly compounded by inner conflict.

We have already demonstrated helpful techniques. These include those that take the coachee to an outer perspective on their issue. This could be to ask them to adopt the third, or "observer", position on their situation in order to seek clarity. Another method is the one I adopted with Julian, when I asked him to imagine being me, the coach. In front of him he has someone with his issue. How will he advise and help this person? This is an example of the contrived second position. Another variant of this, as used with Judith, was to ask her to imagine that she was a colleague of hers. How would that colleague see the situation? Each of these methods assists the coachee to take a view less influenced by the emotional energy that may weigh on them because of their psychological association with the issue.

Where there are two conflicting elements in an issue, it can also be helpful to help the coachee explore their conflict in an emotionally associated state.

Linguistic tip
But

When a coachee uses the word "but", the coach must be aware. "But" may be followed by a negative statement (often a limiting belief) that undermines the coachee and as illustrated by Jane when she said, "I have given brief presentations to small groups of colleagues and prospective customers which have been friendly and easy and well received but ..." "But" can also prelude the expression of an inner conflict or contradiction. In that case, the coach will wish to consider highlighting that contradiction to help raise the coachee's conscious perception.

Sales manager and driving problem

Steve had a speeding ticket and had then been surprised when the HR director subsequently summoned him to his office. He found that his line director was also there. Steve had a reputation for driving fast and the directors had decided to give him a stern warning. Another ticket would mean the removal of his car. In effect, if Steve were unwilling or unable to afford a chauffeur, he would be out of his job. In spite of this serious danger, Steve was still often driving fast. News of this had quietly reached management and so, three weeks after his first warning, Steve was provided with my time.

My first job was to see if he would engage with the coaching assignment with free will. If he would not so engage, then I would extricate myself and report to the HR director as per my contract. In either scenario, Steve would have realized that he was under pressure. This is not the best arrangement for a coach to start with. When there is a perceived issue between coachee and coach, it is the duty of the coach to approach it first before engaging in the contracted work. Having introduced myself, I continued thus:

ANGUS: Steve, there are at least two ways that you can engage in this meeting. You can try to get through without achieving any useful result. You could choose to engage with me in order to trust that something useful might be learned. I doubt that I could teach you anything, but I may help you to find skills you didn't know you had and use this effectively in your work. Or maybe there are other options available to you.

STEVE: I could walk out but know that wouldn't go down very well.

I did not reply but merely gave him my absolute attention, as before, in order that what he had just said might sink in fully.

STEVE: I could try to outwit you, play the game. If I fail to convince you I guess you would report back.

ANGUS: The content of what goes on here will remain private between me and you. I am in the service of this company specifically to help you with an issue that the company wishes to see resolved. If the company did not value you and your contribution, I would not be here. My contract with your management is simply to report on the whether we have made progress or not. If you agree to engage fully, I am going to offer you the possibility of making a shared statement, provided that it fulfills the needs that I have in reporting to ethical and professional standards.

STEVE: You win.

ANGUS: *Can you contradict that?*

STEVE: I could win by keeping my job, driving slower but being bored as hell two or three hours a day; but you would win too by getting me to play the game.

ANGUS: Whether you win or lose is entirely up to you. My job here is to support and encourage you. There is no winning or losing in that. What you achieve interests me but your choices will determine what happens here. If our session is constructive, it is because you choose to be constructive; if it is destructive, it is because you choose it to be so. What is your choice?

75

Steve agreed to work with me. I wanted him to explore what it was he gained from speeding and what boredom meant to him when driving at normal speeds.

ANGUS: What does driving fast do for you?

STEVE: It reflects my work rate, fast. I like the adrenaline rush.

ANGUS: Instinctively, how do you *experience* that adrenaline rush?

This question does not necessarily mean Steve has to specify *kinesthetic* information about his state.

STEVE: My brain is active, I am having to make decisions quickly and react, I'm in control, I feel quicker and faster than the rest, and I'm keen to get to my next sales call.

ANGUS: And the negative aspects of driving fast are?

STEVE: I may lose my license if unlucky. I would then lose my job and find it hard to get another like mine. It would be a disaster, as I've just taken on a mortgage.

ANGUS: What about being bored two or three hours a day?

STEVE: I spend twelve or more hours a week traveling in my car. When I drive slow, which I can, I get restless; soon the speed picks up and I am pushing the pedal again.

ANGUS: Are you in control of that or not?

STEVE: Sometimes yes, sometimes no. If the road is clear I will make a go for it; at other times it just happens.

ANGUS: Sometimes it is in your control and you make a go for it; other times you are not in control. What is not being in control like for you?

STEVE: I hadn't thought about it. I know I have a problem that could get ugly for me. But I had not thought about it as a weakness of personal control.

Again, I left a considerable pause for that to sink in before asking another question.

ANGUS: You said earlier that when you drive fast [reading] you make quick decisions and react fast, that you are in control. Now you seem to be saying that sometimes you exhibit a weakness of personal control when you drive fast. *How do you resolve that?*

STEVE: I can't. If I thought it was a personal-control issue I might be able to do something about it.

Linguistic tip
How do you resolve that?

When there is contradiction in the coachee's statements, they reveal inner conflict. It is surprising how often the person is not aware of the contradiction. Both statements can be parts of an established pattern of thinking. Usually there has been no thoughtful challenge to resolve it until this opportunity. The coach is advised to address such contradictions as they arise:

- by questioning (as the example shows)
- by statement (merely repeating the two contradictions without adding any question and then waiting)
- by challenge

By using the interrogative "how?" I am inviting the coachee to remain in an analytical frame of mind by inviting logical thought.

In this example, a suitable challenge might be, "If I hear you correctly you say you are in control, and, if I hear you correctly, at the same time, that you exhibit a lack of personal control. That's interesting."

ANGUS: What are you saying? Is this your personal-control weakness issue or not? If it is your personal-control weakness issue, might you be able to do something about it or not?

STEVE: I'm unhappy that I cannot control this problem …

ANGUS: *Up until now* at least.

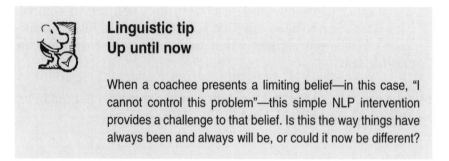

Linguistic tip
Up until now

When a coachee presents a limiting belief—in this case, "I cannot control this problem"—this simple NLP intervention provides a challenge to that belief. Is this the way things have always been and always will be, or could it now be different?

I remained silent, giving my full attention. Two or more minutes went by while Steve thought deeply.

STEVE: Sorry. It is my problem. I want to get it fixed now. I don't like the idea of being unable to control myself. I'm just stuck with the boredom. I can't imagine being able to deal with the boredom. The boredom gets me.

ANGUS: Are you saying that, up until now, the boredom is more powerful than your own self-control?

STEVE: Unfortunately, yes, I am.

I again stayed silent to let Steve allow this to sink in fully. Steve was hunting for solutions and came up with the idea of doing a skilled-driving test. He had previously thought about high-speed instruction but now thought that, if he could concentrate on safety and control issues instead, he would be less bored. He agreed to try this strategy and I agreed to request funding for it. We had almost run out of time, so we both worked on a statement to the HR director. We agreed to have another short meeting to see if we could help him unhook the pattern of "boredom transforming into speed", since boredom might still arise even with some advanced driver training. At our next meeting I introduced him to the **"Pattern breaker"**.

Pattern breaker

The "pattern breaker" ties one behavioral event with a new one in order to break the pattern of experience. It works! I remember a stressful time when, while driving, I had a tendency to scratch my head. Using the pattern breaker, I found that if I moved my hand off the wheel toward my head I could say, "I do not need to do this any more" and the behavior could be stopped. Even now, if I move that hand off the wheel, I am reminded automatically of that same process and rediscover that I have a choice. Other interruptions of the pattern can include (internal) shouting and sounds or a fast alternative action, such as a sharp pinch.

ANGUS: Just before you push the pedal down, what happens?

STEVE: My concentration starts to go.

ANGUS: Anything before that?

STEVE: Just boredom. No, I drum my fingers on the steering wheel, turn the music up, and then speed up.

ANGUS: So the first thing you notice is your finger drumming on the wheel?

STEVE: That's right.

ANGUS: Let's imagine you are in the car now, this seat back is the wheel. When you start the first tap, can you think of anything that will distract you? It might be a sound, a shout or something.

STEVE: It's a loud shout in my head, "No! I am in control!"

ANGUS: OK, will you run through this now? Tap the wheel and then make the shout, "No! I am in control!" and then, if you will, add another phrase, in your own words but something like, "That was not me, I do not do this."

Steve came up with the pattern-breaker reaction, "No, I am in control!" followed by, "I no longer do that." As it happened, Steve needed the pattern-breaker device for some time until the advanced-driving bug caught him. Now his mind is busy checking his speed, improving his precision in both road positioning and speed control, and scanning for hazards. He is, apparently, an exemplary driver.

Inner conflicts are sometimes amenable to exploring what I call the leader and follower elements of inner conflict. This involves a process that the NLP fraternity sometimes calls chunking up and chunking down, a process for finding out key psychological drivers and inhibitors within an internal conflict. The process does not always lead to resolution but invariably improves conscious perception and opens up areas for research and action. Here is an example.

Promotion possibility—go for it or not?

Jon is an executive in an IT business. He had been in his current post for just eleven months. An opportunity at the next level of seniority had come up in another department, in the same building. Jon had been procrastinating over his application and, if he did not act quickly, the deadline would pass. Most coaching assignments do permit the subject of job satisfaction/internal promotion, and this assignment allowed such development.

Leader's question and follower's question
Chunking up and chunking down

The leader's question is: "What does [that] do for you?"

The follower's question is: "What stops you [from ...]?"

The leader's question (McLeod, 2000), repeated over and over (and reflecting the coachee's language) is designed to find the overarching motivator for achieving a target. In the

> same way, the follower's question is used to elicit what is at the core of resistance to change.

Having talked over the issue, I asked Jon the **leader's question** ("What does [something] do for you?"). I also used reflective language to help keep him emotionally associated with his material.

ANGUS: What does the promotion do for you?

JON: More money and self-direction.

ANGUS: And what do more money and more self-direction do for you?

JON: Greater freedom of choice.

ANGUS: And what does greater freedom of choice do for you?

JON: It's a feeling of wellbeing.

ANGUS: And this feeling of wellbeing, what does that feeling of wellbeing do for you?

JON: I feel taller, cooler, happier.

ANGUS: And, when having a feeling of wellbeing, when you are feeling taller, cooler, happier, what does feeling taller, cooler, happier do for you?

JON: I get ... I have a warm feeling inside my chest that lifts and fills me.

ANGUS: And this warm feeling that is inside your chest is lifting and filling you. So what does that do for you?

JON: It's the best way to be.

ANGUS: And this best way to be, what does this best way to be do for you?

JON: I can do anything.

ANGUS: And this best way to be when you can do anything, what does that "I can do anything" do for you?

JON: That's it! When I have this warm feeling, I feel I can do anything!

During this process, Jon had been increasingly engaged. Observers who watch a coaching session and hear the repetitive nature of the phrasing can think it rather contrived. However, when they experience it first-hand there is no longer any doubt about its effectiveness in helping to maintain a focused state. The exact repetition of the language is designed to maintain state and is wonderfully effective in all coachees. I have never known anyone resist the language, even though some people in an audience do sometimes think it odd.

Jon now had a compelling reason to lead himself toward his target of being promoted. Now it was time to find out the inhibiting side of his issue by asking the follower's question, "What stops you?"

ANGUS: Jon, you said you want to apply for the new job. So, what stops you?

JON: I don't want to let my boss down **and** I'm nervous about what it will be like to fail my application.

Here were two separate issues and I decided to offer them by **splitting lines of questioning**.

ANGUS: What stops you going for the new job *and* not letting your boss down?

 Splitting lines of questioning

Coachee: I do not want to let my boss down and I am nervous about what it will be like to fail my application.

Where the coachee comes up with two quite separate issues in answer to the follower's question, I find it helpful to split the

> lines of questioning and deal with just one at a time, as in the example, so the coachee has total concentration within each issue independently. When the coachee has come to find the key inhibiting issue to the first issue (and we hope an insight how to move beyond it), the coach can come back to the other line of questioning.

JON: I can seek his advice and support and anyway leave my post in good order.

ANGUS: So what stops you doing that?

JON: Nothing.

I started the second line of questioning:

ANGUS: What stops you feeling OK if your application fails?

JON: Losing face with colleagues.

ANGUS: You application has failed, so what stops you keeping face with your colleagues?

JON: Lack of bravado.

ANGUS: What stops you having more bravado?

JON: Nothing. If I thought about it, I can do it. I will tell people what I am doing and why, how I think my chances are, and will discuss with some of the them the consequences for me of winning or losing the appointment.

ANGUS: Do you have some actions, then?

JON: I will see my boss right after our session here. He's expecting me anyway. After that, if I have his support, I will talk first with Brian and Jenny over lunch today about my plans. I will get some feedback from them about my chances and about the consequences of getting or losing the appointment, and for my relationship with them, too.

ANGUS: And how certain, zero through ten, are you to discuss this with your boss right after this session?

JON: Ten.

ANGUS: And how certain, zero through ten, assuming his support, are you to discuss this with Brian and Jenny at lunch today?

JON: Also certain. Ten.

The leader and follower questions are excellent at helping a coachee find the prime motivators for action; as a consequence, Jon saw his issues through successfully.

Work-life quality

Dawn works very hard as the most senior director in a progressive corporation. She tended to get bogged down in her work. She wanted a better work experience. We had explored the tasks she undertook and how she prioritized them. It was clear that there were still times when the task-load became too much and she hated the experience of the treadmill.

ANGUS: You say that you dislike watching your life consumed by tasks at work but that as the leader of the organization there are a certain number of tasks that have to be done by you.

DAWN: I hate it when life is being consumed in tasks, when I seem to have responsibility for everything. If I had something more like living a satisfying life at work then the issue of more private time for me may become less important.

ANGUS: You suppose it's possible that the other issue of having more private time for yourself might be less important?

DAWN: That's right. I don't know, but see it could happen.

ANGUS: Let's explore, then, what these states are like: of having life consumed in tasks at work and of living a satisfying life at work.

DAWN: OK.

ANGUS: When the tasks are consuming you, and you seem to have responsibility for everything, what is that like?

DAWN: It's weighty, irritating, pushy.

ANGUS: And when the tasks are consuming you and it's like weighty, irritating, pushy, what is that "weighty, irritating pushy" experience like?

DAWN: It's a closet, it's crowded with people, paper, books, boxes, well lit but not organized.

ANGUS: And it terms of experiencing this state of being in the closet crowded with people, how perfectly are you in that state?

DAWN: Ten. I am here in the closet.

We explored this metaphor of the closet some more before asking the feedback question, and I had many choices of how to proceed. It was very clear that Dawn had powerful visual representations of her state and that these dominated her experience. In repeatedly talking about her "experience" of her state, all the descriptive material she was offering, while in that state, was visual. I decided to explore a more positive way of being.

ANGUS: And, when you feel like you are living satisfying life at work, what is that "living a satisfying life at work" like?

DAWN: It's rare but it's like being in my porch at home. It's wonderful looking at the trees. First, I am mentally restful, and then I become physically restful. That is very important.

ANGUS: And that being in the porch looking at the trees when you are mentally restful and now physically restful; what is that being in the porch like?

DAWN: Wonderful, I can see the trees.

ANGUS: And if there was something about the trees and about being mentally restful and physically restful that is representative of how this is, what is that *representative* thing like?

DAWN: A big green tree.

ANGUS: Do you experience that big green tree now?

DAWN: Totally, it's wonderful.

ANGUS: OK, let's come back to the room.

We spent some time reproducing the big-green-tree "state" and it was very quickly anchored.

Because Dawn was so exquisitely visual and so flexible in moving into and out of state, I decided at our next meeting to offer her a technique for changing her experiences of being in the closet at work. This is an NLP tool called the **SWISH pattern** (see for example Hall and Belnap, 1999) and involves the automatic linking of visual images *and* the states that are associated with them. The idea is to change a negative pattern of "being" into a (visually represented and desired) new experience. She was willing, and so we started by checking that she could revisit the two states easily and with high reality.

 ### SWISH pattern

The SWISH pattern is an NLP tool devised to help the coachee replace a negative experience with a positive one, using visual submodalities. The word "submodality" is NLP-speak for variants in experience. The SWISH pattern is simply a trigger-and-shoot mechanism for changing emotional state using visual images as the tools of change.

The SWISH can be offered to highly visual coachees who have a habitual experience that they dislike and would like to change. It depends upon the coachee's having real emotional association both with their current pattern (in visual representation) and with a preferred state. The SWISH deploys habitual association to create the second experience when it is triggered by the first.

In Step 1, the coachee is invited to enter the state that they dislike by returning to a recent example and seeing the (cue) image (within a border) and experiencing as much as they can. When this is complete, the coach invites the coachee to "clear the screen." This is repeated to get to scores eight and above (scale 0–10).

Step 2 sees the coach invite the coachee to imagine a pleasant picture (target image) of how they would like their experience to be. The coach encourages the coachee to alter the submodalities of that experience toward an even more comfortable and positive experience using illumination, color, brightness, tone, back lighting, distance and texture, for example. This is repeated, as above.

In Step 3, the coach explains that the target image will be shrunk down into the corner of the cue image and it will expand and brighten as the cue picture darkens and fades away. The coachee confirms they have understood and whether their subsequent experience approaches that reached during positive state in Step 2.

Step 4: The coachee repeats Step 3 more rapidly to the word "SWISH" and their responses are checked after some repeats.

Step 5: The coachee is asked to future-pace the experience by imagining a future time when a similar event could trigger their experience again. If the SWISH does not work, repeat the process.

ANGUS: In your own time, I would like you to return to the big green tree state for me.

DAWN: I'm here.

ANGUS: I would like you to do whatever is necessary to make this big-green-tree state as real and empowering as possible. That may mean both seeing the big green tree but may mean more than seeing as well: hearing and feeling.

DAWN: I'm at ten here.

ANGUS: When you choose, could you shrink the big-green-tree image down to a small dot and place it somewhere of your choosing in the image of being in the closet?

DAWN: OK. I see the closet and am here, I can see the small dot down on the right.

ANGUS: When you choose, I want you to allow the dot to expand rapidly to replace the closet image with a "SWISH" and be back in the big-green-tree state.

Dawn did this and then I asked her to make her vision blank. I waited for her state of alertness to change and then asked her to give her attention back to the room. I checked with her to what extent she had attained the two states (zero through ten). She then repeated the process of shrinking the dot and superimposing it onto the closet image about ten times or more, eventually doing it very fast and being able to score a nine or a ten for each state. We then tested the SWISH to see if it had been installed. I asked her to imagine the closet image and then asked her if anything happened. It did. As she conjured up the closet image and began to have an awareness of its negative state, the new image washed over it and she felt in her big-green-tree state, at Level 10. If this had not worked, I would have invited her to go through the process some more times before retesting. Dawn was still automatically triggering her metaphoric state a year later, and to useful effect.

With highly visual and spatially creative people like Dawn, the SWISH pattern can be quite quickly learned and installed. As with all "anchored" states, the anchor can be uninstalled by an association of a neutral experience of now (for example) with, in this case, the big-green-tree state and repeating it until the image of the big green tree no longer has the state change associated with it. The SWISH will then no longer work.

Work–life balance

Another useful way to explore inner conflicts is to explore the possibility of experiencing both sides of the conflict at the same time. This was useful for Fiona, a working mother who felt compelled to achieve at work but was limited by the time she could give to it while having some sort of family life. When at work, she wanted to stay and clear her desk to feel effective. She then felt guilty around the time that her children finished school and she was still at work. She wanted to be at home with the kids but, when she did go home, she felt guilty because there was always more to do at work the next day. The inner dialogue that accompanied this conflict reduced her feeling of performance at work and irritated her.

I said to her, "Fiona, if I hear you correctly, on the one hand you want to stay at work late and clear your desk but on the other hand you want to go home and be with your kids."

Fiona agreed and I asked her if she could imagine being at the office feeling effective and clearing her desk. I invited her to make that experience as rich as possible by using all her senses. Further, as this state became more real (say, five out of ten and rising on a scale of zero through ten), I asked her to extend one of her hands from her body straight in front of her, palm in. I suggested to her that if the experience started to reduce, or if she wished to reduce that experience of her own will, she would withdraw her hand again. Fiona chose the right hand and got to about six out of ten. When she had done enough, she withdrew her hand and I invited her to check some detail in the room and tell me how "present" she now felt. Fiona repeated this process several times until the movement of the hand was anchored to the experience. We checked this by asking her to extend her right hand, palm in, and see what happened. This time, the movement of her hand triggered the mental state rather than the other way around. She experienced the same state as before. If she had not, we would have tried repeating the process several more times before testing again.

We repeated the same process for the left hand but this time for the other state: "When you choose," I said, "imagine being at home with the kids after work and feeling entirely happy to be with them."

Using the left hand, Fiona explored this state, each time extending the hand as the state increased or maintained in intensity, and withdrawing the hand when the state reduced in intensity. Ultimately we were able to check the anchored state and she extended the left hand and instantly experienced the state as an automated response to the movement.

I then asked Fiona to return to the right-hand state, and she was immediately able to do that. Finally, I asked her to extend both hands slowly so that she might experience both states simultaneously. Fiona slowly extended her hands, palms in and hands about a shoulder width apart. Sometimes she withdrew her left hand a little and then would extend it further again. Her eyelids flickered as she concentrated on holding the two states at once. Eventually she had both hands extended and seemed calm. I invited her to move her hands together until they were touching, at her own pace. Within a minute, Fiona had both hands together.

Fiona told me afterwards that every working day she had experienced nagging voices in her head from about 4 p.m. onwards. A week later she was able to tell me that those voices had stopped. In the immediate aftermath of this exercise, Fiona made some decisions about her work and how to organize herself differently. It also meant engaging in dialogue with her husband, and this resulted in a flexible timetable so that he would be home by five at least two evenings a week. On those evenings she would work later, coming home to tuck the kids up in bed and kiss them goodnight.

Influencing

Lack of influence is a common frustration for managers. Their ideas may be taken over or stolen from them, and, when they have special knowledge that could be useful to the team, they may be ignored. They can be overlooked for promotion too. Sometimes this is because they are valuable in their role, sometimes because they do not seem capable of operating at the next level. At other times promotion does not come because they have not been given opportunities to shine. We will look at examples of coaching where a major feature has to do with influence. This will give us some insight into typical ways of helping people improve both their thinking and their impact at work.

I wish to give the paper

Diane had worked hard in the technical marketing division of a large manufacturing conglomerate. Her market-research skills were well developed and she often prepared important information in a form that was suitable for presentation by senior managers. Sometimes this would have a strategic influence on the direction of the division. Her name never appeared on the paper and she was never asked to present the findings. In most cases she did not mind, but an opportunity to present at her own professional body had come up. Her boss, David, was not a member of that body and she felt that she should present the paper herself. When she had broached it with David he had said something like, "Let's think about it. You haven't done this sort of thing before, have you?" But David did not expect an answer and quickly moved the subject on to something else. Diane felt that there was little chance that he would change his mind.

We started with second positioning. Diane was to take David's perspective at the meeting at which she raised the subject of presenting the paper. What Diane perceived was this:

DIANE (David): I value Diane's work immensely. I am most interested in what people do, not who they are. I am busy and do not like change in my department. I like things to run smoothly and efficiently. Diane is notable in being wholly reliable. She wants to present a paper but she does not carry the company by her presence in spite of her technical competence. I have never seen her present something like this.

We also explored the "third position" (observer) in the context of the meeting and Diane added these new perspectives:

DIANE (observer): Diane has little impact with David except by the delivery of her work. She does not look professional enough in David's terms. She is too informally dressed and too readily involved in her subject. She does not take in the bigger scene or widen discussion enough. She looks like a small player.

When Diane came back to the room and our interaction, she took on board these perceptions and decided on some changes in her bearing and dress. These included wearing darker and more tailored clothes. She thought that this would provide her with a feeling of increased gravitas. She felt that she could enhance this if she assumed a sense of "authority" in her area of expertise and by being more dispassionate and critical about her work.

ANGUS: What is David's preferred way of receiving information and acting upon it?

DIANE: We're email-based. David gets over three hundred a day but his secretary, Stephen, funnels stuff and prioritizes everything for David. I know that he also has a special folder, which is where David starts—that's for anything that Stephen can't immediately deal with.

ANGUS: So, if you wanted to get an idea and action from David, what might be the best way to do it?

DIANE: By email. It's possible too that I could get Stephen to bring it to the top of the pile by putting it in the special folder for me.

ANGUS: And what sort of language and information does David best respond to, do you think?

DIANE: I don't know. His stuff is all couched in corporate language, relating to aims and objectives, targets, values, and that sort of thing. Are you saying I should ask him again but in a way that he likes?

ANGUS: Would that make a difference?

DIANE: I think it would. If I get some of his stuff together that would help, but I don't feel he'll reconsider.

ANGUS: If there was another way to get David's confidence that fits in with the corporate objectives, values, and that sort of thing, *what might that be?*

Linguistic tip
What might that be?

This question is designed to help the coachee think outside the box. For those who have experienced this NLP intervention repeatedly it can also be one of the most annoying questions! Use with care! It assumes that the coachee knows the answer even though they may have said that they are stuck and do not have the answer. Miraculously, in many cases the coachee will come out with a solution or new perception as a result. A similar question is, **"And if you did know?"**

DIANE: The company wants to see greater sharing and involvement. "Cross-fertilization" is a current buzzword. I could offer to give a briefing to other departments on the same research to widen the understanding of where we are, what's happening in the competition, and the options for where we might invest in development. If I did it right, then David would support me. He would never give a briefing himself—he considers himself too high up the tree for that.

We explored the language and format of an argument that might be compelling for David. This would contain key phrases and links that he used in his own communications (where pertinent to Diane's case). She committed to a schedule of actions and to speaking with Stephen over lunch to get her mail prioritized. She would find dates for the internal briefing when David might attend too. If he thought that departmental heads from other areas might come, he would be certain to want to be there. She also decided that she would ask Stephen to make her an appointment to see David in order to speak specifically about her briefing and to get David's advice on which elements to highlight.

Diane achieved all her immediate actions. Her briefing was well received and discussed at length. David was there. Although she did not give the talk at her professional body, David invited her to travel with him for his presentation of her material and she had some consolation that he gave credit to her at the beginning of the presentation and included her name on the visuals. In discussion he referred to her several times for clarification and interpretation. Supporting him, she referred back to David and his department as well as providing stimulating comments that continued discussion well past the allocated time. There has been a real shift in their relationship for the better.

In the case of Diane, there was an issue of image that seemed to be important in achieving a new perception from Diane's boss. A change of sartorial style and bearing contributed to that. As in so many other issues of influencing, the area of communication was also vital. David preferred the written word.

Communication is often a vital component in issues of influencing. Another is understanding both the needs and drivers of others. This is not the same as getting the style of communication right (to make it accessible and interesting to the recipient(s)). Needs and drivers have to do with the motivating factors that maintain interest and may initiate an action process as well. One can intellectualize about these needs and drivers but this is no substitute for second and third positioning to gain insights. Now I detail an example where perception and communication were important parts of an issue of influencing.

My new product idea is being ignored

John is a technical manager in a high-volume manufacturing business in decorative panels and fittings for the commercial and domestic market. He had developed a simple means of varying process conditions that would allow a wider range of colors to be incorporated into the panels without compromising speed, and would have minimal cost implications. He had also established that, although the company's products were present in the DIY market, these were stored unattractively in the heavy end of the shopping areas and that volume turnover was low. By introducing color, he thought, it would be possible to repackage the product in smaller units for use by unskilled DIY shoppers. They could refresh kitchen cupboard doors for example, adding value to the product's worth and potentially increasing turnover. When he put the case to Bruce, his sales VP, John was told that the cost of running a manufacturing line on a different product was prohibitive and the volume investment too much. Discussion ended and John felt the project had received inadequate airtime.

ANGUS: What do you know about Bruce's preferred way of communicating?

JOHN: Bruce is a people person and very engaging. He can be very short with junior staff and impatient. His presentations are on overheads, very traditional except that there are never more than three bullet points, no descriptive information, and each bullet has as few words as possible.

ANGUS: So, assuming he likes this style of communication, what might be the best way of communicating with him?

JOHN: Have a meeting with a specific objective. Be brief. Maybe show or give him a presentation that is based on bullet points; no more than three per page.

It's one thing to communicate in a suitable style—it's another to motivate. I asked John to second-position Bruce in the situation where he and Bruce had discussed his project idea and it had been turned down.

JOHN (Bruce): John does not understand all the ramifications of developing new sales lines: the risks, investments, politics, and commercial arrangements. If he wants to talk about these technical issues, he should talk to the technical consultant and not to me. We have some bulk sales in large DIY stores. It's not a very significant part of our turnover, so I don't see the point of developing another product that is specific to that sector.

Having come back to the coaching session and taken on board this new perception, I asked John whether he still thought his project idea had value for the business.

JOHN: I've done some market research on refurbishment for the DIY sector and it's huge and growing. However, if you look at the products, they lack visual impact and are not well labeled. The average shopper would not know what to buy and what else they would need to do the job—I anticipate something that a first-timer could pick up and immediately see how much they needed, what other tools and fixings are involved. Even ten percent of the market would be a fiftyfold increase in our sales in this sector.

John later experienced the third perceptual—or observer—position.

JOHN (observer): Bruce regards sales as very much his own show. If the CEO wants new products or initiatives, Bruce makes sure that everything flows from him, not his staff. He is most interested in his own profile and raising overall turnover and profitability. He might accept ideas from John but is impatient, as John is too focused on technical stuff.

John provided some more information from the observer position and then came back to the coaching session. Having taken on board these insights, I asked John what he thought motivated Bruce.

JOHN: Bruce is motivated by ownership of sales and by opportunities for making stepwise increases in sales performance.

ANGUS: In communicating your ideas to Bruce and having these perceptions of what we think motivates him, how might you be advised to prepare your case?

JOHN: The case should be in the style we discussed before but I will now leave out my name on the front. He's not good with computers so, in addition to the paper copy, I'm going to give him an overhead set with his name on the front page in case he wants to discuss with his people. I'm going to put the overall sales potential right up front, including the source references. That's just for the paper copy. He'll take more notice of the market-research literature than he will of me. I'm going to ask for a very brief meeting, just a few minutes. I'm going to tell him that

I have some data that looks exciting but don't know what to do with it.

ANGUS: And, if that meeting is taking place, how satisfied are you?

JOHN: It's my best shot. I've been frustrated knowing that we're missing this opportunity. The technical folk know where this comes from so I will not go entirely without recognition even if I'm overlooked at the top. If it fails I'll let it go.

John's approach worked. Bruce apparently said very little, but raised his eyebrows when he saw the huge sales potential even with market share modestly presented. The technology became driven by sales and after a slow start rolled out through several big players in the DIY market. Since then, other manufacturing companies have emulated the products. After restructuring, John was eventually promoted to a new post as product development VP.

Chapter Three
Drivers for Change

Here we look at areas of change work and many of the techniques that help to stimulate sustained change. The use of these techniques, or tools, is illustrated by examples. We will see that many of the interventions of change and some of the motivators for change involve very personal material, even though the goals may be business ones. Such issues preoccupy the minds of executives and reduce their ability to perform. Coaching them to deal with such issues specifically and generically is a huge contribution to performance. I have chosen examples that are based on business goals (rather than life goals) but many of them involve motivations that come from outside the arena of work.

Wealth, living standards, and life expectancy are now radically higher in commercial nations. Executives are able to make lifestyle changes earlier. It becomes increasingly important, therefore, for organizations to help link business goals with personal targets. Almost all this work is being done outside of the work environment by numerous "life coaches". It will not be long before companies will offer employees life-target coaching at work. This will not be entirely altruistic: if companies will help harness the passions of their staff to develop both their work goals *and* their longer-term personal plans in one cohesive strategy, they can expect to gain commitment and dedication to work at more productive levels. Strategies involving life plans may necessarily involve an optional exit strategy from the company, including succession planning that involves the outgoing executive. Commitments at this level work both ways. How many organizations are brave enough to enter into dialogue with their executives about their plans for leaving, and to discuss, and involve them in, succession plans?

Internal dialogue and self-judgments

Many people experience a life saturated with internal conversation in their heads. Sometimes this dialogue may spill out into conversation with self-depreciating comments, "I'm not sure I should be doing this"; "I'm not good at that" and so on. If the level of stress associated with the negative dialogue is high, the individual may be motivated to avoid potential failure. This may manifest in inactivity or focus on secondary matters. High-achievers who exhibit limited abilities in certain areas sometimes have their inner dialogue to blame for their inconsistency. They are either striving or avoiding and find it hard to find a balance.

Inner dialogue can also reduce listening skills and prevent a good understanding of other people (and those people's motivations). When one's mind is busy on internal issues, it is not available for other work. At the most dysfunctional levels, people can become out of touch socially, even though they may exhibit exceptionally high (or low) skill sets in specific areas.

For those of us who aspire to be coaches, the busy head is not helpful. The most important feature of the coach is an ability to give the most exquisite attention to the coachee. Self-doubts, worrying about silence, being anxious about which question or coaching tool to use all get in the way of best attention. These quotations (Luke 4, Matthew 7) are advisory:

- "Physician, heal thyself"
- "Judge not, that ye be not judged. For with what judgment ye judge, ye shall be judged: and with what measure ye mete, it shall be measured to you again. And why beholdest thou the mote that is in thy brother's eye, but considerest not the beam that is in thine own eye?"

Where inner dialogue is manifested by the coachee or seems a likely component of a limiting pattern, then the coach should act. We have already looked at the pattern breaker. In the example given there, the coachee was trying to stop a repeated behavior. If a coachee experiences a repetitive negative inner dialogue, then the pattern breaker can be used for this dialogue too. To summarize, each time the phrase comes up, the coachee will say to themselves, something like, "That's not me. I don't need that any more." Pinching oneself at the moment the phrase comes up may enhance the effect. This will help break state and prevent the mindset that can flow from the negative internal dialogue and pattern.

Another method is to look at the submodalities of the experience and to change them. Yet another is to look for a metaphor that may represent the inner dialogue and then play with evolving or replacing the metaphor with another. Let's look at examples.

Negative voices when my sales report is due

Theo was stressed at the time of his written, monthly reports to the senior directors. It was his immediate boss, Matthew, whom he was most stressed about. Theo was getting no positive feedback from Matthew, only new targets, new directions, and off-the-cuff ideas about forecasts that were much higher than Theo imagined realistic. Theo's negative feelings about writing reports caused stress during the month but especially at the end, not just because the results were never acknowledged (even if above target) but because he dreaded discussing it with his boss. At this time, Theo would hear an internal voice. There were several typical sentences:

- You are not going to make it this month.
- You will not get the report done on time.
- You're failing. You'll be out.

It is quite common for the voices to be in the second person ("You are" rather than "I am") and may not have the person's own voice. I invited Theo to recall a recent episode and to enter as well as he could into that scenario, in the present. He said he was achieving a nine (out of ten) score.

ANGUS: **Where does the voice seem to be coming from?**

THEO: It's here behind my right shoulder. That's weird, I never thought of that before.

ANGUS: And do the other phrases you hear sometimes, [repeats phrases], do they come from behind your right shoulder there?

THEO: Yes they do.

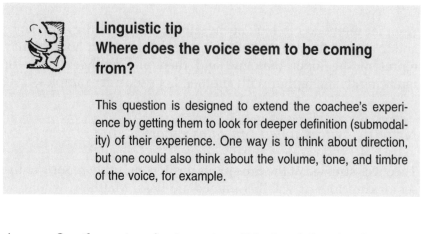

Linguistic tip
Where does the voice seem to be coming from?

This question is designed to extend the coachee's experience by getting them to look for deeper definition (submodality) of their experience. One way is to think about direction, but one could also think about the volume, tone, and timbre of the voice, for example.

ANGUS: So, the voice that's saying "You're failing"—does that voice belong to someone?

THEO: They're my words but the voice is not mine. I think it may be my father's voice or Matthew's voice. They're both very similar.

I then asked a question to see if Theo could flex the submodalities of his experience.

ANGUS: So, that voice which you hear behind your right shoulder, is saying, "You are failing" and it sounds like your father and Matthew. Can you move that voice and change it? Can you make it small or muffled? Can you make it far away?

THEO: It won't budge but I can make it tiny, like a mouse squeak.

ANGUS: And that voice is now saying "You are failing" like a mouse squeak behind your right shoulder. What about that voice now?

THEO: It's stupid and insignificant. I feel free to make my own agenda.

Theo went through this process several more times, each time checking on how he was experiencing the squeaking voice. His negative stress associated with the voice had been broken. Our session was almost over and, as each voice seemed to come from the same source and have the same characteristics, I hoped that the reframing of his experience would work for the other voices too. It did. By finding a new experience of the voice and by engaging mental activity in an alternate mental process, Theo had broken the pattern. There are many ways in which this can be done to provide a more positive (and sometimes funny) experience for the coachee. Voices can be made into cartoon voices, shapes can be stretched into arrows (and shot away), and people can be pumped up and exploded.

With Theo I might just as simply have asked the classic metaphor question: "What is that voice like?" I might have received the same answer, "It's here behind my right shoulder", or I might have had a response including a representation of that voice. This might have been a picture, sound, or totem; animals are common. These can be explored by asking the coachee to change their experience of them (submodalities) or by comparing (and linking) the negative representation to one that is welcome and desired.

I have voices about the state of my desk

Julie had a similar issue about voices but in relation to her desk. Work in progress stood in piles and prevented her from using the desk without taking the piles off, starting work, and then replacing them all. She desperately wanted to attack the work and sort it all out but could not make a start. I asked her the question, "So, the voice that says, 'I'm useless'—what is that voice like?" And she replied:

JULIE: It's like a wooden beam. One end is on my desk and I can't get past it to work. It's solid, heavy, dark oak with iron banding and big iron buckets.

ANGUS: And this wooden beam that is iron banded and has one end on your desk, with big iron buckets—*what else about it?*

JULIE: It's nailed down and my hands are under the base.

Linguistic tip
What else about it?

The question helps the coachee to delve deeper into their symbolic world.

ANGUS: When you're ready and in your own time, I would like you to imagine a new state of being with your desk where everything is sorted out. What is that like?

JULIE: There's sunlight pouring down in yellow and gold and flakes with happy faces.

ANGUS: And this state of being, with your desk all sorted with sunlight pouring down in yellow and gold and flakes with happy faces—what else?

JULIE: The flakes are just coming and coming. It's great?

(She smiles.)

ANGUS: And the sunlight is pouring down in yellow and gold and flakes with happy faces and it's great. How are you experiencing this "it's great"?

JULIE: I'm warm and feel light. I can work again. My hands are free to work.

The next question looks for a relationship between the two experiences.

ANGUS: And how is this experience of feeling warm and light, with hands free to work and the sunlight pouring down in yellow and gold and flakes with happy faces—*how is this related to* the experience of the beam on your desk with the—

JULIE (interrupting): There's a rainbow. The nails in the beam are flying up the rainbow and the beam is shrinking to nothing. The paper is going and the flakes are falling.

ANGUS: And what about the rainbow that takes the nails up?

JULIE: It's my heart. The rainbow is coming from my heart. I had it all along.

(She smiles.)

 Linguistic tip
How is this related to ...?

This question attempts to find a connection between the "present" state and the future desired state. If the coachee has symbolically explored both states, then they will invariably find a connection that links them.

We checked that Julie was motivated to engage in the issue of the desk and she set herself a target of four days to complete the task. She was totally confident about the task and could visualize herself doing it, her rainbow radiating from her heart.

For the uninitiated or those who are not visually creative, these metaphors can seem odd. In fact, the majority of coachees have metaphors and many express them in their language even without linguistic encouragement to do so. Metaphors and stories are hugely motivating in organizations too where whole teams can construct metaphors and stories that coexist with their vision of performance. There is nothing wrong in being a little skeptical about metaphor; there is something wrong about not being flexible enough, particularly in today's competitive and demanding work environments, to try something that is demonstrably powerful and works.

Emotions

Emotional intelligence or EQ (emotional quotient) has become a talking point since the publication of Goleman's book (1996) on part of the subject. In essence, the turning of attention to EQ has to do with the notion (Patterson, 2000) that EQ + IQ = Success

Research is beginning to show that people who have a good mix of both EQ and IQ (intelligence quotient) tend to be more successful in their career than those who have outstanding IQ but limited EQ.

Interest in EQ started many years before Goleman's book was published. The expression "emotional thought" was coined (1948) by Leeper as early as 1948 and "emotional intelligence" appeared in 1966 (Leuner, quoted by Bar-On, 2000). This interest has led to a number of psychometric instruments for assessing the EQ of individuals.

Emotional intelligence provides better self-awareness and self-regulation. High EQ also hones your senses and this leads to greater success in relationships and in influencing others. Emotions are critical to motivation and hence of great interest to coaches because they are essential to help coachees move to committed targets.

When people have too much emotion attached to their issue, this can get in the way of moving forward. At other times individuals will have insufficient emotional attachment to make motivated commitments. Let's look at both these dynamics.

Overemotional

A high level of emotional distress can get in the way of finding a rapid solution to an issue. Emotions are designed to take over from logical thought under stress; they are mind–body states (McLeod, 2002c) and, without logic, decisions, if made, can be poor. Emotional distress also lowers effectiveness in communicating with others. In these situations, the coach may be well advised to encourage the coachee to learn ways of looking at the issue from another, more "dissociated", perspective. We explored this with Julian earlier. There are a number of options available for new perspective and these are called *perceptual positions*:

- first position (holistic experiencing of self, looking out)
- getting in their shoes (second position)
- thinking of someone else in a similar situation (contrived second position)
- the observer (third position).

The level of emotional connectedness with the material is likely to be lower as one goes down this list. When wanting to reduce the coachee's emotional engagement to work with a more logical and dispassionate state, then err toward the third position.

Examples of all of these are to be found in Chapter Two.

The observer position, making sure that the coachee is far enough away from the situation (to make it comfortable for them), may help. You may recall Mary, who was pushed up against a window to get away from the boardroom table where a scenario was being replayed in her head. In a smaller space, the coachee, if inclined to the visual, can be asked to make the scenario smaller (as if further away), or, if auditory, might make the scenario quieter and more remote. This playing with the submodalities of the situation provides the coachee with a level of mental control over their experience that they may not have previously enjoyed.

Where the coachee is highly associated, the coach may notice that breathing rate is changed and skin tones, particularly in the face, neck, and upper chest, may be affected. In these circumstances, the novice coach may be stressed, too. If the coachee's breathing is too shallow, the coach can encourage normal respiration (and improved mental state in the coachee) by breathing deeply (slowly and audibly) a few times. If that does not help, the coach may overtly invite the coachee to breathe more slowly and deeply by saying, "I notice that your breathing seems very shallow. I think it may be helpful for you to breathe more deeply and slowly. Would you like to try that? We can do it together if you like."

Rapid, shallow breathing has the effect of reducing pCO_2 (the partial pressure of carbon dioxide in the blood stream). Low CO_2 levels affect the heart, further compounding the experience of anxiety.

The coach can demonstrate how the coachee may alter their state at will, by breathing appropriately, and proceed to ask the coachee to do the breathing and then try to go back to the issue and state as before. This time, their experience of it is likely to be better and their level of internal control improved.

Another thing to watch out for is specific bodily tensions associated with the state. We saw earlier that, when Judith shrank down about an inch in her chair, she showed no obvious emotion. When I asked her to exaggerate that movement she burst into tears. There was a powerful internal association between the body movement and her emotional state. We can use these associations positively and to good effect in offering the coachee positive states anchored to body sensations. A properly installed "anchor" can be fired at will and trigger the positive emotional state associated with it. This may seem slightly odd but the fact is that most of us have numerous negative "anchors" that are triggered by events in the external world: think of common sensitivities to particular phrases or insults. It is much more useful to be able to install or uninstall anchors at will rather than react automatically (and inappropriately) to particular stimuli.

My job is going

Jennifer is a senior VP in a major IT consultancy. She was an effective manager and had been with the business through its development and mergers over many years. She believed that she might not have a role in the company because of a rumor that indicated that her whole division would be closed down. The international headquarters had made other cuts and so it seemed a real possibility. She suddenly felt very vulnerable because of her age. As a dedicated worker with poor work–life balance, she thought her world was collapsing. Her intense anxiety undermined her feeling of confidence. In my experience, executives at the highest level sometimes become as frail, as confused, and as unconfident as the rest of us; it is easy to forget that they are human too.

I did not think that referral to a counselor would help with Jennifer's confidence *and* keep her functional at work. As I have counseling training and experience I felt confident to support her "as coach" within her professional setting. In situations such as this, the coach must be aware of their strengths and limitations. Coaching, rather than counseling, would normally suggest that the coach encourage dissociated observation of the issue in cases where the coachee is highly emotional.

As well as a classic breathing incompetence when describing her feelings, Jennifer also appeared to be pulling her shoulders in and squeezing the two smallest fingers of her right hand into the palm. I could see an opportunity for a dual strategy using anchoring. This might help her to detach the mental state *and* the physical representation of it in her body. If we were lucky, she might anchor a preferred state in a way that would make it impossible to maintain her physical attachment to her issue. This might involve, for example, anchoring the positive state to her little fingers but in a different way.

It is one thing for a coach to have what seems a clever idea, but the coachee, as far as possible, should still lead the course of the session. Instead of drawing her attention to her fingers, I asked her what her experience of the tensions in her body was like. She took the clenched fist of her right hand and placed it against her lower sternum. "And if that experience had a more specific point where it exists, where is it?" I asked. Jennifer took the middle finger of her open hand and placed it at the base of her sternum.

As we have seen, it is good to check with the coachee that they are fully returned to the room after leaving a particular state. I asked distracting questions but Jennifer confirmed what I thought. Her issue was still very present. I thought we might look at a preferred state and one that might get her brain working in a different way, to distract her from the issue.

ANGUS: Jennifer, can you find a time and place where you felt particularly happy, content, and safe?

JENNIFER: Yes, a deserted cove on a Greek island. I returned day after day and skinny-dipped in turquoise waters. It was wonderful.

ANGUS: Can you modify that experience now but keep it wonderful? Change the colors as you wish, the light, add trees, a breeze, the sound of favorite music, anything you want.

JENNIFER: OK, I have colored fish jumping out of the water and orchids in the trees. It's not as bright as it was but still warm and comforting.

I remained silent a while and left Jennifer with her state before inviting her to move the orchids and change their smell, to raise or lower the sea and increase or decrease any movement in the water. She did this and became more obviously relaxed. By now, with her right hand open on her lap, her breathing normal, color returned to her neck and face and the tension left her jaw.

ANGUS: Of all the experiences that you are exploring, can you choose just one that is most wonderful for you?

Jennifer repeated the exercise, each time returning to the room but remaining relaxed. We introduced the physical act of placing the middle finger of her right hand on the base of her sternum. As the intensity of her experience was maintained or increasing, she maintained that contact and pressure. As the intensity was reduced or reducing, she took away the finger. In his way, Jennifer was able to install an anchor for her preferred state. I saw her some days later and she was able to fire her anchor by the simple thought of moving her finger to the base of her sternum but not actually doing it. I still see her from time to time and her anchor is apparently in good service.

In this case, Jennifer had come to me with a negative anchor at the base of her sternum. She made no reference to my own observation about high muscle tone in her right hand. Just as people can have negative thoughts and states associated with visual metaphors, many of us also have associations with physical anchors. A breathing dysfunction is common, tension in the jaw or neck, too. In spite of these observations, it is preferable that the coach invite the coachee to notice where any physical anchor may be. Working with the coachee's perceptions should achieve a higher level of efficacy and motivation.

Lacking feeling

Sometimes a coachee is stuck with an issue and there is high dissociation from their emotional experience of it. In that event, it can be helpful to encourage them to be more emotionally associated. The feeling will provide motivation, which will help them to decide whether to run away from or to deal with the issue.

Lack of feeling can dull motivation (which is dominated by emotion, whether consciously perceived or not). Low EQ can also result in interpersonal problems because people can lack insight into both themselves and others. This can also lead to poor sensitivity. At its extreme, a manager might respond to a secretary's distress over a badly cut finger with, "Oh, I suppose that means your typing will be slower." The language is likely to be factual and typically, there is an absence of emotional expression and body-centered words.

Examples of body-centered phrases include:

- I feel that ...
- My heart is not in this ...
- This report disturbs me.

But they are more likely to come out like this:

- It is noted that ...
- I am disinclined to ...
- The report is disgraceful.

Another linguistic clue is that the individual may not use the personal pronoun, especially if rattled. Their conversation can be littered with phrases like these:

- "One finds that the market's usually dull at this time of the year."

111

- "You [meaning I] don't expect to be asked such a question."
- "You [meaning I] don't sign off reports just because you're asked to do so."

Let's look at some coaching examples.

Managing an additional department

Rob works in aviation. When I saw him, he ran a large engineering department and was being pushed to take on another as well. First, he did not want the extra work and, second, he did not want some of the people in that new department. He had previously moved two of them out of his area because he could not "understand what their problems were."

ROB: You don't want to take on responsibility that dilutes your management effort, do you?

ANGUS: Are you asking me whether I want to take on responsibility that dilutes management effort?

ROB: No. I'm saying that you don't want to take on respon—

ANGUS: You mean to say, "I don't want to take on responsibility …"?

ROB: I thought I said that?

ANGUS: No. You said *"You* don't want" when I think you mean, *"I* don't want." Is that right?

ROB: It's the same thing, surely.

I noticed that Rob had firmed his jaw and his eyes went down and defocused. I waited over a minute for any response but none came. He was preoccupied. I had been hoping that he might realize the implication of his language without my needing to be explicit about it.

ANGUS: Is the issue of responsibility mine or yours?

ROB: It's not an issue but the question is mine, certainly.

ANGUS: If the question is yours, could you say, "I don't want to take on responsibility that dilutes my management effort"?

ROB: I don't want to take on responsibility that dilutes my management effort.

Again, there was a long pause; the personal pronoun had produced a degree of association. This was reversed by the time he spoke again.

ROB: You don't seem to understand the importance of the problem. It's not something that one can take on at this time.

ANGUS: I want to understand you fully. Is the problem something that "one" has to take on or is it a problem that you must take on?

ROB: It's me of course.

ANGUS: I'm sorry to be pedantic about the language you're using. You're talking about a problem that you say is clearly important but have been referring to it as if it were my problem or someone else's problem. I would like you to consider using "I" and "my" instead.

ROB: It's easier to think as I spoke before.

ANGUS: Has thinking fixed the problem for you?

ROB: No it has not.

ANGUS: So, if you agree, go along with me and see whether a different way of approaching this problem will help. Let's go back to what you said before the silence. You said [reading], "I do not want to take on responsibility that dilutes my management effort." Could you do that again?

Rob repeated the sentence and again fell silent. I said the sentence slowly and quietly again, exactly as he had said it, and waited. He was still within his issue. I said it again, more slowly and quietly. He responded, anger in his voice.

ROB: He's a complete swine, you know. I hadn't thought that Brian was involved in this but I bet he is. He's a pre-merger man. The little-company people have always resented our taking them over. This new job is just to wind me up, get his own back.

ANGUS: *You may be right, Rob*. This new job may be just to wind you up. Brian could be behind it to get his own back. Can you think of another possibility?

Linguistic tip
You may be right, Rob

Creating doubt about limiting beliefs: I said, "You may be right, Rob" although it seemed unlikely. The point of this is to restate the perceived reality and to question it while still giving credibility and acknowledgment to the coachee. The clause "you may be right" has a good balance and can help the coachee re-evaluate their (limiting) belief.

ROB: The department they want to foist on me is a disaster area. Brian probably hopes I'll make a mess of it and spoil my copybook with the CEO.

ANGUS: Could the company possibly hope something else, other than that you'll make a mess of it?

ROB: The company knows I can manage that department. Brian should, too. I run eight reports and eight hundred in my department; this new area is only two reports and fifty-odd people. I'm going to agree to take it on for six months provided I have a free hand on structural changes and HR agree to walk alongside to help carry the can. After that, one—I mean I—will be too busy in my own patch to keep on with it.

I have no idea what happened that caused Rob to arrive at a number of speculations. It was clear that gaining some internal attachment, or association, with the issue created both new perceptions (whether right or wrong) and the motivation to do something useful. After future pacing, Rob saw his strategy through. Encouraging more emotional association with his material and challenging his limiting belief led Rob to new conscious perception and a committed strategy of action.

Low EQ can sometimes manifest in poor prioritization skills. The coachee is avoiding something that has negative feelings attached to it, not because of a lack of know-how but to avoid the associated emotion. This may have been a component in the case of Rob, who was stuck with his decision making until he had some real contact with the emotion attached to his issue.

Sometimes this avoidance manifests in **displacement activity**. In order to avoid the negative emotion, but stay busy, the executive finds other things to do. This has two immediate comforts: avoidance of the issue/emotion and placing the mind's focus on something else. As we have seen, coaches may offer similar techniques to help with state change, as illustrated by Jennifer. In the case of displacement activity, this strategy is unhelpful because it is subconscious and unproductive. In coaching, we aim to develop conscious perception and choice. The novice coach or mentor will try to improve the coachee's ability to prioritize instead of dealing with the emotion. Because emotion has such motivating (and demotivating) effects, the skills of prioritization are unlikely to be used or sustained. The emotional motivation/demotivation needs to be addressed too. Let's look at an example of successful interventions.

 Displacement activity

Displacement activity (see for example Carver and Scheier, 2000) describes those impulsive behaviors that manifest automatically (subconsciously) to refocus mental attention and avoid emotional processing. Originally, the term was applied (Lorenz, 1966) to the mechanism of avoiding aggressive feelings, but now is used more broadly to embrace "negative thoughts." There are many manifestations of this in the world around us and the types of activity are as broad as human nature but can include the following:

- finger tapping
- scratching
- chewing
- hand wringing
- driving too fast for road and traffic conditions
- humming
- excessive cleaning or desk tidying
- very long telephone conversations
- continual use of music or TV
- inability to sit still

Angela O'Connell (2003) reminds me that sometimes a conscious decision to divert energy can be made by distracting oneself and placing attention elsewhere. Distraction can provide relief where anxiety is high but it will not solve the issue. It is important, therefore, to return to the issue (if likely to be repeated) with a more resourceful state. Good distractions for the purposes of reducing stress include slow breathing, meditation, and visualization of pleasant experiences.

My priorities are awry

Chuck had to research the case for a new prospective business deal for his divisional MD. Time was passing and little had been done. Chuck told me that his regular work was also piling up and he was firefighting. It looked like a prioritization issue and, at face value, it almost certainly was. Two things signaled another possibility. First, he was physically uncomfortable, almost agitated, when talking about either the research work or his divisional MD, David. Second, the activity he was talking about seemed mostly to be quite trivial. Because he seemed most unsettled when talking about David, I asked him further questions.

ANGUS: What do you think about David?

CHUCK: He's a very able director and has an ability to turn huge bits of business. Sometimes little happens and then, bang, he produces something massive.

ANGUS: Do you like David?

CHUCK: Is that relevant? I respect him.

Both Chuck's statements were made with minimal eye contact with me and with little modulation in his voice. I asked him if he would mind looking at me when he replied to my questions. He agreed. I asked him the same questions again.

Again, he found it very difficult to maintain eye contact, his body became more agitated, and there was slight narrowing of the eyes, shallower breathing, and slight tightening of the jaw muscles.

ANGUS: You respect David. Why do you think you're not satisfying him by doing the research for him?

CHUCK (agitated): I don't know.

ANGUS: I'm sorry to put you on the spot. I'm trying to help you reach your objective. I'm confused: is this about doing the research, David, or your workload?

CHUCK: I have too many things to do.

ANGUS: Like the forecasting review which you said is not needed until quarter three? Which is more important, the research needed now or the forecasting review needed in three months?

CHUCK: The research work of course.

ANGUS: But you chose to do the review instead.

CHUCK: I know it sounds stupid, but I did that to clear my desk a bit.

I seemed to be failing to get Chuck to feel attachment to his issue, so tried going for some objectivity (in the contrived second position) with my next question.

ANGUS: Let's imagine that I have an important report to research but instead write a review that isn't needed for some months instead. What would you advise me?

CHUCK: Pull you finger out and get prioritized.

ANGUS: You do have this situation. There is an important report to write and you've done a review not needed for months instead. The best advice available is, "Pull your finger out and get prioritized."

CHUCK (quietly): I guess I don't want to do it.

ANGUS: You said, *if I heard you right*, that the issue is about your workload and not about David or the research work. If there were a reason that had to do with David or the research, what would it be?

Note the invitation to extend his thinking outside the box.

CHUCK: I stay ahead of the game. David has sprung this on me and I don't like the direction he's taking, or the abuse of my time. This isn't really my responsibility: I'm just best qualified to do the job.

ANGUS: David has sprung this on you?

CHUCK: I make my own way. I work hard and get ahead of all targets. It's not fair that I am now directed like some lightweight.

Chuck had colored up, his speech harder in tone and more clipped. He went on to explore more emotional content. A barrier had been brought down and the channel was now open, not just for me, but essentially for him, to begin dealing with the real issue.

Linguistic tip
If I heard you right

An expression like this is used to gain clarity about the coachee's issue. A statement made without this introduction may give the coachee the sense that they have been mis-heard or misjudged. The expression of doubt leaves room for the coachee to correct and embellish as they see fit. Accurate reflection of the coachee's language will, anyway, show that they had your attention and the issue is just one of understanding. Another expression might be, **"Let's see if I have understood you properly"**.

Authenticity

A lack of emotional intelligence can also manifest in poor authenticity, or "congruence". If someone lacks authenticity, an observer might disbelieve them. By contrast, someone who exhibits authenticity is believable. Where we believe and trust, we are most likely to follow.

We are all familiar with the pronouncements of politicians who say one thing and quite clearly mean another. Correctly, many people did not believe President Clinton when he said, "I did not have sex with that woman" in reference to one of his interns, Monica Lewinsky. In UK politics, Prime Minister John Major had a habit of shaking his head while attempting to convince the public about his policies. Spin, or, more correctly, political lies, are willful and we have come to expect them. Few politicians appear to believe what they themselves say, let alone one another, and there are so many examples of "do as I say, not as I do" in high political office that I do not even need to illustrate them further. It is no wonder that political parties are dynamic hotbeds of intrigue and power struggles. Those with integrity stand out, head and shoulders above the rest. Unfortunately, the gray-suits dominate.

Organizations would do well to ignore the strategies of the gray-suits and seek honesty and integrity in their teams. In organizations there are also those who are willfully manipulative and do not intend to change, unless punished. Coaches can help their corporate clients change the culture that permits such behaviors. Coaches can also engage with those who exhibit these behaviors and encourage them to change.

I work with teams and team values. In the early days, it was quite normal to find that senior executives easily gave their commitment to team values, then went back to work exactly as before, manipulating communication and working in cliques to promote or destroy unwanted strategies. I now use a methodology with teams that I call *value imprinting*. Having agreed core values, the team works together to define those characteristics that should be observable if the values are held. This produces a wonderfully impactful list of behaviors. Impactful, because individuals suddenly realize that their colleagues know when they are behaving contrary to expectations. I then ask executives to score themselves privately on their current performance on each of those behavioral dimensions. Having identified their failings, they are empowered to make changes supported by their coaches. It is extraordinary that so many senior executives think themselves opaque to psychological typing. In fact, they are often transparent to their colleagues. If we can help them understand that transparency, they can be motivated to change.

Other issues can cause lack of authenticity. Executives may be unbelievable owing to lack of emotional intelligence or because of internal conflict; sometimes it is simply that they do not truly believe themselves. When executives are unbelievable, they find it hard to influence and engage teams in a motivating way. Coaches get to work with such issues only if the executive's motivation to change is significant enough to force the issue or if the employers are willing to demonstrate leadership.

My team is underperforming

Bella was about 45 and all her team were under half that age; none had been in the job more than two years. The department Bella was running was only four years old but she had been with the company for almost twenty.

When performance targets started to slide in her department, she responded by increasing the number of team meetings, highlighting weaknesses and strengths and bringing focus to strategies that came, unwelcome, from above. These strategies were those of the marketing director, to whom Bella reported. I was unaware of any of this until Bella had gone into the third perceptual position (observer) and told me that the staff did not believe that Bella was committed to what she was saying. Further questioning (back in the first position) showed why.

ANGUS: If someone you respected enormously gave you some very good advice, would you take note of it?

BELLA: Yes.

ANGUS: I have some advice from someone you know and respect. In team meetings staff do not believe that you are committed to what you are saying.

I could have continued talking, asking for the impact of the statement, but thought it best to leave the statement to take hold in her consciousness without getting in the way of that, allowing the power of silence to do its work.

BELLA: These are not my strategies and I don't believe in them. The results speak for themselves.

ANGUS: Is there a solution to this?

BELLA: I can speak with Warren and tell him the strategy's not producing results, but he's likely to tell me it's due to my leadership. I think he knows that I'm struggling with my team.

ANGUS: Is there another way to be with your team rather than struggling, and could this help?

BELLA: I could meet with the team and involve them in exploring what's working and what isn't. Usually I just tell them because they're young and have little experience. In fact, they have a wealth of customer contact, more than I do, and should have some insights into what can be done better. I could report our initial findings to Warren and invite him to a further meeting. If he is still convinced on his way, at least I'll be more a part of my team than outside it and I hope they may give me more support than I have now.

ANGUS: Can you imagine how Warren will experience and react to this idea?

BELLA: He'll be OK about it. He likes to dominate, but if things are below target then he'll descend on me and try to find out as much as possible. He's very busy and may even be grateful, rather then threatened, that I've taken an initiative to provide him with improved information.

I moved to future pacing here, as Bella had been talking about the team meeting with conviction.

ANGUS: If you will, imagine that you're having the meeting with your team. What's your experience of this meeting?

BELLA: I'm an insider, not an outsider. I'm not carrying the portfolio for someone else and hope I can encourage my team to come up with ideas and supporting information that might produce an adapted strategy we can all believe in.

I invited her to check out the third perceptual position.

ANGUS: The meeting is going on. When you move away and observe what's going on over there with Bella and her team, what's happening?

BELLA: There's more energy. It's more dynamic. Some of the team are leaning forward. I'm putting ideas up on the board and the initials of those who bring up the ideas. They can see I'm involving them and giving credit for their input.

ANGUS: And what is similar or different to how it was before?

BELLA: Energy and involvement. Bella is a team player, not an outsider.

It turned out that Bella was pretty motivated by her idea and established an action plan, made commitments to it, and, with later modifications, was successful.

Negativity

Many younger executives will wonder why negativity deserves attention here. Negativity, doubt, negative internal dialogue, lack of motivation strike most executives at some stage(s) in their career. It does not take an inherent weakness of character to fall into the trap. Circumstances, particularly in industries where retention of staff is short and takeovers are rife, cause tremendous pressure. Restructuring in difficult markets dominates corporate finance and contributes to the "interesting" lives of many executives. It's not a question of *whether* they will fall into the negativity trap, but *when*. Middle age often triggers a period of negativity and reduced effectiveness. Sometimes, displacement activity develops at the same time. In an effort to get away from the bad feelings, executives can find other outlets for their attention. The coach will notice negative beliefs in their language and will challenge contradictions and perceptions related to those negative beliefs.

Positive listings

When I was on a senior executive outplacement program with a leading City firm in London, one of the many interventions that I and all other executives were asked to complete was a list of at least fifty positive actions and successes. Interestingly, these were to be from both work and private life and to run from earliest memories to the present day. In the context of possible career change, the coaches there wanted their executives to explore *all* motivating experiences from their life, since any one of these might trigger a new passion for a job-search strategy. In executive coaching, this breadth of positive listings and going back to early childhood may be excessive, but I encourage coachees who suffer from negativity to include positive experiences. I also ask them for a separate list of positive personal qualities. If they cannot find at least ten positive personal qualities, I ask them to think again. Listings may include:

- positive experiences
- positive actions/successes in work
- positive actions/successes in private life
- skills learned
- positive personal qualities

When these lists have been produced, the idea is to try to gain a commitment from the coachee to review and consider each point on a daily basis, preferably linked to another activity that is done every day. Here is an example:

ANGUS: So, you have breakfast every day and can find time to review and consider your lists?

CHARLOTTE: Yes, breakfast is quiet time for me.

ANGUS: Looking ahead to tomorrow, then, imagine having your breakfast now, the lists are with you. You are reading and reviewing?

CHARLOTTE: Yes.

When we checked out her certainty level for doing this action on the following morning and each successive morning until the next session, she was totally sure.

It is also possible to augment the listings by finding a metaphor, totem or other positive anchor in times of negativity. A useful technique is to add another useful resource: positive affirmations.

Positive affirmations

Positive affirmations can help a coachee to counter negative states. Positive affirmations comprise specific personal qualities and may be linked to a target. Examples are:

- I choose to act confidently

- I always achieve what I want
- I succeed in my goals
- I always choose to start the hardest task on my desk first

The language of the affirmations needs to be that of the coachee but is best personalized like those above, with the personal pronoun, "I".

Ideally, the coachee totally believes these affirmations to be true or, if not the case now, that they are achievable. The coach asks the coachee to experience the affirmation holistically. What is that believable state like now? What does the coachee experience? How perfectly, zero through ten?

The coach will ask the coachee for a reasonable commitment to the affirmations. This will involve going through their affirmations several times each day for an agreed period. The times are preferably linked to some other habitual event. Future pacing and getting feedback on the coachee's expectation of success, preferably above a score of eight, helps ensure that action follows.

Acknowledgments

We cannot ensure that coachees get positive acknowledgment from the outside world, but we can coach them to take better note of their achievements and to acknowledge them. Today's executives are likely to be tasking at very high levels. Decisions and actions flow from one to the other without a pause, especially in the most demanding and stressful environments. While the buzz is good and results flow, this may be fine. In the real world, however, effective as we are, things can go awry.

It is very easy to start noticing failure rather than success and get depressed about it. The failures may provide useful strategic information about resources, knowledge, and direction but should not be allowed to damage personal performance. One technique to offset that is the habitual use of self-acknowledgment. What we are saying is that, when the result of some effort pays off, the individual will get strength and confidence from a short pause to acknowledge what was difficult, how they persisted, and how they won through. Examples might include:

- I was going to avoid that call but the outcome was a success
- I had misgivings but my report was well received

These acknowledgments build into a databank of personal resource that can carry us through hard times. Without the discipline to do this, the resource is lacking when most needed.

In all these interventions, there will often be a reason for the coachee to want to take action in order to avoid their negative state. The coach can help highlight positive reasons for change, too.

COACH: I would like to tell you about some strategies that may make your experience of work easier and more productive. All or none of them may appeal to you. Do you want to hear about them?

The invitation is placing all the power of direction and choice with the coachee.

Limiting beliefs and rules

There are numerous examples in this book where limiting belief forms part of the block to coachee performance. These include the statements:

- It's bound to be difficult for her
- I'm unhappy that I cannot control this problem
- I failed last time
- I'm sure that Alan won't see my argument properly
- It's certain to be rejected

Big language clues are in the words "must", "should", "ought", "duty", "always", "cannot", and "never". Negative language relating to the world of the coachee also highlights the potential for learning and intervention. We have seen the use of many interventions. Let's look at some typical statements that characterize limiting belief, together with suitable interventions:

I always fail when …	Can you contradict that?
I can't do …	Is there a time when you could?
I should do …	Who says?
I must go and …	What other options could someone make?
There is only one way to …	Who says?
It's always the case that …	Is it really always the case?
I can never …	Up until now?
It's my duty to …	What if it was not your duty?
I am [negative statement] …	Might anyone close to you think differently?
I have no choice …	If you had a choice, what would that choice be?
I ought to do …	Who will notice and does it matter?
I have to do [something] before I can do [something else] …	Is there another way?

Note that the questions or challenges may relate to the individual's expression directly or encourage some detachment. Examples above that encourage emotional distance include the questions "What other options could someone make?" and "Might anyone close to you think differently?" This latter is chosen because the statement related to a statement of identity. A question that challenges the coachee's self-belief about their identity may best come from encouraging a new perspective from the second or third perceptual position.

The list above is not exhaustive. Neither are the responses supposed to be all-embracing. I encourage the coach to think through such examples and come up with carefully worded phrases of their own that may have the same effect. I can vouch for the effectiveness of these interventions (when I use them in a given context and with a particular individual) and I hope you may have success with them, but I do not wish to prescribe language that does not sit easily with my reader.

Lacking compulsion to change

Individuals often have inner conflicts about wanting something but not taking action to accomplish what they want. We have explored strategies for helping with inner dialogue and the use of the leader's and follower's questions ("chunking up" and "chunking down" respectively) that may help. These strategies can often lead to compelling reasons to change the status quo. We can sometimes gain further insight into compulsion to change by considering the ideas of Gregory Bateson and adapted by Robert Dilts into what we now call the "hierarchy of logical levels".

Hierarchy of logical levels

The hierarchy of logical levels is a helpful model (see Bateson, 1973) that helps the coach to pick interventions that work at an influencing level.

The model suggests that, as we move toward *environment*, the *dominance* of each level increases and, as we move toward *purpose/vision, influence* increases.

Thus, if a coachee is talking about a need for behavioral change, the model suggests that we work with them at "higher" influencing levels in skills, beliefs and values and so on. We know that the pattern breaker depends on replacing one behavioral pattern by changing the trigger pattern by substituting another behavioral pattern. This does not limit the usefulness of the hierarchy model. It does mean that, if we want to give up chocolate, we would probably be more successful to think about our values about weight and health than to throw some away.

Looking at the model from the top, we can all think of examples where a clear vision about purpose was so compelling that somebody changed the course of their life in a spectacular way. Sometimes these people of vision collect followers, too. Cults and political groups are rife with examples. I like the actions of the Bulgarian-born American object artist Christo, who wrapped up the Reichstag in Berlin in 1995, and performed the incredible feat of placing a massive orange curtain across Rifle Gap in Colorado. These projects, supported by his colleague Jean-Claude, found enormous support from technicians and engineers and required remarkable technical and political skills to achieve. Many people have supported these projects without reward, even though the outcome appears, at face value, to be inconsequential in human terms. His vision galvanized people into action against huge odds.

People sometimes surprise us by seamlessly changing profession and adopting a different style of dress, manner, and language. Identity and purpose can lead to major change. This change may be achieved elegantly when the vision is greater than the challenges that delay it.

When the coach identifies an issue at a particular level, they can target their questioning at the higher levels and hope to find influencing information that will inspire their coachee to motivated action. Here is an example.

Changing role, changing job

Coaches sometimes get involved in support for downsizing initiatives as part of a raft of support structures. Tim had hung onto his job, making sure that the bulk of his team, a group of twelve senior managers and almost two thousand people, had found jobs or other suitable exits from the company. All his senior team had placements and only a handful of staff had uncertain futures other than him. An outplacement agency was marketing Tim for a similar senior role elsewhere.

Tim said he felt he was managing his move efficiently but that his heart was not really in it. He felt devalued and psychologically damaged in having his efficient operation pulled out from under him. He had been offered other roles in the corporation but wanted to leave. The company had been helpful in providing out-placement, a financial handshake and impeccable references.

ANGUS: What do you want to do most of all?

TIM: I'm basically a project manager. I can use those skills any-where but would like to work in a related environment where I can use my network.

ANGUS: So, let's put you in a new role in a related environment using your network. Are you happy?

TIM: I can't say that I am.

ANGUS: In working, what do you most value: say, the three most important things?

TIM: Making things happen, helping people, influence.

ANGUS: In this proposed role in a related environment, using your network, does that allow you to do that?

TIM: Sort of. It's all about money first, so helping people becomes simply a fact of doing the best I can to look after my people. I failed last time.

ANGUS: Can you contradict that you failed?

TIM: I still have four people to find jobs for.

ANGUS: Out of two thousand. Can you contradict that you failed?

TIM: I couldn't have protected them from what happened. I've done my best by them and some are happier to have moved on. For others it's been very traumatic. In many cases I haven't failed.

ANGUS: In making things happen, helping people, and having influence, *what is most important?*

Linguistic tip
What is most important?

This question invites beliefs, values and purpose, all at the
high end of motivated change according to the hierarchy-of-
logical-levels model.

TIM: I realize that it's about helping people first. It used to be
money and power. Now it's people first, then the other two are
equal. I've been headed in the wrong direction, haven't I?

ANGUS: You want to help people, then make things happen and
stay influential. Are you headed in the wrong direction to do
those things?

TIM: Yes. I would rather be in an industry having an overall purpose to contribute. We just contribute a product line. I could
work in a large charity or in healthcare. Money is no longer an
issue. I have a small fortune in shares.

Working at the influential level of purpose made direction and
action a lot easier for Tim. Once he had more closely defined his
options, we were able to look at the ecology of those options in
terms of his purpose, his skills, and his needs and wants from
work. He found a new direction for his considerable skills where
he was able to have more positive human impact.

Walking the logical levels

The hierarchy of logical levels can be walked, like a timeline, to
provide a framework for giving a coachee a positive experience
that may inspire them to take action. This is similar to the timeline
but uses progress through the levels from environment upward.

Presupposition that Robyn is a success

The presupposition that Robyn chose was that she could have the identity of a director and perform well as a (newly appointed) director of the corporate board. As usual, the language used by the coach is one of invitation and the use of tense is specific and consistent.

COACH: Thinking about your presupposition and the board, in a moment I shall ask you to step into that environment. And, having found yourself in this environment, where and when is this happening?

As with the timeline, the coach stays with the coachee, pausing to take notice of their state, checking if necessary and allowing silences to be with the coachee while they integrate their experience as fully as possible.

COACH: When you're ready, and in your own time, step forward into the behavior level. Notice your actions: what are you doing and saying that is different and what is that experience like?

The same procedure is used to step the coachee forward through capabilities and skills. At this level in the hierarchy, the coach may ask what additional skills or developments are proving helpful at that level. Afterwards the coach will encourage the coachee toward the beliefs and values level.

COACH: When you're ready, step forward into the beliefs/values level. Notice some of the other beliefs and values you now have. How is this different?

The coachee may need more time to integrate at this level, they may not. If in doubt wait and test later, if necessary getting feedback from the coachee.

COACH: When ready, and only when ready, step into the identity level. How do you experience this identity fully? How is this true to you and who you really are? Make it as true to you as you possibly can.

The final step into purpose is often associated with connectivity to others and the system in which the coachee operates—the ecology of purpose. The coach's language can reflect this.

COACH: When ready, step into the purpose level. How true to you is this purpose? How does this presupposition support your purpose and vision? How is this helping you to connect with your colleagues and support your business?

As with the timeline, it is helpful afterwards to "clear the screen" and take any learning back to the present to look for motivated actions that the coachee may wish to take. When Robyn did that, she expressed a great clarity and determination for action.

Unsettled in HR

Ian was senior VP of HR with responsibilities within greater Europe. He could not put his finger on it, but felt unsettled. His corporation is one of the great names in his industry with high added value—his budget was extraordinarily high. He had been in the job a little over four years. His unsettled demeanor had started after the arrival of a new boss. The new CEO had a very traditional view of HR. Although it had not yet affected policy, Ian felt sure that it would. Ian was much more progressive in outlook. He wished to make a positive impact on the organization and its people.

ANGUS: Ian, if you will, I want you to go on a *journey with me into the future*. Step by step and at your pace, we are aging and the years are spinning by. With each blink, another significant leap into the future has been traveled. We are going to go beyond this life and keep looking back until we are far enough to be objective but close enough to see everything we need to. You will be able to understand the relevance of your life.

Linguistic tip
Journey into the future

Detachment from the emotion around an issue can help find rational ideas that can move a coachee to new conscious perception. When we journey well into the future, the proximity to short-term issues is given greater perspective; objectivity is raised. It is also a good place to seek the answer to questions about life purpose, the most influencing level of change.

I checked with Ian to sense how he was moving. I could have invited him to walk a timeline but, as Ian is highly flexible and open to new ideas, I was confident he could work well without moving from his seat. He was relaxed, head slightly back and to one side, eyes closed, breathing very slowly.

ANGUS: *In a nutshell*, what do you most want Ian to be remembered for?

IAN: Sustained change in people and in teams. Open advocacy of personal development for his staff. Loving well.

ANGUS: And, knowing what you know about Ian, what advice have you?

IAN: Move out. Find a smaller company and an inspirational CEO who is committed to developing people as effective individuals rather than people who task. Money and status should be devalued.

Ian returned to the room and our session. As he did that, I was hoping that his current CEO might appreciate the loss of his VP. Maybe it would be an advantage to the company in the longer term. Ian's heart did not seem to be with the new management.

ANGUS: Ian, the best advice there is in the universe is written on this page. It was written by someone who instinctively knows you and what you are capable of. This person can predict a certain future for you, based upon what is written here. Do you want this advice?

I read the advice to Ian, at a pace and delivery that emulated his own. He breathed deeply twice and came alive like a tiger from sleep. Something powerful and motivating had got into him and he would soon be leaving to take his real passion somewhere where it would be more effective. With luck, his existing company would find someone with a passion for the work needed there, too.

Out of interest, you may like to know that Ian moved to a smaller corporation with a relatively small budget per capita and where management staff retention is only three years rather then the seven he enjoyed previously. The real light still burns in his eyes and he is working with his CEO on truly innovative change programs. They are unafraid to speak of personal development (in the work context) for the critical contribution it makes to executive effectiveness.

Not feeling like a senior manager—totems

A totem is a significant symbol. We have already seen how metaphors can be powerful allies of change. An attachment to a powerfully motivating totem can also play its part in change.

Louise looked younger than her 29 years. She dressed well and one might easily have guessed that she was at high school. In fact, she was managing over a thousand people in a male-dominated industry that was fraught with union intervention and dispute. Her business center was ahead of any other units nationally. Although there were many other young women in senior roles elsewhere in the business, Louise was probably the only one with such exposed line responsibility. In terms of the hierarchies model, she had all the skills and capabilities of her role but seemed to be struggling at the identity level in the context of work. The phrase "in the context of work" is important. Issues are invariably context-specific. Usually, executives have functioning strategies in other contexts. In coaching them, one can rely on these other experiences to bring their attention toward working strategies of their own. I decided to explore the area of identity in the context of work. Later, I might need to look for a more compelling level of change, at purpose and vision.

ANGUS: You say that you don't feel like a senior manager. Is there one way a senior manager should feel?

LOUISE: I guess not. There are lots of different characters at my level but they all look comfortable being what they are.

ANGUS: You say they look comfortable. Does that mean they are comfortable being what they are?

LOUISE: Maybe not.

ANGUS: So, if a fly on the wall was looking at you at work, do they say you look comfortable and that you are comfortable?

LOUISE: They say I'm too young, too "pretty", that I'm effective but don't look the part. If they were very perceptive they would know that I'm uncomfortable.

ANGUS: And are those observations realistic, that you are too pretty, effective, that you don't look the part, that you're uncomfortable?

LOUISE: Yes.

ANGUS: And which of these, if any, is most important to you?

LOUISE: My effectiveness.

ANGUS: And after that? Is being too pretty, not looking the part, or being uncomfortable most important?

LOUISE: I can't do anything about being too pretty and wouldn't wish to. I could dress differently, although the way I dress doesn't seem to inhibit me. I'm most concerned about the discomfort I feel about not looking the part.

ANGUS: Could dressing differently help you look the part and feel better?

LOUISE: I have thought about it, but my clothes are part of who I am. I don't want to change what I wear at work.

ANGUS: ***What is your ultimate purpose*** in your role?

LOUISE: To run a smooth operation. It's dynamic and unstable but the operation runs effectively in spite of that.

Linguistic tip
What is your ultimate purpose?

Inviting an answer to this question is looking for higher-level motivators. In terms of the hierarchy of logical levels, purpose is higher than identity and thus may help in the change process.

ANGUS: Your purpose is to run a smooth operation? And if there was another ultimate purpose in your role, what would that purpose be?

LOUISE: To make a difference to the people who work for me.

ANGUS: And as you are now, with or without a feeling of discomfort about whether you look the part, do you run a smooth operation and do you make a difference to the people who work for you?

LOUISE: My team is happy and I make a difference to each and every one of my managers.

It was important to check that Louise's issue at the identity level was aligned, that she was authentic (or congruent) with her values:

ANGUS: So, in having the values of running a smooth operation and making a difference to all your team, does who you are and what you look like support those values?

LOUISE: Absolutely.

ANGUS: If there was something that represented a successful senior manager, who looked the part and felt comfortable, who ran a smooth operation and made a difference to every single one of her team, *what might that something that represents it be?*

LOUISE: A dolphin. The dolphin is in harmony with its environment. It protects and nurtures, it is perfect in doing what it does. The dolphin leads and is totally comfortable with its environment. It can leap out of the water and can enjoy a bigger vision. It can play. Nothing is less than perfect. It has grace.

ANGUS: So where is the dolphin?

LOUISE: In my heart, at the core of me.

ANGUS: You are at work managing, running a smooth operation and making a difference with your team. In your heart, you have a dolphin that is in harmony with its environment. Is this similar or different than you experienced at work before?

LOUISE: It's different. I feel light and part of the bigger show. Some of the other senior team don't look like dolphins but they are too. It's what is inside that makes us who we are, what we do as managers. I can look down and the dolphin is there. I feel like it always was.

Louise bought a small dolphin brooch that she took to wearing or carrying with her. The dolphin remains for her a powerful symbol of effectiveness and harmony.

There is no doubt at all that Louise gained more grace and respect following this session, with increasing influence at all levels.

Linguistic tip
What might that something that represents it be?

We shall return to totems later, but you may see from the example that the animal totem had powerful symbolism for Louise. The question is constructed to invite any symbolic representation that the coachee might have. Totems can also be things. A sword once turned up as a powerful metaphoric symbol with one of my coachees.

New business venture

Adrian had been very successful in a business that then failed. He was left with debt. A slow personal recovery followed over a couple of years, nothing really taking off. He had a multitude of skills and business experiences that offered him choices but made it hard for him to commit to any one direction. All seemed to offer potential but nothing seemed to truly inspire him. I had coached him previously, and a visual stacked anchor (one anchor linking with another) that had been used then had been of major help to him ever since. He returned to me with his new issue. One of the key elements of compulsion for Adrian was at the level of vision.

ANGUS: *Where do you want to be in three, five, or more years' time?*

ADRIAN: There's a place on the coast that I wish to live.

Linguistic tip
Where do you want to be in three, five, or more years' time?

Asking the coachee to move their thinking forward a long time ahead can help get new perspectives on their issues as well as providing compelling targets. The question may also

> help with a step change to higher levels of thinking at the levels of identity, values, and purpose.

ANGUS: So, those years are behind you. What is living here like?

Note the use of the present tense to encourage Adrian with his experience.

ADRIAN: There are three or four empty houses in need of renovation, one in particular that I want, although any of them would be perfect. This one is a two-story house with a long path to the front door, very overgrown with shrubs and trees, like a hidden garden. You can see the sea from there and sometimes you can hear it.

ANGUS: So you have made it to your house, it's yours, maybe you have a key. What is this like?

ADRIAN: The front door has history etched into the wood. Seeing it and knowing that it will open for me is fantastic. I am here, seeing the door and my hand outstretched to open it, the sun illuminates everything like crystal and is warm on my back.

I asked Adrian to come back into the room and he returned to the **visualization** several times, each time scoring ten on perfection. He was motivated to return to this visualization after our coaching session, and, whenever we spoke after this, he invariably referred to his vision and the steps he had taken to reach it, including the side turns, explorations, and successes that made it more realizable day by day.

 ### Visualization

Visualization can be a powerful motivator for change. Shelle Rose Charvet avers that, where an individual wishes to change a compulsive disorder, such as overeating or smoking, a visually represented future desired state is vital.

Shakti Gawain (1982) says that there are three compelling elements necessary in forming a successful creative visualization and these are *desire*, *belief*, and *acceptance*.

By desire, Gawain means a clear sense of purpose; her belief element is an empowering statement that says "I can"; and, when she writes of acceptance, Gawain means a full appreciation of the ramifications of achieving the target. A target that does not take account of the cost to close relationships (for example) is not "well formed" and therefore dangerous.

The NLP trainer Sarah Frossell (1998) writes of her colleagues on her MBA degree course, many of whom lost their homes and had traumatic family lives because they had not fully anticipated the price that achieving their outcome would have in other areas of their lives. In visualizing targets, we must make sure that the ecology of that target is properly considered and understood.

This visualization, along with the feelings of warmth, became a key part in Adrian's success. After seeing and experiencing his dream, he knew for certain which venture to plug for, which could be run part-time from his new home. Adrian is now on the verge of realizing that visualization. After only four years his business is a success. Expansion and joint ventures enable him to work part-time from the coast, coming to the city twice a week. I never had any doubt that he would make it and neither did he. His passionate description of his visualization, repeated and embellished at each revisitation, also created a positive anchor for me!

Motivation

There are numerous models for motivation that can be applied wholly, or piecemeal, in coaching. Whatever model(s) is/are chosen and whether by process or by experience and/or instinct, the whole issue of motivation is hugely personal to the individual. Unfortunately, many executives do not understand their motivation and make mistakes in choosing the right job and organization to work in. Because motivation is so personal, it is useful for the coach to have the widest possible understanding of the most common factors and to look even wider if necessary.

Personal factors of importance to motivation may include the need for any of the following:

- dynamism
- ownership
- working alone
- internal leadership (toward strategies)
- internal following (away from strategies)
- certainty
- working with others
- positive feedback
- clear procedures
- choices
- compelling target or goal
- stimulation by the fear of failure
- influencing others/organization
- feeling secure
- risk
- a progressive career path
- tangible rewards
- visible rewards/status
- family and friends' support
- direction
- cajoling
- self-determination
- leading others
- feeling part of a team/organization
- a team/organization vision
- fitting into the cultural norm (matching behaviors, identity, or solution)
- difference/uniqueness (mismatching behaviors, identity, or solution)
- changing and demanding role
- familiar role
- being a big fish
- being a small fish
- being noticed
- being gray
- clear corporate messages

The list is deliberately made up of needs rather than wants. Almost everybody wants more money but not everyone needs or is motivated by it. In my work with people and teams, it appears that organizations need to wake up to the power of self-motivation and encourage their staff to understand their motivation and to communicate it with others.

There are simple motivational models that stimulate learning. Many models have just a few dimensions—in the case of the hierarchies model, just six. Shelle Rose Charvet uses five motivation traits and I use a model illustrated in my book, *Me, Myself, My Team*, which has motivational (and cultural match and mismatch factors) with over thirty dimensions. All these models are helpful in encouraging:

- staff to be more aware of the factors that influence and motivate them
- managers to encourage their people more effectively
- teams to self-distribute tasks for the greatest possible effectiveness

These are traits of highly effective teams. On top of the need for a high level of skills and encouragement to be the best, people are encouraged to distribute efforts where most effective and where the team is most efficient.

To complicate the inner world and the relationships of the individual executive, it is common for larger organizations to make strategic changes that unsettle the staff and typically undermine the constructive work of managers and HR people in creating motivated teams. Here is an example. Some time ago we were supporting an organization with the Ask Max mentoring service via email (see Chapter Nine). The project was working very well until a major restructuring took place. At exactly the moment when individual support was needed, many staff felt alienated from corporate support structures and wanted to leave the organization. Our remit with the organization did not include helping their staff to leave it. Both we and the staff were frustrated. The situation was exacerbated because of the regulations requiring a thirty-day cooling-off period. During this period a veil of uncertainty fell over the whole business, further unsettling staff. To make matters worse, an external consultancy (with a record of indiscriminate weeding of whole departments) was employed. This same consultancy required staff to reapply for any available position as if they were newcomers to the organization.

The coach needs to have a clear idea of the culture in which their coachees work and the structural and cultural dimensions that are in flux.

Other management changes that are implemented universally can also create motivational problems, as we saw with Philip. A new purchasing audit system required him to invent data and forced him to work in a way that did not meet his needs to do quality work. In the twenty-first century we might have expected organizations to manage information more flexibly and still achieve useful data. The coach may need to ask the right questions to learn to what extent these strategic factors are linked with their motivation (and performance).

These questions can include ones such as:

- What frustrates your performance?
- To what extent do [the changes] affect your colleagues and your effectiveness?
- What would help you perform one step higher than you do already?
- When are you most productive?
- When are you least productive?

One of the most basic factors in motivation is typically overlooked in organizations but is one of the most common. It is *dynamic preference*.

Dynamic preference is a measure of the number of projects that an individual ideally works with at one time. Of course, there are related dimensions, including the preference for the overall length of projects, the number of strands (complexity) in the projects, and many of the factors highlighted above. However, if you explain the idea of dynamic preference to a coachee, you very quickly get a picture of what it is that they prefer. Why is this important?

Here are some possible new roles for you. Each of them will persist as a three-year appointment. Do all of them appeal or not? How motivated could you be to function at peak performance with these working scenarios?

- Three-year research job on one aspect of your current job and experience that may lead to a PhD
- Fifteen individual projects lasting between one week and one month. All have specific requirements for completion and involve steps that are out of your line control
- Six projects running between one quarter and one year at any one time. These are largely self-determined but regular weekly reports are required

It may be that you could function in all these roles, but would your motivation and performance be different? If your motivation is lower but you feel that you would perform well in spite of that, at what cost might be your frustration? Might it affect your work and personal relationships? To what extent might this further affect your ability to work to a high level?

Managers and coaches rarely ask questions about dynamic preference. The personality profiling that might provide some insight is often missed or not acted upon. Coaches do well to be open to the concept of dynamic preference where motivation is an issue. Companies can provide training in project management, but if an individual is working well outside their dynamic preference, there will be problems.

Too much going on and losing track

Betty is highly effective and had a track record of succeeding in all her previous roles in her company. Her new job was exciting and dynamic and continued the same levels of stress that she enjoyed. There was a difference: instead of running two or three projects for the executive chairman and a number of smaller "firefighting" activities, her new role had much more emphasis on project management with up to twenty projects running simultaneously. Many of them stimulated her with need for "firefighting", but she was finding it hard to maintain pace with all the projects and felt "thin on the ground".

ANGUS: Betty, this "thin on the ground" that you experience, what is that "thin on the ground" like?

BETTY: I'm trying to hold spinning plates in the air but there are too many. I can handle big heavy plates but these are too numerous and too light. I'm burning up, running from plate to plate.

ANGUS: Is there any way you can keep all the light plates spinning?

BETTY: Some are crashing down. Now I have about eight rather than the sixteen. I can manage them.

We discussed dynamic preference and it was very clear that Betty would be able to manage six to eight projects, even if much more complicated. With new insight into her dynamic preference, she decided to discuss the issue with the chairman. He was pleased and together they restructured her job.

Meta-programs

I earlier referred to the work of Noam Chomsky when discussing *limiting beliefs* and introduced briefly his three filtering mechanisms: generalization, deletion, and distortion. The founders of NLP extended this work (Bandler and Grinder, 1975) to help elicit and facilitate an individual toward greater conscious perception. Cameron-Bandler took this work further (1985) by looking at behavioral patterns that manifest because of these filtering processes—she called them "meta-programs" (see for example Hall and Belnap, 1999). Hall and Belnap give more than eighty examples of filtering processes in their book. All these filters enable us to function without being swamped with information or crippled by a need to have cognitive processing in familiar circumstances. A small number of them have been identified as "motivation traits" and hence are of significance here, and will be referred to again later.

One of these (NLP) meta-programs is the idea that individuals may have, in any specific context, a preferred motivation for "moving away from", or "toward" issues. Here is an example.

Going for double

WARREN: I have to get the proposal done but hate the audit process. I'm already late. I'm due to see my boss in two days and he will be very upset if I have not made progress.

ANGUS: Will your boss getting upset prompt you to action?

WARREN: If I haven't done anything by the time I meet him, then he will throw a fit. I will have to do something. Most likely I will get more anxious about it as the meeting gets closer and will go mad trying to put enough together to look like I am making better progress than I have done.

ANGUS: What else could happen to urge you to start the proposal?

WARREN: My boss asking about it beforehand; his boss asking about the project; his secretary asking for my draft; running out of time until I get freaked.

Warren was providing me with "away-from" features. I wanted to link these to consequences to see if that would provide him with motivation to act.

ANGUS: Do you want any of these things to happen to you?"

WARREN: No.

ANGUS: And would you prefer to avoid all those things or not?

WARREN: Yes, they're all disastrous.

We had isolated the things that Warren wished to avoid and so I thought we might explore positives that he might be motivated to move *toward*.

ANGUS: So, in preparing the proposal, what could be, or will be, good?

WARREN: If I do a good job it will go forward without much editing or changing in the pricing.

ANGUS: And?

WARREN: We may win the business.

ANGUS: Anything else?

WARREN: I don't think so.

ANGUS: If there was something good other than "being accepted without significant change" and "maybe winning the business", what would it be?

WARREN: My boss could ask me to lead the presentation. I haven't led one so big but have experience of fronting presentations.

ANGUS: You've mentioned three reasons why doing the proposal might be a good thing for you: doing it without significant modification; winning the business; and the possibility that you could be asked to lead the presentation? Of these, or any other, which one is the most compelling?

WARREN: You mean which is the most appealing?

ANGUS: Yes.

WARREN: Leading the presentation.

ANGUS: And do you have any influence over that?

WARREN: It's not my choice, if that's what you mean, but there are things I can do to make it more likely. I could pull out the overview and key information to prepare a draft slide show. If my boss likes it there's a good chance he would ask me to lead.

Now, Warren had explored both "away-from" and "toward" motivations for making progress. I then asked a question to encourage *future pacing*.

ANGUS: And, imaging that conversation with your boss, showing him the proposal and the slide presentation, maybe even making the presentation to the customer, what is most appealing to you?

WARREN: Being asked to do it.

ANGUS: So, imagine if you will, that you are being asked by your boss to do this presentation. How is that?

WARREN: It's great. It's double the value of anything I've done. *There would be at least three of us there* and I will be leading the team even though not the most senior.

 Linguistic tip
There would be at least three of us there

Language and **emotional association or dissociation**: The fact that the coachee language is not in the first person does not necessarily mean that they are emotionally dissociated from their material. In this case, Warren was very attached to the experience: alert, engaged, and positive. The coach must always remember that the information they observe is never good enough to provide certainty about cause and effect. It is only by getting feedback from the coachee that we can be certain of the etiology of the behavior.

ANGUS: So, in your own, time, when you come back into the room, as before, and look around and think about the proposal, what next?

WARREN: I can't waste any more time. I'm going to focus on the presentation while I prepare the proposal so I can lift bits straight out. I will keep it all simple and make it easy to understand the main benefits of our strategy.

ANGUS: In the time scale you have available, what rating do you
   give your success in preparing both the proposal and presentation in time.

WARREN: No problem now. Ten out of ten!

Warren did what he had committed to and he showed how har-
nessing the double motivation of "away-from" and "toward"
strategies, and future-pacing his actions, led to success.

Lacking feedback

Joanne works for a major IT business. The company is organized
upon matrix principles and attracts self-starters. Line-manage-
ment skills are frequently weak and not rationalized. People are
hired for their past record of achievement and given a desk. After
that they sink or swim, finding out where the person they report
to is, who they need to communicate with, and where the influ-
encers are. HR is simply a fragmented library and facilitation service to those managers wishing to spend their budget on training
and development—many do not. There are no standards or proto-
cols for meetings and actions arising from them, all depend solely
on the convener and his or her personal methodology.

Joanne was fortunate that her manager was prepared to spend
money on coaching for those reporting directly to him. She had
been with the company for four months. Joanne had found her
way around and had explored a number of networks where her
skills could be applied. When she was clear about a need, she
would start work and then lose momentum. The framework was
there but she could not put the flesh on the bone. Something was
not quite right. Ten minutes into our session, the following dialogue took place.

JOANNE: My plans get started and look great and then I get stuck.
   It's like being in a vacuum, just floating.

ANGUS: And where is this stuck thing, floating in a vacuum?

JOANNE: It's in my head.

ANGUS: And *what else* is there about that stuck thing, floating in a vacuum?

JOANNE: It needs to get out and be touched by others so it can fly back on a breeze.

ANGUS: So, what next?

JOANNE: Others are breathing and scribbling on it and it's getting clearer like a real thing that people want from me. Now there is enough for me to move on and it's coming back. I can see the writing.

ANGUS: And how is this different from before?

JOANNE: I know it's OK. I'm not working in the void. Now I know it's OK I can press on again.

ANGUS: And what makes that difference? What's it like?

JOANNE: Letting the thing out of the vacuum in my head, sharing it and getting feedback. It's like a light channel working two ways.

Joanne appeared to have a need for external feedback in order to be motivated with her projects. On the face of it, she was in the wrong organization. Luckily, she had met two other women who seemed sympathetic and were able to open two new channels of dialogue where there were means of mutual support in each case. Joanne got her feedback when it was needed.

The preference for external feedback contrasts sharply with the bulk of employees in that company who are self-referencing (for feedback). These individuals use their own measuring sticks to decide whether what they are doing is successful. Joanne was one of many people who need more external feedback to function.

These two preferences are defined within NLP as *meta-programs for external reference and internal reference*. As with all meta-programs, the preference may appear only in certain contexts. The coach must suspend judgment about the "character" of an individual in order to give good service to the coachee. The coachee may operate from different preferences in different contexts. Just how critical this understanding is is highly stressed by Shelle Rose Charvet, who promotes the creative use of meta-programs in organizations and in coaching.

The coach can gain understanding about the coachee's preference for internal or external reference by asking a question in the context of work such as: "Think of something you recently achieved in your job. If you will, take me through the decision process that led to your success."

Decision making has a measuring system associated with it so that the individual knows when something is OK. If the above question does not reveal key information, then try another question: "In making [that decision], how did you know it was the right one?"

Managers often expect staff to be motivated in the way they themselves experience motivation. This is a very common and serious mistake and one that whole companies often suffer from. It's no wonder that a culture of kicking and bullying at the top is emulated by executives several layers down.

There are many models for exploring people's motivation and all of them (including my own) must fall short because we are dealing with individuals and not morphs of our own making. The basic drive of people as expressed during coaching often surprises me in its richness and variety. Managers who (through lack of training and development) fail to understand that their staff are stimulated differently from themselves are severely inadequate. We must open up to reality if we are to let our people perform. The more we understand about their preferences, the more we can communicate and mould tasks to stimulate and motivate them to success.

I want to highlight further issues that affect motivation that are described in the language of meta-programs. These are *procedural* and *options* preferences and *big-picture* and *small-picture* preferences. These will be illustrated below by coaching examples.

My boss doesn't make sense

Wendy works in technology. Owing to corporate restructuring, she was managing three instead of two areas. Wendy also gained a new boss. She preferred information that had logical tie-ins, moving from step to step; she had, in meta-program terms, a *procedural* preference. Her boss, Ian, was quite different. He was creatively brainstorming all the time, looking for new slants on everything and bouncing ideas back and forth like a ping-pong ball. He liked choice and was an *options*-preference person.

The difficulty for Wendy was that in meetings with Ian she could not see the wood for the trees. Ian was planting new ideas all over the place without letting her see a logical direction and sequence of thought. In her work, it was mainly her methodical attention to detail that was critically important to providing value to her role. In questioning Wendy, I wished to appeal to what was logical and procedural:

ANGUS: Is there a method that you might share with Ian that might satisfy his thinking preference and also help you structure your thoughts?

WENDY: If I knew how his ideas fitted my work direction, then they wouldn't seem so random and I might know how to give weight to them and in what context. At the moment they're coming at me shoulder-high like bullets. I have no idea what most of them are about and why or when they may be important to Ian.

ANGUS: So a system that allowed you to fit those ideas logically onto an overview of your direction of work might help?

WENDY: I guess so. If I could have a picture, grid, or timeline to hang things on, I might at least make sense of it afterwards. As the moment I feel I'm failing Ian because, when I get to my office, my notes mean nothing.

ANGUS: In thinking about a picture, grid or timeline, what do you think might work for you and Ian?

WENDY: I like the idea of a timeline. I can put on established actions as I see them now and ask Ian where his ideas might fit.

ANGUS: And do you think he might respond to that?

WENDY: Yes, if he feels I'm doing it to make more use of his advice.

Wendy decided to try this device with her boss. She was successful.

The big-picture/small-picture preferences can also be a motivating or demotivating area to explore in coaching.

My team doesn't spring to action

I also coached Wendy's boss, Ian. Not only was he a free thinker but he also had big ideas about where he was hoping to lead his team. His ideas and visions were way ahead of those in the corporate five-year strategic policy. The policy had a business plan that supported the direction. Ian had additional ideas that needed to be selected and worked on by others to find fruition. Ian was fond of strategy meetings that for him meant letting his staff think outside the box and look further ahead. In doing so, he was leaving his managers behind. He was aware of this.

IAN: The business is growing, but in a loop. The answer is in bespoke processing, where we can capture more value added. The market isn't fully developed for that but it will be. If we've learned anything from the past production issues it is that we need to be flexible and adapt more quickly to market and technical issues.

Ian's ideas seemed rather vague; they needed more detail for his staff to know where to place their efforts. I asked Ian if he could capture his targets *"in a nutshell"* and whether I might write these down on the large board in our room. He agreed.

IAN: We need more flexible manufacturing and working practices to adapt faster to market and technical issues.

I invited Ian to write this statement down on the board but he was happy for me to do this. I wrote down his broad statement, low down on the right side, where he indicated.

ANGUS: What needs to happen to arrive at the target of "flexible working practices"?

IAN: Using our production overcapacity to trial new products would help.

ANGUS: And if the left hand corner of the board is now, and knowing that the target is down on the right, where or when will this be happening?

Ian got up, took a pen, and wrote down at the middle of the board. "What else?" I asked. Ian stayed at the board adding this and other new steps between the two extremes. Not only were we putting more detail into the target, but were also ordering it to provide a process as well. When a coachee has a process, you can be more confident that success will follow their commitment.

In a similar way, we explored the other goal of flexible manufacturing. This entailed short-term purchases and longer-term capital investment. When we were finished, I asked Ian to put time-based milestones on the board, too. He did this rapidly and was all set to ask his secretary to copy it all, but I had another question that would look for behaviors that might result from the policy decisions.

ANGUS: When we have more flexible manufacturing and working practices adapting to market and technical issues, what will your people be actually doing differently?

IAN: We could be producing five or six products in a week rather than one a month. There'll be increased automation in quality control, perhaps a full SPC system and more modern handling and demarcation of stock. There will be less stock, too. Our suppliers will need to tighten up deliveries or be changed, perhaps on a JIT [just in time] basis.

ANGUS: And how do you imagine your people will experience their new working environment?

IAN: They should feel more confident and able. They will be communicating much more frequently and enjoying that extra contact and team involvement in making new things happen rather than firefighting the process. They will be happy to say "yes we can", too!

ANGUS: If you were to describe to your team what you will be producing, the new production cycles, the investments in plant and quality, and if you were to describe what you envisage that they will be doing, would that make a change in your team?

IAN: Yes.

My last intervention was not very "clean" since I was making a suggestion, but Ian had already invested a lot in this exercise and I was responding to both that and his energy. We had not changed Ian's preference for big-picture information and communication, but he had learned a new way to express his ideas and plans in a way that was clearer and more motivating for his team. It was, apparently, a critical step in his development as a senior manager.

Compelling targets

Compelling targets should be in the first rank of motivational factors. As we have seen, what is compelling for one person is not necessarily compelling for another. The tools we have used so far help to unearth issues and targets and, further, to have the coachee think about ranking their motivation to achieve them. I have maintained so far that I like to have coachees attain a score of eight or above in their confidence of achieving their targets but that benchmark is mine, not theirs.

In the case of Brian, we used a timeline to help him get a real sense of his target in the present. In addition, we then explored some objective information around that target. In the coaching environment, it is not always easy or convenient to run a timeline by actual physical walking, but it can still be done in the coachee's mind to useful effect. Objectivity can be explored by asking the coachee to mentally fly over their timeline. Sometimes, the coachee has identified a target and their enthusiasm for it is already tangible. Then it can be simpler and faster to ask the coachee to go to that target, in their own time, supporting their experience by using the present tense to assist them to hold their state.

Magda had been frustrated by the eagerness of a colleague to steal personal kudos from their combined effort. Magda had arrived at a solution that suited her but one that would need some courage to fulfill.

MAGDA: I want to use the skills I've learned here to seek Judith's cooperation in experiencing what it's like to be in my shoes.

ANGUS: And have you control over this outcome?

MAGDA: No, but I'm happy to explore other solutions if she refuses, but I think she will do it for me.

ANGUS: If you are happy, let's look at what those other solutions might be and explore the one you've identified.

MAGDA: Please.

ANGUS: Imagine, if you will, an opportunity when you will ask her whether she's willing to engage in this meeting. I would like you to be in this meeting now, as perfectly as you possibly can. Where is Judith, how is she looking, where is the light coming from, how do you feel, what is your breathing like? Is she speaking or are you?

I waited some time while Magda sat quietly, eyes closed.

MAGDA: Judith's leaning on the windowsill. I think she's anticipating something from me. I can't quite make out her face.

ANGUS: Develop your sense of everything you find it easiest to capture here. What she is wearing, whether you can smell any perfume, hear the telephone, voices. The hum of a fan, a typical movement that she makes when with you.

MAGDA: Judith's fine. I can ask this question and deal with her response whether positive or not. I think positive.

The aim of my questioning was to try to encourage a wide range of experiencing into the situation. Magda had used sensory language in talking with me and I reflected that in talking to her. The language is designed to gloss over things gently, not steer the coachee down a particular line. Magda had noticed that she could not see Judith's face and I steered away from that toward the things she might more easily construct in the experience; the face might come later, when her experience was more real.

ANGUS: How real is this experience, zero through ten?

MAGDA: Nine.

ANGUS: And could you make this better? And, if you could, how can you do that now?

MAGDA: Judith always fiddles with her watch when nervous. She's doing it now. That helps, too.

ANGUS: So, when you are ready, and in your own time, ask your question.

Magda was able to experience asking her question and her level of certainty about asking it was subsequently ten out of ten. We then explored the scenarios evolving from the question depending upon Judith's level of cooperation, and then rechecked after that whether her certainty in talking to Judith about her issue was still as it was.

This checking phase in coaching is important. When a new layer of issues or perceptions is explored, it may change the motivation to achieve the original target or even change the target itself. It is the job of the coach to make sure that targets remain as compelling at the end of a session as they may have been in the middle.

Compelling targets or vision make decision making so much easier. If we are fearful of issues, such as failure, we tend to steer our direction away from confrontation and move away from peak effectiveness. If we have a compelling target, we tend to steer toward that target and our performance improves. Those without targets tend to move toward and away from a line of direction and outcome. This may appeal to those who are weak in planning and focus. They may still meet their corporate targets but will take longer to get there.

Chapter Four

Coaching Contract and Practice

Now we look at the different ways in which coaching comes about, ethics, and terms of reference for coaching practice. We will also set out the needs for preliminary communications in advance of coaching work and post-contract follow-up. I also indicate some of the key elements of importance for setting up coaching or mentoring activity.

Freelance coaching

I typically work for an initial number of sessions with each individual. This is dependent always on the willingness of the coachee(s) to move forward after the first session. Necessarily, within teams, that raises the issue of alternative coaches should there be some interpersonal resistance in the coaching relationship that cannot be easily set aside. In my case this has not yet been invoked but it does happen. The number of sessions varies but I usually set out for six and may settle for five, sometimes even four.

Most of my work comes from individuals within companies at a senior level who want coaching for themselves. Other work comes to support other management initiatives. Sometimes, managers are contracting for themselves and all or part of their immediate team. This is often the case where there are new jobs that may clash. I may be asked to coach each person in those overlapping posts with an option to meet them in joint sessions, if needed. Occasionally we are retained to continue at the next level(s) down an organization.

I am also retained to coach other coaches who typically have a dual agenda: first to experience a different style of coaching and, second, to deal with a performance or leadership issue of their own.

Employing external coaches: strengths and weaknesses

If the organization has made the right choice, then the external coach provides objectivity and focus to coaching that is rarely available internally, because of the huge demands of modern management. The external coach will often be balancing the individual's direction and performance against the strategic needs of the organization, whether overt or not. The individual can be encouraged to face issues that will provide them and the company with best value in terms of the organization's development. External coaches more easily gain the trust and confidence of a coachee. As a result, coachees are often far more willing to express much more, including their motivations, and thus progress faster to more compelling targets. External coaches working in teams can collate valuable and general information about key motivators and demotivators in the organization's structure and in its culture and support policies.

The problem of using external coaches can be cost and the lack of flexibility over timing of sessions owing to financial issues. The financial issues for coaches arise where only one or two people are to be coached and sessions are short. This is not financially ideal for the coach and can be prohibitively expensive in fees and expenses for the organization. It's for that reason that many of my colleagues try to establish two-and-a-half-hour sessions as the norm. Clearly, though, these do not necessarily suit all individuals, many of whom are excited but exhausted after an arduous hour and a half. If the company and individual are flexible, extra time can sometimes be agreed for support by telephone and billing takes place as normal.

When working in teams, I sometimes offer longer initial sessions so I see just two executives on one day and then, on a flexible basis, move to see four people in one day. I see both individuals and sometimes have longer sessions but with two staff members concurrently. This is a useful set-up where there are issues between departments, historical conflict, or a need for separation of a corporate function because of the onerous responsibilities and duties in running it.

Coaching can sometimes appear expensive until you set the cost against the salary of the individual being coached and the relative investment in that individual. A good coach is much more motivating than a more powerful vehicle and the effect will last through the working life of the individual, not just the first few weeks. Companies also realize that independent coaches do not earn fees all the time and are not remunerated when marketing and developing their business or investing in their own personal and professional development.

External coaches have the advantage of being exposed to solutions and efficient methods from outside the organization's culture. They bring fresh challenges and their experience and vision can be highly motivating to others. Often, organizations retain former staff to coach existing staff. Owing to lack of training and experience, what the executive gets is mentoring, which is highly limited in its impact compared with true coaching. Where experienced ex-employees do have such training and experience there are very useful benefits in using them as coaches, even though their breadth of experience and solutions from other cultures may be limited. Where they excel is knowing the strategic influencing paths to success, and, by informed questioning, they can help their charges to find highly effective solutions.

Internal coaching provision

Internal provision typically works on standard mentoring practice rather than true coaching. In these situations a more senior person (or HR executive) offers mentor solutions and advice. If a coaching model is used, then a high level of executive learning becomes possible, sometimes limited by two main factors: limited breadth of experience from other cultures and the level of trust available within an in-company relationship. However, with suitable training and experience and a selection process that allows the coachee to change the coach, there is scope for very good coaching to be undertaken within organizations. This is of special benefit where coaching is offered in support of management-change programs that have been rolled out internally by the same team. In selecting a coaching team, beware of staff who understand a lot about change programs and training but do not exemplify the qualities of personal change personally—a coach must be someone open and authentic in their willingness to help others and in developing themselves.

To whom is the coach responsible?

Sometimes I am engaged to coach senior managers on their own volition and from their own budget. In that case, it is quite usual for me to have no contact at all with the human-resources VP. I often work, therefore, without a formal agreement with the corporation. In this case, both my coachee and my client are, to all extents and purposes, the same. I agree directly the terms of reference for working together, negotiate fees, expenses, and so on. These are set down in my letter of engagement.

The issue of responsibility is more complex when the external coach is engaged in work for an organization. Then, the work undertaken will need to meet the organization's expectations as well as the coachee's. Just occasionally these can be in conflict. In this event, it is vital to have set out the terms of reference for coaching and to be clear on the limits of engagement.

An obvious area of potential conflict is where the coachee wants help to find a better role inside (or outside) the organization. Unless these parameters have been properly set out in advance, the coach can be seen to be making influential decisions "on the hoof" and this is counterproductive to healthy coaching.

Where coaches are internal, it is similarly important to set the parameters of engagement and make clear what other provisions are available to support the coachees—for example, counseling. The independence and confidentiality of the material discussed and the keeping of any notes needs also to be set out and should rightly be available to all coachees to maintain transparency and to underpin trust.

Selling coaching internally

Individual coaching should be seen as an investment of significant time and money and too many senior managers worry excessively about how a particular individual will take to coaching. Typical comments include:

- Tom will feel singled out and failing
- Helen is more likely to take to an internal mentor than an external coach
- Ashok would feel like he needed counseling
- Julian will feel like a problem rather than a solution to our challenges

This projection of feelings is invariably oversensitive. They would rarely occur if the procuring manager had coachee experiences of their own.

Where management confidence has been gained, external coaches are invariably asked to help sell the assignment internally. In attempting to frame the concept of coaching for an individual, managers should be able to communicate at a more positive level. Thus, reframing the above statements for the individuals concerned, they might say:

Tom, we want to invest in your increasing success by providing you with your own personal coach for six weeks. If you find it useful I would be open to considering more sessions later on.

Helen, I want you to shine more brightly in the organization and believe that having your own personal coach will provide you with a safe environment where you can further stretch the limits of your ability.

Ashok, it's only top VPs who usually have access to a personal coach but I wish to extend this bonus to you. Think of it please as further investment in you and in the company's future.

Julian, you're in a unique position to help us sort out relationship issues between the divisions and to help us work better as a team. I need your help and realize that this is a colossal and open-ended task. I've taken advice at the highest levels and we've been lucky to retain a heavyweight personal coach who will be available to you for four months with two half-day sessions per month. I hope you will want to participate and then report to me on how we might move our communications issues when that period is over.

These are positive ways of selling the coaching assignment and of course can be tailored to suit the preferences, motivations, and aspirations of the individual.

Letting coachees know what to expect before sessions

My experience is that coachees are very willing to go along with all manner of interventions. However, it is important that coaches have thought through what they feel best for both their clients and coachees in this phase of any contract. The coach seeks to reduce any stress associated with the session and to increase the likelihood that the coachee will concentrate on the session's performance target or issue. There are no hard and fast rules. Too much information out of context can be alarming. So can too little information. I prefer to leave the level of information needed to the individual. In the absence of any desire to know more, I restrict the communication to essential points such as the length of sessions and the need for an issue with which to work. If they want to know more, then the HR department or I provide it. In any case, at the first session and after introductions, I always take a couple of minutes to set the scene.

First meeting: preparing for work

When undertaking client work it is often the case that I have had limited contact with the coachee, or sometimes none at all. In this case, it is even more important to establish a working level of rapport before the session begins. I recommend establishing a mindset that assumes that this is not part of the session. The session will start when the coachee accepts an invitation to begin.

First, I introduce myself using my whole name but no title. I never offer a business card except in exchange. I always offer them any seat in which they may be comfortable and the possibility of moving it. My own briefcase, notes, and so forth are placed in a neutral position that does not take ownership over any chair. The normal banal greetings and chitchat work best. I do not wish to introduce discussion about politics or issues of corporate restructuring. Acceptable subjects are those that any two executives might engage in as a preliminary to a meeting: their journey, the weather, how they are today, and so on.

Instinctively, I am invariably leaving short silences (not forced) that give the coachee potential to stay with the introductory process or to start work in the session. If I sense a reluctance to start rather than a lack of obvious rapport with me, then I will tackle that directly, with something like, "Are you happy to start our coaching session shortly?"

The coach must always face issues that impact on the quality of the dynamic *before* engaging in any other issue.

Scene setting and recapping expectations

The scene setting or prologue will depend on the engagement criteria. I may have to set the scene in the corporate context before attending to my methods. Only then will we go to the issue that they have brought to the session. I reaffirm the commitment to the number of sessions and length of them. If it is appropriate to the terms of my engagement, I also mention whether or not the sessions can finish early. When I set out my own stall, what follows is representative:

COACH: As you know, I am here to support you. I don't have magic powers and will not be telling you how to be a more incredible manager than others at [name of organization]. I am here as a catalyst to help you to deal with issues and reach targets using your own talents and abilities. The rate at which we work doesn't matter to me. I am, however, interested in your success, and the degree to which you excel in these sessions is again entirely up to you. I will work at your pace. What happens in this room is confidential to us. If we feel it useful to provide specific feedback to the company, then we can do it together and agree it together. I believe you have already been provided with a mechanism to provide feedback on my performance.

There are typically small breaks and pauses in which to invite interruption. I then say, "You may wish to know what I do." If there is agreement, and there invariably is, I continue.

COACH: I shall be asking questions and challenging you from time to time in order to give you an opportunity to learn more about yourself and what works most effectively for you. There may also be silences and these are in your control. I do not mind whether they last a few seconds or ten minutes if they are useful for you.

I may also invite you to move around the room, write on this paper or the board, and I will probably challenge you in new ways to gain new insights. All of these things are quite normal in coaching. All I am offering you is gifts—questions, challenges, and silence—and whether you accept these gifts or not is up to you. I have many more in my bag. At times I may make notes. These will remain private and confidential to us and, if you wish to have them when our sessions finally end, you may do so.

I may, occasionally, give you the benefit of my own experience or share a story with you. I may provide you with articles if appropriate. I am [am not] available for email and [or] telephone contact and here are the times when you might call me. I'm flexible about finishing times but hope that we can agree to keep our appointments and to starting on time, as a commitment to the work we are going to do here.

I don't mind whether you work on an issue that is small for you, one that is more challenging, or one that is a major step. Again, the decision is yours. I shall think no better or worse of you. Do you have any questions before we begin?

The prologue is best if it is personal to the coach and reflects their own style of engagement. In any case, it will need to be clear about confidentiality, will need to mention the taking and ownership of notes (if used), and will need to agree that decisions on direction, interventions, and pace are for the coachee. If the coach uses their own stories and metaphors, then the coachee must be prepared for this (see "Transference" in Chapter Eight). From an ethical stand-point, I insist that the coachee be fully aware of the relationship the coach has with the company and the form of any reporting.

My invitation to start the session might be as follows:

COACH: OK, if you're ready, shall we make a start? [Watching.] Why don't you tell me what you want from this session and the two hours we have?

Logistical needs for coaching sessions

In setting up coaching, I much prefer to work outside the organization's premises but this is not often achieved. The reason for this preference is not personal: it comes from a knowledge that many people relax better on neutral territory when talking about issues related to their working environment, maybe find greater objectivity too. In any case, the needs for a working space are the same. It should:

- be away from communal (noisy) areas
- be lockable
- be isolated from the vision or hearing of others
- be comfortable, adequately lit, and have at least three identical chairs
- have board or flipchart, pens, and paper
- have water and glasses
- have no telephone (or have one that can be unhooked)
- have a notice on the door giving the date and times and "no admittance"
- have secretaries informed about noninterruption
- have cellphones turned off
- have space necessary to do timelines and perceptual position work

- have uninterrupted space between the coach and coachee
- have a watch that it is easily visibly by coach and coachee
- have cloakrooms that are nearby

When working in my own rooms I also use colored hula hoops that the coachee can select and use to represent the present and future for timelines. Coasters, place mats, pens, etc. do just as well.

Behaviors during coaching sessions

Many coaches never get out of their chair after an initial greeting. There is nothing wrong with that, but those of us who use boards, large sheets of paper, perceptual positions, role play, timelines, and other interventions requiring movement need to be natural and considerate of the coachee's needs. If in doubt, ask. If you are considering the use of perceptual positions, the dialogue might go rather like this:

COACH: In that scenario, where you are with Donald in that "difficult meeting"? And, in reliving that meeting here, where would you and Donald be? You can move any chair and the furniture, including the one I'm sitting on.

(Coach gets up and stands.)

With timelines, I am typically standing just to the side of the coachee and within a few inches. I am rarely looking directly at them but trying to capture and sense as much information about their state as possible. This proximity has never afforded any difficulty for my coachee. If a coach is unsure of how close they should be, then I advise doing group work with other coaches and inviting as much feedback as possible. The process can be wholly sensory or instinctive—it does not matter which, as long as the coach supports the coachee's state. Training and work at practice groups helps enormously.

The coach needs to provide good attention at all times. If the coachee is reticent about an intervention or a suggested tool, then simply offer other choices. Note taking can be a distraction and looking at the clock annoying. I warn my coachees that I may take notes. I use a silent propelling pencil with a soft lead or a pen that does not click or scratch. The watch is placed where I can easily see it without turning my head or making any gross movement, if possible so the coachee can see it, too.

Eye contact needs to be natural and flexible to the needs of the coachee. Some people are very disturbed by prolonged and direct eye contact. The coach should be as natural and comfortable as possible but open postures or overintensity (leaning, looming, staring) can be distracting. I do not wish coaches to be entirely gray, but the most important thing a coachee should notice is the quality of attention and the skillful ability to demonstrate that their issues and language have been heard and understood. Anything that detracts from that is best left outside the coaching session. This would include the wearing of inappropriate clothing for the culture, inappropriate physical contact, and encroaching on the coachee's space.

Remember, too, that posture copying by the coach can be particularly annoying to coachees. If you are making conscious decisions about mimicry of posture, then you are almost certainly attending to the wrong thing. Keep your attention to attending to and listening to the coachee as a first priority. Any mimicry of posture should be fluid and natural.

Watch out for tiredness. Where training and development in soft skills has been limited, coachees may find sessions both stimulating and tiring as well. A pause for breathing and stretching and a refreshment break may be both welcome and helpful.

In long sessions of over an hour, bear in mind that a change in position and pace may be offered and useful. A refreshment and comfort break should be offered when appropriate.

Recently, an experienced coach told me how tired they become in coaching. I sense that the closer one evolves into an authentic coach, at all times, then the easier and less stressful coaching becomes. I guess that also means that the coach will be familiar with emotional material and unstressed by it rather than detached. Detachment might lower the coach's stress level, but will not be useful for the coachee.

Neutrality

The novice coach, especially, needs to maintain a neutral emotion through the bulk of the coaching session. There are exceptions, some of which are dealt with in the next chapter, but for now it may be useful to illustrate why this neutrality can be important. First, however, what do I mean by neutrality?

Neutrality is the ability to maintain good attention and support the coachee without mimicry or copying of posture or expression. Examples include smiling because the coachee is smiling, raising eyebrows in response to raised eyebrows, laughing in response to an inappropriate laugh. These views vary from the "pace and lead" philosophy of NLP and I make no apology for that. Coachees are not our friends: they are entering a professional relationship that demands a different approach. We shall also see that the common NLP view of "rapport at any price" is not appropriate to professional coaching practice. Both NLP resources are useful in coaching but must not be prescribed, as they often are in coaching courses.

When we respond to these tics and expressions subconsciously, we are in effect saying, "Yes, that's OK, and I want to be in your gang." The coach needs to be alert. Tics and expressions may anchor emotions for the coachee that are inappropriate or unhelpful. Here are examples.

ROSALIND: The presentation was a disaster. I was the only one not to get any applause. [Laughs.]

JONATHON: I've made rather an ass of myself. [Smiles broadly.]

In these cases the coachee may be improperly aligned (emotionally) with their issue. By maintaining exquisite attention but not responding (by smiling or laughing), the coach is leaving a question mark over that possible misalignment without necessarily having to deal with it overtly. It may be socially acceptable to laugh but it is not appropriate to laugh at calamity in the coaching context.

Sometimes the coachee will then express that lack of alignment:

ROSALIND: Of course, it's not at all funny. In fact, if I thought about it, I would cry again and I really don't want to do that now.

COACH: So Rosalind, is there something you want to change because of that experience?

If Rosalind had not responded, the coach could decide whether to be more direct:

COACH: Was not getting any applause funny for you?

That is a more difficult intervention to make if the coach has just laughed at that situation. In fact, it is more difficult to appear serious and concerned at all, and an opportunity to help the coachee may be lost.

Many coaches pay no heed to neutrality in their practice—sometimes out of ignorance and sometimes out of choice because they feel that it is more important to be honest and "natural" than to be contrived. This is a weak argument but one with which I have sympathy. Coaches are always contriving to behave and question in ways that are learned rather than natural—why should this skill be any different? In practice, my coaching is mixed. Sometimes I do nod or smile but I do modify my behavior where those behaviors would help imprint lack of authenticity in the coachee (incongruence). Whatever you choose to do as a coach, let it at least be out of intelligent decision, not ignorance.

Empathetic projection and expressed sympathy

Empathetic interventions by the coach can be a distraction and bring the coachee's concentration away from their own issue and toward that of the coach. Strictly, expressed empathy (information about the emotional world of the coach) is not helpful. We shall see in the next chapter—in relation to "provocative coaching" (PC)—exceptional variations on that traditional approach.

However, what of sympathy? I have found that sympathy, simply expressed, can be cathartic when a coachee is holding onto unexpressed emotion. Clearly, I am now moving into the interventional world of the counselor. A coach without training and experience in counseling is best advised to leave these interventions to specialists. I advise any coach without such experience to avoid sympathy for any unexpressed emotion that they believe they perceive in the coachee. A simple intervention such as "It must be very hard for you" can trigger weeping and emotional collapse when the subject is holding back feelings. Unless the coach is trained in counseling, it may be safer simply to acknowledge or to reflect, accurately, what has actually been expressed by the coachee (if in an authentic way).

COACHEE: It's been very hard for me.

COACH: Yes.

Or:

COACHEE: It's been very hard for me.

COACH: It's been very hard for you?

Alternatively, let them know of any other support available and ask them to observe the situation that was difficult from the position of observer (third perceptual position) in order to help the coachee attend to more logical aspects of the problem than the emotional ones.

Pacing and leading

The concept of pacing and leading comes from NLP. The idea is one of coach alignment with the coachee to establish good rapport, then moving ahead. Earlier I provided numerous examples of the linguistic elements of coaching that encourage rapport and help the coachee to feel that that they are being heard and attended too, without judgment. There are other components, some of which are highlighted below, and others under "Mindsets for the coach" in Chapter Six. An example where the coach moves the pace forward and leads is that of Adrian, below. Reflective language showed him that he was being heard and attended too. I wished then to lead him to an experience of his future desired state, as if it were happening in the present.

ADRIAN: There's a place on the coast that I wish to live.

ANGUS: So, those years are behind you. What is living here like?

Note the use of the present tense to encourage the coachee with their experience as if it were happening in the present. I invited Adrian to change state and have a fully developed experience of the future in our session. Here is the example of Dawn. The language I used copied her own.

DAWN: Wonderful, I can see the trees.

ANGUS: And, if there was something about the trees and about being mentally restful and physically restful that is representative of how this is, what is that representative thing like?

DAWN: A big green tree.

ANGUS: Do you experience that big green tree now?

DAWN: Totally, it's wonderful.

Note the use of the present tense to help maintain the coachee in state.

Breathing

Breathing deserves a special mention outside the context of pacing and leading, where the degree of emotional association about an issue is distressing or unhelpful. I make one slow intake of breath and make an out breath from my mouth slightly more audible by pressing my tongue to the roof of my mouth. The effect on a tense coachee can be transformational, irregular breaths moving to deeper and more regular intakes. Typically one then notices a change in skin tones and physical relaxation.

Exquisite attention

Give your attention fully to the coachee as a first priority. Some NLP training organizations often see the skill of pacing and leading the coachee as a primary-level ability. I disagree. I feel that the ability to give exquisite attention and the skill to reflect accurately what you have heard are prime factors in developing and encouraging the coachee to work with you.

A great way to develop skills in listening is to experience and to coach in nonintervention contracts. These silent contracts are some of those we run in the course "The Power of Silence". Participants experience silent coaching as both coach and coachee. This provides rapid learning in what works and what does not and the feedback from these observed sessions is greatly influential in encouraging coaches to refine these skills.

Sensing

One of the four pillars of NLP is sensory acuity (the others are flexibility, well-formed outcomes, and rapport). In coaching, the ability to raise one's awareness of the coachee's state is vitally important. It is important also not to rush to conclusions (see Chapter Eight). A coachee who has what appears to be a nervous cough early in the session may simply have had a piece of candy go down the airway and be suffering the consequences.

Sensing, listening, watching, and increasing peripheral vision all help to gain information about the coachee's state and especially about a change in that state. Try to be slow to make a judgment about its significance. You can always ask the coachee to tell you the significance of what you perceive.

COACH: I notice that your middle finger seems to be restless. What is that about?

COACHEE: Oh, I tend to do that when my blood sugar goes down. I need to eat something. Thanks for reminding me how hungry I am.

Typical body signs may give clues to a change in the coachee's state. Whether you are right or wrong about the significance is largely irrelevant. The coachee can tell you exactly what it is. It may be a tightening of the jaw, coloration in the neck, a slowing of breathing rate. You do not even have to highlight it:

COACH: Something seems different about you since I asked about your boss. What do you think or sense?

What is significant to the coach may not be significant to the coachee. They will have their own map of significance. Asking an open question helps them to pinpoint what is significant to them.

A note on eye cues

In NLP, a great deal is often made about eye cues. The suggestion is that information can be gained from the eye movements of the coachee. This is correct, but unfortunately the statistics for eye cues, even for skilled practitioners, do not provide a great deal of confidence and hence the aspiring coach has a poor chance of being correct about the cause and effect. Ordinarily, one might ask the coachee for confirmation of the cause, but a word of warning to prospective NLP coaches: eye cues are usually very annoying to coachees and can put them on their guard. The emphasis on eye cues has done NLP and its coaches a disservice by highlighting a technique that is seen by many as being intrusive and manipulative.

Instinct

Instinct is one of those intangibles that some people have and others do not. It is not a critical gift to coaching but can be supremely elegant at times. At various times I have been accused of having extraordinary instincts, homing in on a critical leverage point very quickly; but I am sure that it is not finely honed for all individuals that I encounter. I suspect that my instincts depend partly upon a matching of emotional and cultural history with those of my coachees but regret that I have no evidence for that statement. There are others who have the most extraordinary instinct and seem to demonstrate it elegantly with a whole range of individuals.

I am sure that instinct is improved by one's own emotional development.

Another factor that may be important is a genuine interest in people and a desire to support them in a way that is wholly pertinent to them. This selflessness of spirit provides a sound basis for exquisite attention and for the provision of a "safe space" in which the coachee can accelerate their progress. The founder of provocative therapy, Frank Farrelly, has the view (quoted in McLeod, 2002d) that, "It is crucial to proceed with a twinkle in the eye and affection in the heart." "Heart" is a good word: it conjures up a sense of real care, or love, for others. The twinkle in the eye must bring a feeling of confidence in the coachee and the sense that you have an empathetic fellow traveler on your journey. Coming from this state (of being), it is little wonder that Farrelly helps his patients to miracles.

Reflecting back issues and language

The skill of remembering and reflecting language can be learned. Some coaches find it harder than others. I sometimes use notes when the flow of associated information from the coachee is rapid and prolonged. Coaches can develop their own style of reflection. Where linguistic memory is weak, the coach can reflect more frequently. These twin skills of exquisite attention and accurate listening are key to establishing the potential for a high rate of progress for the coachee. Without these, any amount of pacing and leading will be relatively fruitless.

Ending sessions

I am flexible about the length of sessions provided my contract with the client allows it; invariably it does. This is contrary to most psychotherapy practice, for example, where the strict session length is often seen as a means of underlining the contract/boundary between therapist and client and instilling discipline and commitment in the latter. In coaching, I am more interested that the coachee might feel that they have made progress and be considerably more motivated to action than they were when they arrived. I invariably ask the coachee what actions they have agreed to take rather than tell them, and assist in that process as necessary. Sometimes I have actions too.

COACH: If I heard you correctly, you also said that you will be reading those positive listings at coffee break.

COACHEE: Yes, that's right, I'll be doing that!

COACH: And this evening I'll email that article I promised you.

Where the coachee has brought issues with emotional attachment, I invariably ask them to reflect on the level of progress "of state" that they experience:

COACH: Before we finish, I wonder if you'd like to reflect on the measure of your state when you came here today and what it is now, as usual, where ten is the highest that you consider it could be.

It is a gift to me to have this feedback and may contribute to the coachee's feel-good factor by acknowledging my small part in their achievement. Of course, the last word has to be about confirming arrangements for the next session.

Out-of-session work for the coachee

Occasionally, where a new intervention is being practiced or some preliminary work will save time in the sessions, I will ask the coachee if they would like to do some work between sessions. Examples include anchoring, where a coachee may have an idea about stacking one anchor over another, but, owing to other commitments, we have to end the session. Another is the writing of positive listings. The coachee will usually undertake to bring these back to the next session or email them to me by a certain date. Yet another example is when we are dealing with values and beliefs.

A coachee can set these down at home and save session time. Similarly, the coachee can prepare the way for a session that will revisit their map of strengths and weaknesses. This too can be done at home. In all cases, it is important to make sure that these targets are as measured, realistic, and as certain as any other target. We want our coachees to feel that they are building experiences of success, not failure.

Subsequent sessions work for the coach

As well as any mind-setting activity that the coach may do before a session, it is vital to have private time to review the previous session. Where I have a sequence of sessions, I will review the notes for each coachee prior to the sessions, sometimes an hour or more previously. I particularly note any actions that we have agreed (for either of us) and their issues and targets. Where the coaching is linked to a team-development issue or target, I will review these also to see whether any change of direction needs to be offered to the coachee. I summarize these (if not already done earlier), typically on a new sheet.

Chapter Five

Developmental Models

Many coaching methods are based upon specific approaches. These include the GROW (*g*oal setting, *r*eality checking, *o*ptions and *w*hat/when/whom) model favored by Whitmore (2002), integral coaching (Shervington, 2002), conversational coaching (a methodology of Shelle Rose Charvet first facilitated for the Coaching Foundation Ltd. in Hurley, Berkshire, UK, in November 2002) and solutions (brief-therapy) coaching (De Shazer, 1985). References to some of those organizations offering information and training are provided in the appendices.

In addition to specific coaching models, numerous management-change models can be applied, in part, to coaching. It is unrealistic in one book to cover all such disciplines, particularly when they are treated in numerous specific texts. My exposure to such models also includes transactional analysis (see for example Harris, 1995), provocative therapy, clean language, SCORE, PROGRAM, symbolic modeling, emotional intelligence, and alpha leadership (Deering, Dilts, Russell, 2002). Where I have found an approach particularly useful, from my own experience of using and observing such approaches, then I include it here. In some cases, I am unaware of any other available resource that makes a connection between the model I have chosen to illustrate and the actual practice of coaching.

Flexibility of coaching approach in organizations

Every model has its benefits and application. Individuals who are looking for individual coaching may prefer one model to another. In the corporate context, however, I maintain that it is usually better to meet individual needs by being flexible.

Where an employee is resistant to a particular model, it is unlikely that they will make best progress in coaching. A flexible approach will be better. One can set a framework for this with the organization.

Sometimes a model is chosen by an organization because a strategic decision has been made to disperse the model generally throughout the team. This can occur where, for example, a personality-profiling instrument is being rolled out through an organization—MBTI is just one typical example of that. If a pan-team model is being implemented, and where there is individual resistance, I would still hope to convince the client that a wider set of interventions (taken from different models) would be best for those individuals. We would then trust that we might encourage those employees to gain confidence in the preferred model, by stealth, once progress had been made.

We will also cover some background to the psychology of communication and learning by considering individual preferences. I hope that this will improve the coach's ability to join up with the coachee, or, in NLP terms, establish a working level of rapport. Notice I write "working", not "high" or "exquisite". Very high levels of rapport are not necessary for coaching. Challenges can risk rapport but, once trust and confidence have been established, excellent coaching results may be obtained.

Clean language

David Grove developed a series of questions called "clean language" that reflect much of the coachee's language and make minimal assumptions. I have explained that it is better to ask a coachee what they "experience" rather than what they "see" or "feel" since these make assumptions that may not be true for that coachee. The argument for using Grovian interventions is similar. The coach brings to the session their own map of the world complete with insights and prejudices and a preference for communication that is likely to be different from that of their coachee. Clean language offers a specific set of interventions that are "cleaned" of many of these limitations. The result is that the coachee is exquisitely maintained in their material and they find their own solutions in the most motivating way. Lawley and Tompkins have studied Grove and found that, over 80 percent of the time, he used nine "basic clean questions". These are categorized into two subsets:

Developing questions

- And is there anything else about [client's words]?
- And what kind of [client's words] is that [client's words]?
- And that's [client's words] like what?
- And where is [client's words]?
- And whereabouts [client's words]?

Moving-time questions

- And then what happens?
- And what happens next?
- And what happens just before [client's words]?
- And where could [client's words] come from?

The developing questions help the coachee to enrich their symbolic awareness. The moving-time questions translocate that awareness in order to connect to a wider symbolic inner world. To the uninitiated, David Grove's questions can seem limiting to the intuition of the coach and of doubtful effect. In practice, these questions and the additional "specialist questions" are enormously powerful in helping the coachee to maintain their state and in assisting them to develop their metaphoric experience of both their issues and their solutions.

Symbolic modeling

No contribution to coaching would be complete without reference to the outstanding work of Penny Tompkins and James Lawley (2000). With its basis in clean language and its focus on coachee metaphors, symbolic modeling offers a powerful skill set for personal change and development geared to compelling targets. In its overt use, symbolic modeling may not appeal to all managements. However, I use several of the interventions and the language patterns of symbolic modeling in my work and have never encountered any resistance to them during a coaching session, even though the language seems to many observers to be contrived. Do not be misled by the language constructs: they are powerful keys to unlocking motivated change. The examples of coaching given in this book are highly influenced by such language constructs.

The core of symbolic modeling is in both clean language and accurate reflection of the coachee's language. These language patterns work, rather like trance, to help the coachee to remain suspended in their symbolic world without the external distractions offered by the well-meaning coach. Symbolic modeling encourages and maintains the coachee in that world and helps them to devise symbolic solutions to their performance and personal issues in unique and highly compelling ways. Symbolic modeling is also easily amenable to a wide range of coaches and highly effective even in the hands of the initiate.

Trance

Intervention using clean language often appears to help the coachee into a state like that of trance. Audiences may be amused by stage shows where suggestions under the effect of trance are used for titillation, but we are speaking here of something quite different, established and valuable.

Lawley and Tompkins (2002) describe the effects of trance thus: "Clients naturally develop heightened states of self-absorption (trance) indicated by fixed focus of attention and slowed speech." They go on to quote David Grove: "Every time the client goes inside, as in a daydream, he is going into a trance. It can be very effective to use these facilitatory states in producing neurological changes."

While trance is not a prerequisite of coachee progress using the above models, it can and does occur. It is a useful state in which catharsis (quantum insight) frequently occurs. The experienced coach and counselor need not be afraid of trance or trancelike states and the coachee need not be aware of the label "trance" for the state they have just experienced. In the context of good professional coaching, trance is not induced by suggestion or by using a mechanism of trance induction. Trance, where it results, comes when the coachee goes voluntarily deeper into their symbolic world. The coach, by exquisite use of the coachee's language, is merely a reflective instrument, assisting the coachee to go where they wish to go. The effects can be profound. Age-old blocks to performance may be shed permanently and tantalizing targets can be reached by deliberate effort in spite of the risks that may have been perceived before the coaching intervention.

Conversational coaching

Shelle Rose Charvet has been developing her ideas about "conversational coaching" and many of these came together during 2002, when she delivered a one-day event for us called "Conversational Coaching" in Berkshire, England. I feel sure that this material warrants a whole book to itself, so will concentrate here on just one area that I think especially useful in the context of coachee targets. As background for my reader, Rose Charvet's methodology reflects her considerable skills in NLP questioning and interpretation in the area of NLP meta-programs and particularly those identified in the LAB ("language and behaviors") profile. She uses the nonvocal-communication method of John Grinder to set up the background to her coaching and follows this with an appraisal of the coachee's present state and desired state (target) in terms of the LAB-profile meta-programs, including both "working" and "motivation" traits. Necessarily, this is specialized material, but those trained in NLP, and particularly those trained in the LAB profile, will be familiar with this background. For others, I refer you to Rose Charvet's (1997) book. The book has very little to say about coaching but I hope that a new book will spring from her hand in due course.

The piece that I find most helpful to the lay coach is what Rose Charvet has to say about motivated commitment to goals.

Rose Charvet's goal meta-programs

Rodger Bailey laid out a subset of NLP meta-programs that are called *motivation traits* in his "LAB Profile" self-study kit (Bailey, 1981). Shelle Rose Charvet says that the four motivation traits (meta-programs) that are essential in any goal are the following (given here together with their opposite dimension):

Goal trait	Opposite
Proactive	Reactive
Toward	Away from
Internal	External
Procedures	Options

In the LAB profile, the goal traits are revealed by standard questions made in context. In conversational coaching, they are made more fluidly by the coach in the context of the coachee's goal. The language used by the coachee provides clues about which meta-program is operating, as shown below:

Proactive	Action words, specific to goal only
Toward	Directed, including words such as "get", "find", and "succeed"
Internal	Reliant on self, not others or extraneous facts
Procedures	Clear story showing the essential steps to be taken

Simply asking a question such as, "How do you propose to achieve that?" will provide information; this can be quickly identified by the coach in the light of these four categories of goal trait.

Provocative coaching

Farrelly and Brandsma's seminal book (1974) on provocative therapy highlights a methodology that sprang out of Farrelly's frustration with client-centered practice and the repetitive nature of his patient's predicaments. In many ways provocative therapy is the antithesis of client-centered work. Instead of having the therapist follow the plot of the patient and encourage the patient's free association, provocative therapy encourages free association *by the therapist*. This, coupled with humor, complete honesty in expressing how he saw his patients, and the actual *encouragement* of the patient's dysfunction behavior, yielded phenomenal results in many of his patients. The methods formed the basis of a methodology that has grown significantly in the last twenty years.

The art of provocative therapy is supported by the most exquisite attention (except when a patient is repeating a pattern, in which case the therapist may turn away and drum their fingers or show some other sign of boredom) and the maintenance of an exquisitely safe space for the patient. Needless to say, there are few people with this degree of ability. There are lessons from provocative therapy as practiced by Frank Farrelly that are relevant to coaching practice, including exquisite attention and safe-space.

So often, coaches (and particularly those entrenched in NLP) see rapport as something so important that they dare not risk it. Provocative therapy shows that, in the right hands, the most provocative challenge can be made and propel the individual to an entirely new level of thinking, often breaking patterns that have existed for many years. The level of rapport, as commented upon by the coachee afterwards, is sometimes low. However, the coachee still shows a willingness to go on with the interventions, owing to the level of trust and safety that the therapist engenders. The techniques are particularly suited to people with low self-esteem and those who exhibit long-held dysfunctional patterns.

Farrelly has more than thirty interventions but those below will give an impression of the ideas that underpin the model.

- Solve the person's problems using idiotic ideas: "If you can't write the proposal, pay a colleague to do it."
- Frequent interruption of the individual when they repeat the same issue (it does not matter how).
- Minimize the problem: "Everybody has this problem, so what? Any other problems?"

When I published an article (McLeod, 2002d) entitled "Provocative Coaching," (PC) it was demonstrably tongue-in-cheek. I do not propose that coaching be normally carried out on this basis but wished to explode the myth that risking rapport by challenge is always inappropriate. I also gave a personal example of how provocation can have a healthy outcome.

I recall as a child struggling to walk on tall, homemade stilts and saying something like, "I can't do it, it's impossible!" And got the response, "You're right. Give up and do something else. No one could do it!"

That provoked renewed effort and success.

So, what is PC and when might it be used? I use provocative interventions rarely and never in an initial session. If a dysfunctional pattern is emerging and I think that PC will help, I introduce it at the beginning of the next session and offer it as an intervention strategy without promising to use it. If my coachee agrees and the pattern emerges, I may use one or more PC interventions.

A good coach does not need to use provocative tools but, in the right hands, PC offers useful insights to coachees who may be very stuck. Here are two examples.

Resisting action

Garcia had three or four sessions and we had run up against low-confidence issues in the context of dealing with awkward situations with colleagues. At this session he brought up a similar issue.

GARCIA: I'm sure that Alan will not see my argument properly. It's bound to be rejected.

I could have interjected with, "Can you contradict that statement?" but instead challenged using a PC intervention.

ANGUS: It's obvious then that you should not bother to show it to him. Just let it go.

GARCIA (after a pause): I have to tackle this issue now.

Poor self-esteem

Monika was often self-deprecatory in our sessions. It seemed odd because of her seniority as a group HR director. I doubted that she could behave with her staff as she did with me. She was never as well groomed as her peers in the company and kept referring to that.

MONIKA: I don't look the part.

ANGUS (smiling): Maybe you're right: dressed as you are, what job do you think you might be doing here? Emptying the trash?

MONIKA: I'm not that bad!

ANGUS: How "not bad" are you?

This question challenged the coachee to think through what she had just expressed. She found herself taking the positive view instead of the negative in response to my more negative statement, a helpful start.

Along with our symbolic world, we often carry old phrases and expressions that we use subconsciously to punish ourselves and stay stuck. Challenging such phrases and inviting rational thinking can help the coachee notice them in future and have a different and more positive emotional reaction to them.

The STEPPPA coaching method

STEPPPA is an acronym that helps the coach to be sure that the coachee has reached a motivated strategy for success. There are a number of steps that appear briefly below:

S: Subject brought by the coachee
T: Target objective the coachee may have established
E: Emotional context to the subject and target
P: Perception and target re-evaluation
P: Plan, a procedure of STEPs leading to the target
P: Pace, checking the strategy for realism, and understanding ramifications of success and failure
A: Adjust target strategy or Act

STEPPPA contains the prime elements of establishing and checking that the strategy will be carried out, be successful, and enhance the wider context of the executive's role and life. The steps may go out of order and that (if logical) is OK, but every step is important and it may be risky to miss any of them out.

Subject

Coachees bring a variety of issues, sometimes planned, often arising during coaching itself. The coach needs to check that the subject is one that is permitted within the terms of any contract. A desire to get out of the organization may not be allowable, for example. Has the coachee got clarity about the subject of concern? If not, the coach will help them to arrive at a clear understanding.

Target objective

Very often coachees also bring a target objective but have difficulty in motivating themselves to achieve it or in having the confidence to decide on the "best" way of getting there. The coach will already be assessing whether the target is realistic and within the control of the coachee. If not, further questioning will help the coachee arrive at a target that does begin to meet the needs for a well-formed outcome. It will also need to fit in with the organizational objectives. Where there is no obvious target expressed by the coachee, the coach will return to this issue after "perception" and before "plan".

Emotional context to subject and target

Is the subject something that the coachee has sufficient emotional attachment to in order to want to do anything about it? A question can help: "Zero to ten, how important is it for you to deal successfully with this issue?" Sometimes a coachee may need to reject a subject and do nothing, or simply give the target to someone else. If solving the subject matter does not stimulate them, there is little point in coaching around this issue. If the coachee has established a target objective already, what level of emotional engagement is there with that target objective? Is their experience of the target ambivalent (mixed)? If it is mixed, then the coach will wish to offer help for the coachee to extend their understanding of the target objective. That will include emotional aspects, since emotion is critical to motivation. Where the coachee has not yet established a persistent target, the coach will return to its "emotional context" after "perception" and before "plan". In any case, the emotional commitment to the final stage will also need to be checked.

Perception and target re-evaluation

Perception is a wonderful key for gaining the coachee's investment in their coach and assisting them in learning how to routinely extend their conscious perception. This process will bring them to a wider and clearer view of the subject and target and provide more choices of action. It is the stage where the coachee may find too many choices. Some will have a better fit for their personality and for their organization. At the end of the period of extending and developing conscious perception, the coachee will focus increasingly on targets and strategies that are achievable and exciting.

Plan

The plan will lead to the target. It will be a process, not a series of choices. The coachee may already be motivated to get on with it. The coach will want to encourage the coachee to pause to check that the target is achievable, that the strategy is feasible, within their area of influence and control and that they have considered the wider implications for colleagues, for themselves, and potentially for their families. Does every element of the plan accord with corporate policy and the culture of work?

Pace

Pacing will establish whether the target solution has a realistic chance of success and may provide further impetus for achieving it. The contrary is also possible, in which case the target and/or the plan may need to be reworked. Pacing may occur earlier and even in tandem with planning—a timeline can achieve this.

Adapt or Act

It's important to check for any needs to adjust the plan before seeking commitment. Once a level of commitment has been established, the executive will have invested sufficient attention to the subject and target to want to move on. However, the level of motivation is still a variable, both rising and lowering. The coachee may need exposure to some more perceptual work, further attention to vision, beliefs, and identity to adjust the plan to achieve a highly motivated coaching result. Checking the emotional commitment is crucial and good pacing will have helped. The question, "Zero to ten, how certain are you now to achieve your target by [date/time]?" is also useful.

I will have more to say about STEPPPA elsewhere, but this is not the place to do it. I wish here only to give a new perception on coaching using the STEPPPA model. It enables a systematic means for coaching with a process that makes absolutely sure that motivated plans lead to successful targets.

A footnote on personality profiling models

Emotional intelligence, the Myers–Briggs Type Indicator, and the OPQ are some of the profiling instruments that offer a potential framework for coaching. This is particularly the case where coaching supports a corporate program of that instrument within an organization, in order to improve understanding, communication, and improved team performance. Where personal-development plans spring from the implementation of the program, one-to-one coaching provides a valid and useful support for that too.

Because these models are so numerous, and, frankly, because I am relatively inexperienced in using so many of them, I have not highlighted their use. However, it should now be clear that the tools of coaching as illustrated will enhance any coaching initiative to support these programs. It is true that each instrument may offer a number of new interventions and I have failed my reader by not highlighting them. However, I trust that this book will serve you well in developing your own successful interventions.

Thinking preferences: filters on our world

Earlier, I introduced the idea of meta-programs (from NLP) as a collection of mental filters with which we view and react to the world.

One of the negative aspects of these filters is that they also lead to prejudice and errors of judgment. As a coach, when I make assumptions about my coachee, I am working from my own filters and will make errors. Invariably, many of our filters are different from those of the people we meet. That is why I have put emphasis on coaching methods that, from the linguistic standpoint, are relatively "clean". I may still have an assumption or "intuition", but, instead of donating this observation to my coachee, I ask a more general question to find out what their perception is around my observation. Using these methods, the true coach will not easily fall into many of the traps that await the uninitiated.

I would refer those who wish to gain a deeper insight into these issues to my book, *Me, Myself, My Team* (see bibliography), and to the other references provided. Here is a brief synopsis that may whet the appetite of those readers not already completely familiar with this subject. There are a myriad disciplines that have produced constructs that can help understand how we, and our coachees, are preferentially predisposed to sorting information by filtering and deleting subconsciously. NLP provides much of the background to what follows (representation systems and meta-programs) but the seven intelligences determined by accelerated learning, Belbin, and the Jungian-based Myers–Briggs Type Indicator all offer alternatives that are worth understanding.

Remember, too, that all models always fail some of the people some of the time. They have nothing to do with truth, but serve as temporary realities. The good coach will check perceived reality with the coachee in nondirective terms—not to seek the truth but to help them to extend and improve their conscious perception and reach motivated targets. I hope those listed will provide a starting point for making informed interventions.

Visual preference

"Visual preference", "visual representation", and "visual intelligence" are some of the names given to the intelligent storage, processing, and recall of visual images. People who have highly developed visual preference may be in jobs that use their skills. The language used is likely to include phrases like:

- I see
- I can picture what you are saying
- This looks good
- There's light at the end of the tunnel
- I'll keep my eye on the situation

In coaching, these clues may help determine whether to choose highly visual interventions (SWISH pattern for example). In the absence of such visual information, a visual instrument will not be ideal. Remember also the intervention, "How do you experience that?" This does not presume any particular preference and the coachee will consciously recognize something that is inherent to their own preferences. This will be much more impactful than using the coach's preference.

Auditory preference

A smaller proportion of people exhibit an auditory preference over their visual. Their language may include phrases like:

- I hear what you say
- Sounds good to me
- That went with a bang
- I'd say that …

Kinesthetic preference

The physical and feeling dimensions are important for those who have kinesthetic preference above visual or auditory. Their actions are very likely to be motivated by feelings rather than logic. They may use phrases like:

- I'm going with my gut on this one
- My sense is that we are onto something
- I feel out of touch with this project
- Let's hammer this out finally
- I can taste success
- I'll sniff out the competition

Linguistic preference

Where linguistic preference is highly developed, the individual may sometimes tend to prefer reading and writing to talking. Note that those with photographic memory will have a highly developed visual preference. The meanings of words may be very precise.

Interpersonal preference

The archetypical salesperson can be expected to exhibit this preference. They will be highly skilled in developing communication with many different people.

Creative preference

Creative people are stimulated by new ideas and innovation. They also tend to be bored by procedures, systems, and directories of facts. They often need to have options to be content.

Away-from and toward preferences

People exhibit both preferences but in the work context, for example, some individuals will be disposed one way or the other. Sometimes this is very marked. You will find people whose motivation is invariably to move away from pain. George Forman, the former world heavyweight boxing champion, says (2003), "My best performance was motivated by fear." Others are more frequently motivated to move *toward* objectives.

In coaching, it is worth exploring both preferences when the coachee is looking to define an action or target. If you can help them to find strong away-from *and* strong toward motivations, they will benefit from both the carrot and the stick.

Big-picture and detailed-picture preferences

As with the toward and away-from motivation, many people are highly aware of their preference. People with big-picture preference will tend to gloss over things and provide sketches or overviews without detail. Coaches may need to help them engage in more detail in order to define targets into manageable and achievable tasks without boring them.

Someone with detailed-picture preference may be so involved in detail that they fail to see the larger view. The coach can encourage thinking outside the box and more creative ways of recording and managing information by using, say, mind maps (see for example Buzan, 2000).

Past, in-time, and future preferences

Past-preference individuals are largely motivated (and demotivated) to action by their past experiences. Their language will keep referring to examples. This can be very tedious for people like me, since my preference is very much with now. Future-preference people have so much investment in the future that they do not necessarily fully complete actions in the present. They may not acknowledge their successes and the coach can help them to do this. In-time individuals may also leave things unfinished as they may focus attention on what happens to be in front of them. An extreme manifestation of this was a man who would not look in his in-tray for months on end. If he put signed letters into his tray and a colleague put some sheets over them, the letters would still be there months later. The same was true of work on his desk. He could prioritize, but his interest was invariably distracted to something more interesting in front of him.

Completer/finisher preference

Completer/finishers may exhibit a number of other preferences. They are target-oriented but their motivations can be complex (as for everyone else). It is facile to think that their motivation is the target itself, since the target may be only a trigger for something more stimulating than the achievement of numbers, money, or ego. The coach is lucky to work with someone with a high preference for completing, but their task must be to make sure that outcomes are **well formed**. Sometimes their target orientation can make them insensitive to the needs of others around them.

Convincer and decisive preferences

A friend's eight-year-old daughter had been told to go to bed three times and still sat playing in the kitchen. Exasperated, my friend said, "It's time to go to bed. How many times do I have to tell you?" Her daughter replied, "Four times, Mommy." The adult convincer preference manifests in adults similarly. Coaching can help the individual to recognize their pattern and to find shortcuts if they want to. In defining outcomes, it is especially important to be sure of their commitment; you cannot rush a convincer-preference person and expect motivation.

The decisive-preference person quickly associates with targets but may be more or less committed to achievement. They may also exhibit a wide variety of other preferences. Because they may not be tenuous in their targets, the coach can help them to define the steps to their targets and to get a real impression of the actual tasks and journey involved. In both cases, emotional commitments to the plan and target are essential.

Match and mismatch preferences

Match-preference people look and sort for sameness. Mismatch-preference people sort for difference. Both traits will motivate or demotivate and hence they appear as "motivation traits" in the LAB profile. Because match-preference people are looking for sameness, it can be useful to help them explore sameness in their chosen outcome to increase their motivation. The same is true for mismatch-preference people, where information about difference can be drawn out.

Internal and external preferences

These are also LAB-profile "motivation traits" and, as with other preferences, are likely to be context-specific. Internal-preference individuals tend to have an inner conviction that will motivate them to action, whereas the external-preference person will need third-party support and/or approval. The coach can help the coachee to recognize the importance or otherwise of understanding their motivation in respect of these dimensions.

Procedural and options preferences

These preferences appear in the LAB Profile as "motivation traits". The typical procedural preference is for logical (left-brain) processing, resulting in an attraction for information that develops sequentially. Options people look for choice but not necessarily for innovation (creative preference). They are stimulated by variety and the coach needs to be sure that they can frame their outcomes in procedural terms, or they will be less likely to succeed.

If you perceive a person as being procedural, then questions that keep introducing new choices will produce what Shelle Rose Charvet calls "sensory overload". The coach will be able to help the coachee to find an example where they had succeeded in a similar situation and then ask questions about the steps that led to that success. The most important question for the procedural-preference person is, "What next?" This question appeals directly to the logical procession of thought.

There is nothing inherently wrong in having a preference for options, but in the context of target setting it is important for the coach to facilitate the coachee to a defined plan, or their target will not be achieved. Necessarily, this means helping the options-preference individual to hone in on a compelling (emotionally motivated) target and establish a process for doing that.

Drawing on past resources will help the coachee to find a compelling personal plan for their current issue. When the coachee is unable to think of something in the same context, take another context, perhaps outside work, and break it down similarly. An options person may have difficulty recalling the successful steps that they took. To help, the coach can also ask about the events in reverse order: "So, before you won the order, what did you do just before then that made it possible?"

The coachee may be disinclined to be sidetracked into past events. Sometimes people who have had a bad experience of counseling or psychotherapy fall into this category. Where this happens, the coach can still help break down the issue into workable pieces and help build up the sequence of steps for those parts. We will see that procedures are vital for committed and successful target objectives. A good coach will be listening for procedures language where target setting is on the coachee's agenda. People who are still talking about options when discussing their targets are unlikely to be ready to succeed in them.

Left- and right-brain preference

One of the simplest and widely known models of human psychology suggested by the Nobel laureate Roger Sperry in 1981 (see for example Erdmann, Hubel and Stover, 2000), is that our cognitive processes are largely split into mental activities on the left and right sides of the brain. Thus, logical processing—comparing, organization, structuring, and arithmetic—are all thought to be activities that predominate in the left brain. The right brain is concerned with emotion, expression, creative inspirations, and play. It is supposed, therefore, that the commercial, Western world is mainly populated by people with more left-brain skills than right-brain skills. Using the same theory, we can expect to find more instinct, inspiration, and creativity in the East.

Whether this model is correct or not, it is easy to imagine that there are people who have dominating intelligence on one "side" of the brain rather than the other. In coaching managers in the USA and Europe, I am seeing a small sample of people who were attracted to organizations that operate in logical ways. Needless to say, most of my clients, and their employees, fall into the left-brain category. This can occasionally mean that they are perhaps weaker in emotional intelligence, intuitive solutions, creative explorations, or the ability to "play". When we invite people to be coached, it can be very challenging to those unwilling to let go, to play, and to run with the experience. Having a feeling for the left/right-brain model can help the coach choose interventions and tools that will stretch their coachee.

The left/right-brain model suggests that logical questioning by the coach will help the left brain to develop its processes while the invitation to be creative, to go with experiences, will stimulate the right brain.

But what is the point? Surely logic is the Holy Grail of performance.

We have already seen that emotion is critical to both motivation and effective communication. Emotional expression is the stuff of the right brain. Without emotional intelligence, the manager is compromised in modern management. Similarly, in the fast-changing world of business, more managers need to be flexible and creative in their thinking and behaviors. Stimulating right-brain activity has to be a good way to encourage more flexible thought, creativity, and a willingness to let the mind free up new possibilities.

Coaching interventions starting with the word "how" or "why" may kick the coachee into logical thinking and logical comparing (left-brain activity). This logical response is particularly likely if the questions invoke judgment rather than instinctive response, or where the question opens up wider inquiry through lack of specificity—the coachee has to think in order to work out what is required of them. Where we want logical, objective mental processing (or to appeal to it), it can be helpful to use questions that contain "how" and "why":

- How much improvement do you think they might then make?
- How is that likely to be achieved?
- Why would that occur?

Body awareness and creative mind-play will stimulate right-brain activity, as will questions inviting expression of any metaphoric and symbolic descriptions of their state. Some of the questions we have already seen used that assist are:

- Instinctively, how do you experience that?
- If there were another solution to this problem, what would it be?
- Imagine this happening in the future. What is that experience like?

Of course, there are other things that coaches can do to encourage right-brain activity and intelligence both inside and outside the coaching dynamic. *Timelines* have a logical and procedural base, but they inspire creative mind-play with new activity and ideas. We can invite the coachee to draw or paint their issues and solutions and we can take logical steps and ask whether they would like to set them down on paper, cut them out, and rearrange the steps to see if new ideas spring from what they perceive.

Outside the coaching session, we can encourage the right brain by opening up to creative expression through art, play, instinctive writing, and poetry.

Many people do not know that there are two types (at least!) of writer: the left/right-brain model can also describe them. There are left-brain writers, who prepare a logical scheme for the work, establish the detail to create smaller sections, and then write and pick over the words frequently to check if the manuscript is readable and clear. The right-brain writer marks the page and writes with little or no preparation, typically leaving corrections to the end.

What is inspiring is that the right-brain writer can enter into a state, similar to trance, called "psychological flow" (about 20 percent of the population are able to do this) in which the words flow out but the structuring is left to subconscious processing, free of logical thought. Tim Gallwey (2002) calls this state "Self 2 focus". Thus, we can see that it is possible for right-brain writers to create structures (associated in the left brain) as a subconscious support to their right-brain creativity. Similarly, we know that there are intensely left-brain thinkers who, through a spark of right-brain inspiration, find new and creative ways of solving problems. There is a famous story of Friedrich August Kekulé, the nineteenth-century German chemist, who was struggling with a logical problem of how his analytical data could be interpreted. Up until that point, compounds containing carbon and hydrogen had all been structured in lines or chains. Daydreaming, he found himself imagining snakes twisting, moving, and swallowing their own tails. Thus, the structure of the cyclic, aromatic hydrocarbons were elucidated—by a stroke of absolute brilliance during dreamlike or "trance" state.

It seems reasonable, even logical, to suggest that people who are able to use both "sides" of their brain effectively will outperform those who cannot. I subscribe to that view. In so doing, I am also contributing to the philosophy that good work–life balance makes better and more effective managers. I am also committed to life-long learning for the same reason. By encouraging a wider breadth of imagining, flexibility, and conscious perception, the coach is helping people to be better managers, partners, parents, or friends. Happy people make good executives!

Chapter Six

Coaching Development

We have looked at many typical issues that face the coachee and at practical methods to assist the coachee to move toward their targets. Additionally we have developed some thinking about the way in which coaching is contracted. Here I wish to look at what the coach can do to improve their mindset for coaching and the types of activity and experience that may enhance the coach's competencies.

I shall briefly discuss philosophies that I believe support best practice in coaching. These include "servant leadership" and the compelling work of Monty Roberts (1997) with horses. We will also look at a methodology for coaching in teams or group meetings that is close to the ethos of conversational coaching.

Mindsets for the coach

John Abulafia is an opera director and producer working on many of the world's finest stages. He also helps people to realize how minor changes of attitude, or mindset, can have stunning effects on others (McLeod, 2002e). It's such talents that enable a solitary actor to cause several thousand people to hold their breath, simultaneously, without uttering a word. If an actor can find such impactful, nonverbal expression in their repertoire of authentic emotions, then what negative impact might a coach have after a tedious drive to the session? If a gesture, a look, a slight movement of the head can have such enormous effects, should the coach not take better care about their mindset prior to coaching? Will their own disappointments, frustrations, desires, and hopes express themselves nonverbally, affecting the coaching dynamic? Of course!

Many coaches prepare themselves by anchoring a resourceful "coaching state" prior to a session (McLeod, 1997). You could call this "attitude" but the effect will be an authentic expression of traits and beliefs that the coach already has in their repertoire.

Inner-game coaching

Tim Gallwey determines three stages of conversation in the coaching process using the *inner-game model*. These are conversations for awareness, choice and then trust. Gallwey's awareness phase is simply the step of defining the situation clearly. The choice stage is about broadening the vision of how to get to a future desired outcome. In my terms, this is the development of conscious perception. The last conversational stage, trust, is when the coachee gains greater access to both internal and external resources in order to move from present state to future desired state. Gallwey says that the most important outcome of the coaching intervention is that the coachee should feel respected, valuable, and capable of moving forward. The coach's contribution to this stage starts from the coach's mindset that they trust the coachee more than the coachee trusts themselves. Gallwey makes a clear differentiation between typical coaches and "really good coaches". The best coaches he experienced were those who made him believe in himself, in his value, and in his capabilities (including his ability to learn).

I am in total agreement with Gallwey. But how can the coach manage this? Until now we have looked at the language and tools of change, and the methods I have illustrated all underpin certain values that the coach will have if they are true to the inherent gifts in the methods used. These gifts include:

- respect
- hopefulness
- trust
- patience
- creativity
- openness

Here are some of the unspoken drivers that determine the difference between the coach and the "really good coach" whom Gallwey describes. Achieving this level of coaching requires a mindset that acts as a blueprint for every expression, mannerism, and inference that the coach displays in the coaching dynamic. To be truly effective, the mindset needs to be "at one" or "part of" the real belief and value structure that the coach has in their repertoire—to be authentic. In adopting a mindset, all the coach is doing is to take beliefs and values with which they are already familiar (perhaps in other contexts) and bring these into the domain of coaching. Let's provide an example by asking a question.

A person may display authentic tenderness toward their child, partner, family, and friends but be highly competitive and aggressive in other contexts. If we ask this individual to coach, which underlying aspects of their character would we want them to display?

Mindsets

Values and beliefs, underpinned by one's sense of identity make a mindset and provide the "attitude" for coaching (McLeod, 2002f). Let us start with appropriate empowering beliefs. I write "appropriate" since a belief that "I make perfect interventions" might empower the coach but be counterproductive to the development of both the coach and coachee. Let's look at examples that are appropriate to the coaching dynamic:

I believe that …
- I value myself and my coachee
- I have nothing to prove
- The coachee's solution is good enough
- The coachee's pace may be slow or startling, it does not matter which
- I offer my coachee opportunities for their growth and learning
- I am an instrument for learning and change
- The coachee has the resources necessary for their learning
- Silences belong to the coachee, not me

I believe that I can …
- Offer choices in my questioning (not solutions and instructions)
- Offer permission to myself and the coachee
- Give the coachee my best attention at all times
- Remain flexible in my thinking and actions
- Check the coachee's commitment and their confidence level

When you prepare to coach, the beliefs that you revisit will be in your own words and be authentic with who you are, but in the context of coaching. If you have no faith in a belief, then leave it off your list. It is uninspiring to work from dishonesty and method. The best way is through the depth of your own being. Actors, like my dear friend Jill Greenacre, work from their authenticity, not method, and they are truly inspiring. The best coaches are also authentic and true to their mindset. Here, then, begins the difference between coaches and truly excellent coaches, whatever their chosen toolkit.

Underpinning values and beliefs

Identity is also a factor in the coach's mindset (McLeod, 1997). Useful ones might look like this:

- I am a patient coach
- I am a tolerant coach
- I am a caring coach

Simple affirmations are useful in changing state. One can carefully recite a list of such affirmations. Some coaches use the *hierarchy of logical levels* (see Chapter Three) with one or more empowering beliefs. Having taken on the belief, they walk from "environment" toward "purpose" to install their mindset. This is a method encouraged by Lynne Kerry (the UK-based NLP trainer) in her coaching workshops for Vievolve. Kerry also suggests a methodology for accessing a coaching state involving a seven-step process:

- empty your mind
- get comfortable
- control your breathing (breathe slowly)
- withdraw attention momentarily (focus internally)
- concentrate on one thing (anything at all)
- expand awareness (peripheral vision)
- total awareness (physical and emotional awareness of the space)

John Abulafia recommends the use of a mantra, or empowering sentence, that sums up all the above in one brief line. That line should embrace all the positive aspects for coaching in a personal and significant way. This sentence will carry the key messages about being an effective coach for you. Here are two examples:

- I am an instrument for change
- I am a facilitator helping the coachee to their chosen target

For those with a mastery of anchoring, it is possible to anchor these phrases to a state reached, for example, by walking the hierarchy. Then, merely thinking the phrase before the session triggers and recreates the state.

Other coaches use animal *totems* (like the owl and dolphin) to anchor a coaching state that inspires care, thoughtfulness, and wisdom. The coach takes the essence of their thoughts and feelings about the positive attributes of the animal into the coaching dynamic. All these methods help to create the mindset. In all cases, the mindset is composed of authentic aspects taken from the personality repertoire of the coach.

In the same way, it is possible to imagine a useful mindset for the coachee (McLeod, 1998) and I provide a suggested framework for that in the appendices.

Servant leadership

The work of Robert Greenleaf (Greenleaf and Spears, 1998) is very worth mentioning in the context of coaching mindsets. The great servant-leaders of our time must include Mahatma Gandhi, Mother Teresa of Calcutta, and Nelson Mandela. These are people who inspired from a state of humility, who were optimistic about the human spirit, and who led by example. Of course, they also held clear and inspiring visions of where they were heading. The mindsets of these extraordinary people are largely those that coaches may try to emulate. In my view the aspects of servant-leader that serve the coach well are these, exhibited with grace:

- helps people to be their best

- is tolerant of error and sees mistakes as an opportunity for sustained learning
- encourages and offers choices
- helps people to create imagination, vision, and direction
- places others in a position of primary importance
- understands the greater good and steps aside when necessary
- is uncorrupted by fawning and idolatry and is humble
- is always a pupil of learning

These simple statements hold a wonderful resource for the aspiring and practicing coach.

People whispering

Monty Roberts, "the man who listens to horses", showed the world that the old approaches to communication with horses were inadequate. His radically fast methods have transformed the ability of humans to work with horses. He and subsequently Andrew McFarlane and Pat Parelli have all acknowledged that there are key messages from Roberts's work with horses that are pertinent for managers. I have owned and ridden horses for many years and am astonished and overwhelmed when watching his disciple, Kelly Marks, at work. Her understanding of horses is phenomenal. Roberts and Marks are able to take powerful animals that have become very stuck in their behaviors and radically enable them to change. What is evident is that they do not coerce a horse but instead enable the horse to be exquisitely and perfectly itself.

If we begin our coaching with individuals and teams with the idea that everyone wants to perform excellently and do what they do best, how much better might those people succeed? To what extent are our team members constrained by our inability to nurture and motivate them?

The metaphor of working with horses has more to tell the coach and manager. I suggest these:

Listen	rather than tell
Invite	rather than push
Encourage working with me	rather than against me

Allow them to be their best	rather than resist their excellence
Appeal to their motivations	rather than tell them what to do
Permit them to be themselves	rather than subdue them
Invite them to work with the culture	rather than against it

I hope that the methods and questioning techniques that I have illustrated in this book go some way to encouraging readers to this level of thinking and belief. Coaching without a set of principles like these is not true coaching.

Facilitation

My interpretation of facilitation is that it means to assist people to work with their own resources in a holistic way, in the broad context of their life experience and connections. Carl Rogers states (Rogers, 1967, 1997) that facilitators:

- set the initial culture and trust for exploration
- help to elicit and clarify purpose
- act as a flexible resource
- respond to expressions, intellectual content, and emotional attitudes
- give each individual the time and attention they warrant
- take the initiative in sharing themselves in thought and feeling in ways that others can take or leave
- accept and openly acknowledge their own limitations

Paul Barber, (2002), embracing his depth of experience in Gestalt thinking with humanism and transpersonal psychology avers that facilitators draw from their own personality, acquired store of practical skills, and intuitive wisdom to:

- generate understanding
- liberate and refine new knowledge
- raise personal and social awareness
- educate and empower those involved

Notice again the hands-off position of the coach as servant and inquiring facilitator, not guru or adviser. This is not an omission but an acceptance that the best solutions are those that are motivated and that the most motivated actions are those that belong to the coachee.

In coaching terms, Gestalt emphasizes the cultivation of an authentic "I–Thou" relationship, wherein coach and coachee endeavor to co-create a culture where everything is open to question. In this relationship, robust challenge and experimentation are performed; difference is respected and encouraged; the relationship itself is seen as a metaphoric example that totally illuminates the wider dimensions in which the coachee lives and works.

In the context of the above relationship the coach explores through dialogue and experimentation rather than instructs; looks to the wider inner relatedness of things rather than isolates facts; raises awareness to the options rather than provides ready answers.

As to its values, Gestalt emphasizes holism and organic development, while all the time drawing attention to what is happening in the moment. As Barber writes (2003), "so as to illuminate wisdoms not only of the senses and intellect, but of the soma and the soul".

Coachees do not necessarily need outside influences to feel directed, motivated, and successful. They may, however, need help from a facilitator (coach) to make better use of their own resources and to succeed as a consequence of being more exquisitely themselves.

Coaching in groups

By now, I hope you are fully accepting that the skills of the coach can be more a way of "being" than a package of skills used for coaching intervention. Of course, we are less than perfect and so have needs to express ourselves in ways that would not be helpful in the coaching environment. This is also true of working in a facilitating style within groups. Our needs to be competitive, to appear bright, quick-witted, and decisive can sensibly be left outside the door. Instead, tap into personal characteristics that are supportive of coaching and facilitation.

The language of the coach is largely one of questioning. In groups, the use of questioning to facilitate and encourage creative expression is much more productive, although typically slower than in typical "led" meetings. Questioning is offered to elicit individual ideas and to make best use of all the talents in the team. When individuals feel that they are part of the method, structure, creativity, and direction of the team, then the team benefits from the quality of that participation.

In group, the skills are identical to those of the coach with additional needs for moving attention. These include varying one's attention to embrace the group dynamic; being flexible in order to pinpoint attention for an individual; and then widening to attend to the group dynamic again. Additionally, the coach can encourage group discussion and a consensus of ideas. The coach can nurture the group and individuals toward agreed actions.

This also requires fluid leadership, knowing when the group needs to summarize and when it needs to donate ideas. The coach/facilitator will be as comfortable giving the stage away as taking it back in order to provide a defined process to the group. Thus, break-out groups, group presentations, and brainstorming all contribute to involvement by all participants. Remember, too, that each participant will wish to contribute in their own way and may not fit a corporate model. The coach/facilitator will be open to variables in both expression and contribution and will use methods that encourage and are inclusive.

Whitmore writes (2002) that team coaching has two defined purposes. The first is to encourage task performance and the second to stimulate team development. He uses the GROW model to structure his questioning (*g*oal setting, *r*eality checking, *o*ptions and *w*hat/when/whom), but the underlying principles are similar to those provided here.

My friend Georgeanne Lamont's recent book (2002) provides research on corporate successes that seems to suggest that many managers are a hindrance to performance. Enlisting the involvement of the people who report to managers captures profound solutions and motivated actions that produce more efficient results than those of traditional businesses. Her work also shows the phenomenal potential that working with shared values can have. If these are underpinned by a philosophy that honors and encourages the best from *all* employees, then the scope for massive improvement in efficiencies becomes possible. It seems strange that in a world keen to generate money so little notice has been taken of working models that are so much better than the norm. Involving staff and using a facilitation/coaching model to engage them must be a more powerful approach to teamwork.

Self-coaching

Self-coaching does not have the elegance or inspiration that one-to-one coaching can provide. As part of a balanced way of being and understanding, self-coaching does have a useful part to play in self-development. In essence, this activity is about self-questioning and self-challenge, learning to listen to one's spoken language and the dialogue in one's own head for the telltale signs of limiting belief, negativity, and self-deprecation.

For some of us, the practice and art of coaching makes us more attentive to the clues about our limitations; for others, this is a discipline requiring timetabled episodes of self-awareness and external intervention. The mind is wonderfully efficient at making a fool of its host and so external feedback is essential.

The point of self-coaching is to understand more about one's own sense of reality and the resistances to change. When we understand more about our own issues and resistance, we gain some insight into how some of our coachees may struggle with their own issues. Coaching should not be seen as a set of therapeutic tools for the analyst but as a platform for gaining instinct about people's motivation and resistance. Only a sense of openness on the part of the coach will allow for the learning, pain, and growth that will assist in this journey. It is for this reason that we at Coaching Foundation Ltd. get our coaches to incorporate as much "coachee experience" as possible both during their training and through their professional development and working lives.

Coach as coachee and observer

In our training courses for coaches at Into Changes Ltd. and in practice groups we run at the Coaching Foundation and elsewhere, we provide as much training experience with the coach in "the coachee position" as possible. We also operate groups of three (coach, coachee, and observer) to gain additional insights from a third party as well as that available from the coachee. The coachee position is inspirational for learning. From the coachee position, the coach learns what techniques work best on them. In talking with others, the coach learns that what works for them can be unsuccessful or unpopular with others. This experience is a valuable foil to the enthusiastic use of a superb intervention or tool that has recently been learned. Yes, there are excellent coaching tools, but they are not always the right ones for the coachee. Experiencing this reality rather than learning it by rote is a critical learning step for the ambitious coach.

Changing coaching parameters

We set up coaching sessions where we artificially change the coaching dynamic in order to give our coaches practical experiences of what it is like to be a coachee in less-than-perfect situations. Typically, we set this up with three trainees and a round of three sessions, so that each has the chance to be coach, coachee, and observer. An example is to provide the coach with a card that may say, "Move your chair a little closer to the coachee." The result of moving into the coachee's comfort zone can be offputting and the signals for that may be seen or felt by the observer, too. Similarly, we may ask the coach, "Try to have as little eye contact as possible" or "Try to have more eye contact than you normally would." However naturally performed, these changes can upset the coaching dynamic and reduce the potential for success in that session and the ones that follow it. Other parameters that provide useful learning include these examples of instructions for the coach:

- Quietly tap a finger when the coachee is talking

- Think about a holiday you enjoyed while the coachee is talking
- Tighten your chest and shoulder muscles as discreetly as you can during the session
- Diffuse your focus occasionally when the coachee is talking
- Do not repeat any of the coachee's language
- Use several metaphors of your own choosing to describe the coachee's situation
- Do not leave silences: talk or make interventions to fill them
- The coachee expects a ten-minute session, try to finish it in under seven
- The coachee is expecting a ten-minute session, imagine you have twenty
- Breathe a little more quickly than you usually do
- Adopt a relaxed and very open posture, legs and/or arms quite wide
- Tell two or three experiences that are like those that the coachee describes
- Let your head tilt back very slightly or, if you wear glasses, look under or over the lenses
- Look briefly at your watch three or four times during the end of the session

Coachee and observer feedback provide stunning learning about the major impact that tiny changes in the coaching dynamic make. By experiencing the downside from the coachee perspective, coaches should become more attentive to the needs of their coachees. They learn to adopt codes of behavior that are more likely to encourage rather than discourage work.

Two on one

Placing two coaches with one coachee (where all are in coach training) can be a useful learning experience for coaches. Each coach can intervene at any time. The coaches are told to work as fluidly as possible. It's not a contest!

What happens is that confident coaches with clear ideas about the "best way to go" find that the methods of other coaches may sometimes be better than their own. This is invariably more impactful learning than that from just observing others. Here, the experience is within their own coaching dynamic. Feedback from the "coachee" after each session is also helpful.

Sometimes coachees say that the pace of intervention is uncomfortable. Where the coaches are working fluidly and respectfully of each other and their coachee, the coachee and observers note that instinctive and inspired intervention of one coach can make a breakthrough in the session.

I have never been part of a two-on-one coaching dynamic on a professional basis but imagine that there are circumstances where the approach might be a useful one-off session to help move a willing coachee to a new level of learning. I guess I am thinking of a highly intelligent executive who is using spare mental capacity on pre-emptive thought (about the tools and interventions being used) rather than staying with their own material. The two-on-one dynamic for a single session will help overload the executive's reasoning potential (particularly if trance strategies are used so that one coach is attempting to increase kinesthetic awareness (right-brain) while the other coach is making interventions that require logical (left-brain) reasoning). The two-coach strategy for a single session may be more useful than changing the coach for all of them.

Co-coaching

We promote co-coaching as a means of achieving interim practice, gaining experience of being the coachee and to assist in both personal development and successfully achieved targets. I have adapted the term "co-coaching" from the discipline of co-counseling, where two counselors take it in turns to facilitate each other. In co-coaching, the pair decide on session lengths and agree to bring issues. They tend to meet every two, three, or four weeks with a typical session length of thirty or forty minutes each way.

Co-coaching provides a way to gain exposure to high-quality coaching for a simple trade in time. Changing partners every now and again also provides a wider exposure to the effectiveness of different coaching tools, interventions, and styles.

Practice groups

Practice groups like those we organize at the Coaching Foundation are enormously popular and enjoyed. Our formula for the short sessions is a three-hour slot (including a short meal break) incorporating techniques and practice. We try to extend the exposure and learning potential available by having a very wide exposure to both established coaching methods and to other disciplines. Provided there is a context to coaching and an opportunity to do practical work, then we tend to be open to any new ideas. We also have one-day sessions for more in-depth exposure to new thinking, models, and practice. We attract some of the leading figures in their areas of expertise. Here are examples of the type of session we have run over the last year or so.

The Power of Silence	Silence as an "intervention"
Emotional Intelligence	EQ approach to coaching
Myers–Briggs Type Indicator	MBTI profile and hints for coaches
GROW Performance Coaching Model	Whitmore's approach to coaching
Clean Language	Coaching without the coach's fog
Symbolic Modeling	Metaphoric interventions
Conversational Coaching	Rose Charvet's meta-program model
Provocative Coaching	Lessons from Provocative Therapy
Aligning the Inner Coach	Kerry's Mindset Model
Alpha Leadership in Coaching	Russell/Deering/Dilts 9-part model
Transactional Analysis	TA learning for coaches
Gestalt in Action	Psychotherapeutic lessons for coaches
Status, Secret Wants, Space Walks & Mantras	Abulafia's Impact, Status, and Body Language Workshop

A number of other organizations now offer coaching practice groups but many of these have a particular model on offer rather than a broader perspective. Some of these organizations are supported too by Web-based information and I have provided a list for some of these in the appendices. Of course, there are many training companies now offering "coach" training and many of these are also limited by having a narrow perspective, whether it is NLP or another slant. For that reason, a more independent approach including academic courses can be useful but many of these suffer from the same lack of vision. Others take a wider view of their syllabus and it is incumbent on the budding student to look closely at the course program and seek advice from experienced coaches about the usefulness or otherwise of the course. Ultimately, the practice groups provide the biggest potential for learning without risks to client and coachee.

Inspiration

The coach may have a feeling of rightness about something that they call insight, but it may be something wholly from the world of the coach, not the coachee. These "insights" may concern "perceived" emotions, patterns of behavior, or the best model or tool to offer the coachee.

True instinct or inspiration must come from experience and a broad understanding of self. Perhaps the traits of inspiration are multifactorial, and there may be other nonverbal means of sensing, learned early in one's development, that may bring acute insight into the world of the coachee. The problem is that one cannot know what is in the world of the coachee.

Being "right" is the most useless contribution a coach can offer the coachee. The coach may help to modify the coachee's view of the world but the interventions that create that potential for success need to be made with due caution. Indeed, the coach may be best advised to have the mindset of an inquiring but inspired ignoramus! In other words, it can be very useful to follow instinct, but do not be fooled by your cleverness. Seek confirmation from the coachee and make sure that your questions are open rather than closed and ignore any desire to prove yourself *right*. You may not get the answer you want, but your coachee will get the answer that is most useful for them.

Academic resources

In the appendices I offer contact points for a number of courses available for coaches. Some, like the (UK's) Newcastle College course, are based upon distance-learning philosophy but incorporate a requirement for a log of activity and coachee feedback. I graduated from Newcastle in 2002 and found the scope of the course quite broad for a one-year program requiring just 120 hours of activity. Others include workshops and assessments in role play.

Chapter Seven

Other Coaching Tools and Interventions

We will highlight some of the more important tools that may have been illustrated earlier on in this book but that deserve greater attention. One of the most important of these is context-free questioning, but we will also look in more detail at other types of questioning techniques first.

Questioning

Open and closed questions have been described very thoroughly in sales training manuals for many years. Salespeople are warned not to ask a closed question such as, "Will you buy this or not?" because it is likely to bring the response, "No, thank you." Instead, they are trained to ask open questions such as, "Are you buying one or two of these products?" The hope is that the implied command to buy (one or more items) will lead to the sale.

In the context of coaching, we do not want to lead the coachee's mental attention into that inhabited by the coach! Tim Gallwey says that he had to learn how to teach less, so that more could be learned by his coachees. The best way to avoid 'leading' is to reflect the exact language proffered by the coachee and to ask questions that are as unloaded as possible. The whole philosophy of symbolic modeling highlights these dual skills: unloaded questions and reflective language. You do not have to coach using the symbolic model in order to follow the same principles in your coaching practice. Open questions attempt to open up the world of the coachee without assuming anything about that world. An example is the question, "Instinctively, how do you experience that?" The coach might easily say, "What is your view of that?" but this question assumes that the mental registration of the coachee is visual.

The brain has no consistent means of filtering out irrelevant information from coaches (and elsewhere). Once a word or phrase has been said, it is captured by the coachee's brain. In the case above, some effort may be expended to explore visual information and accept or reject that assumption. Other irrelevant words also tempt the brain to think outside its experience. Often, as seen earlier, we want the coachee to remain in an associated state and these diversions prevent that.

The coach shouldn't work in order to be right about their assumptions: the coach ought to help the coachee develop their view of the world and move beyond any limitations that they may have with their existing worldview. By asking questions and challenging, the coach can hope that the coachee will develop a new worldview developed by using conscious perception. The coach should dump as little as possible into this dynamic. Here are some examples of typical coach questions with the assumptions in italic type. I have also added an alternative question, in each case, that I think may be better. See what you think.

How to you *feel* about that?	What is your experience of that?
Could your boss be *angry* with you?	From your boss's position, what might he be experiencing here?
You look *tense and upset.*	What is happening with you at this moment?
Maybe you have failed but how do you *put that behind you?*	If you did fail, as you say, what, if anything, can you do about that? What have you learned?
You have your target. How do you *reach* it?	What next?
Those were good steps. What is the next *step*?	What next?

Coaches invariably talk too much and introduce too many of their own words and interpretations into the coaching arena. Unless we wish to spring the coachee out of their associated state, we are best advised to limit the amount of assumed experience we communicate by asking "clean" questions.

Context-free questioning

I hope you have gained considerable insight into the constructs of questioning from the examples in Chapters Two and Three. The sections on clean language and symbolic modeling in Chapter Five support these. I now want to turn attention to the concept of *context-free questioning*.

Previously I have referred to the importance of questioning as one of the three principal instruments of coaching (see Chapter One). The others are challenge and silence. I also mentioned that in the case of unhelpful emotional association (with an issue) a coachee might prefer to limit the amount of information that they are revealing. There may also be embarrassment about an issue or a desire to keep corporate strategy secure. The coachee's preference must be accepted. A coach will fluidly move to context-free questioning. This will help preserve the coachee's preference for secrecy and will not bring extraneous stress to the dynamic. Since the coachee's responses tend to be silent or monosyllabic, in the example below I have left out most of the coachee's responses unless they are helpful to the reader.

COACHEE: It's an awkward situation. The individual concerned is highly influential and regarded.

COACH: So, in this situation with this individual, could you bring that event to mind now as if it were happening in this room?

COACH: And if it is happening in this room, have you a sense of where you and that individual are in this room—move if you wish; I can move out of the way, too, if it helps.

COACH: Being in this awkward situation with this individual, how real is this compared with how is was, zero to ten?

COACHEE: Seven.

COACH: If you will, try to make this situation with this individual more real. How are you seated in this situation, what, if any, body sensations do you have? How do they look? What is their posture like? How does the light catch them? How warm or cool is it? Do whatever you feel necessary to make this situation more real, in your own time. Signify to me, if you will, when you are ready.

COACH: What do you really want to say to this individual if you are totally free to do so without any comeback? I do not need to know what that statement is unless you choose to share it with me.

COACH: How would he take what you say, where ten is good?

COACHEE: Zero.

COACH: Are you saying that you would prefer not to say what you really want to say to this individual?

COACHEE: Certainly not.

The coach may then bring the coachee back into the dynamic and check that they are back. There are many possible strategies to be followed including the second and third perceptual positions, all in the context-free mode. Here is another line of exploration seeking a realistic outcome.

COACH: I would like you to consider what, if any, realistic acknowledgment or action you want from this individual. Will you do that and then tell me whether it is an action, acknowledgment, or something else?

COACHEE: Acknowledgment.

COACH: Imagine, if you will, that you are looking through a special telescope at the awkward situation you experienced. You can make the situation closer or further away as you choose. You can hear as well and you can make the sounds louder or quieter at will. You can make the image bigger or smaller, more clear or more out of focus, even dark if you wish. I would like you to be far enough away to take the long view of the situation but close enough to have a clear impression of what is going on. If you are agreeable, could you indicate when you are in that long-view situation?

COACH: What's happening in that situation over there? Is there any advice that you could give that would help achieve the outcome?

The key to context-free questioning is to maintain the language of the coachee where it is offered and to seek their willingness to take a new step. The coach must also test how real any new state is and offer interventions to help them achieve a high level of success. By continuing in this way, specific targets can be reached and a high certainty of success assessed from feedback. The coach may never know what that outcome was.

I have my own example from coaching my daughter Alex. She had been stressed because her examinations were coming up and she had so far done only about ten minutes of revision on one occasion and a little less on another. She was willing to be coached and we walked a timeline in the back yard using two hula hoops that she picked and moved to signify the "present" and her "future desired target." The whole session took about an hour and she was considerably happier afterwards than she had been before. Later we sat down and I asked her whether she would mind sharing the target objective with me.

"I've decided not to do any more revision. I don't believe that I need to revise in order to pass."

I was horrified, imaging what her mother would say when she found out what I had "done" and the impact on me should Alex not meet her own, and her mother's, expectations. I need not have worried. Alex took top marks in three subjects and just one level down in the fourth, ahead of her expectations and desire. Her place at university was assured. Both my daughter and her mother were happy. I was relieved!

Virtual timelines

In Chapter Two we saw that a timeline may be used to help a coachee experience a preferred future and also to gain objective insights into how to move forward. When space is limited or where a coachee shows ability in working with state change, it is possible to conduct the timeline without actually walking it. The language used can be absolutely identical; it remains in the present tense once the process begins. The coach's prologue will need to be different. For example:

COACH: In a few moments, and if you agree, let's go forward in time toward your target. You can imagine moving through the steps that lead to your target and all the necessary points at which new information or decisions are required. Take the time you need at each point to marshal all the sensory components you have about how you experience that. It may include people, voices, images, color, light and dark, and other sounds and sensations in your mind and body.

A variation on the virtual timeline, if the coachee is not fearful of heights, is to suggest that the coachee float or fly over their timeline. Individual steps may be seen as the beacon lights of a runway strip, switching on as the coachee progresses the line. I have had coachees show signs of being in trance during the process of experiencing virtual timelines. From an objective space, this approach can offer a considerable degree of learning and help with motivation toward personal and corporate targets.

Metaphor and symbols

We have seen that metaphor and metaphoric symbolism are powerful instruments of change. In the way we coach, the metaphors and symbols are invariably those of the coachee. However, the coach may also introduce metaphor to help illustrate something that the coachee has identified. A metaphor introduced by the coach can also help where the coachee is struggling with a concept or how to apply their learning. Strictly speaking, this is bringing the symbolic map of the coach into the dynamic, but, where the coach has a highly developed instinctive feel for coaching or knows some of the metaphoric world of the coachee from previous sessions, the metaphor can provide a useful frame for learning. Sporting metaphors seem to be almost universally acceptable where once military metaphor prevailed. Here are some examples:

- You can swing the bat as hard as you like but, if you fail to run, the game is lost.
- You can put huge effort into knocking the ball around the pitch, but it doesn't matter if you can't punch it into the target.
- Tennis is not always about defeating your opponent: sometimes it's about being the best you can be.
- Performance on the last tee can win the round, but, if you tee off on the wrong course, you lose.
- Jibing at sea is not without risk. Misjudge and the boom will take your head off.
- The best football hero in the world cannot win the game on his own.
- You can face the fastest bowler but drop the bat and you're out.
- A big fish may outswim a fishing vessel but a small one will pass through the net.
- The monkey can jump about the tree as much as it likes but may knock all the nuts off.
- Going into bends on the brake is not Formula One driving. Everything must be perfectly positioned and balanced on the way in. It is the controlled use of power on the way out that makes winners.
- You have to be quick and decisive on thin ice, don't you?
- You can't stop a cruising oil tanker in five miles of open sea.

Julian Russell uses a two metaphors that I particularly like, one about a frog and one about a bat:

- The frog does not recognize food unless it is moving. If you put dead flies in a cage with a frog, it starves to death for lack of appropriate information.
- The bat flies blind. It sends high-frequency pulses with ears closed in order to protect them. At that point it is flying forward, both blind and deaf. After the pulse has gone, the bat opens its ears again and awaits the returning information before repeating the process.

Totems and archetypes

We saw how Louise (in Chapter Three) found an animal totem, the dolphin, in response to this question: "If there was something that represented a successful senior manager, who looked the part and felt comfortable, who ran a smooth operation and made a difference to every single one of her team, what might that something that represents it be?"

For her, the dolphin became a tangible totem of her identity and what she aspired to be. She recognized that the dolphin is:

- entirely independent but chooses mostly be stay with its "team"
- graceful both in the water and out of it
- able to fly into the unknown with exuberance.

When a coachee is working with a limited sense of their identity or lack of self-confidence or what they aspire to be, archetypes can also be useful. I often use a line of questioning like this:

COACH: You've been talking a lot about your limitations. I wonder if there is someone alive or dead, fictional or imaginary, in the context of success whom you really admire?

The coachee may come up with any number of ideas. If they do not, then I let it go. It seems that the most useful archetypes are those that spring easily to the coachee's mind or imagination. If they do identify one, I may then ask another question: "What characteristics do they have that makes them so successful?"

The coachee will then list those characteristics and they may include some of the following:

- thoughtful
- charismatic
- engaging
- visionary
- caring about people
- committed
- decisive

I write them down and then ask another question: "Let's imagine that there's someone you don't know, but who for many years has been watching you work. They've been watching you with great care and insight. They say that you are charismatic."

The basis for this statement comes from the philosophy that we sort for information in the outside world that is representative of our own experience. Simply, if we do not have an experience of "charismatic" then we are unlikely to be very good at paying attention to it. Although contrived, this line of questioning will invariably find a number of characteristics where the coachee finds a greater degree of coincidence with their archetype than they thought previously. As a means to boost self-awareness and confidence, they tend to find it useful.

Storytelling

I use stories in my counseling practice and stories work their way into my leadership and executive coaching from time to time. Stories envelop us and allow our imagination to work in a creative way. When we watch a movie, we know what the people look like, how they talk and what they wear. When we listen to a story (or read a novel), the imaginary world is construed by the coachee using the preferences and symbolism of their internal world.

There may be those who say that the coach should not introduce their own material, stories, and metaphors into the coaching dynamic, and I am sympathetic to that view. The world of the coachee is where the bulk of our attention needs to be placed. When we are relating stories, experiences, and metaphors, we are less perfectly listening to the coachee. Sometimes, however, I have an inspiration to relate a story of my own or a favored story that carries an underlying message that may be useful to the coachee. When I think of it, the times when I use these interventions is very likely to be with those coachees who are not expressing much of their own world in metaphor, or relating in an inspirational way. A story given by the coach can allow permission in the dynamic for more creative expression. The story can also make a nice change of pace and bring a new energy to it. It may also help conclude or give new energy to dialogue that is sounding familiar or stale.

Stories allow the listener to enter a state not unlike trance, suspended in a new and different state of being. Over thousands of years, the same stories have been captivating and inspiring people: think of the Greek myths, including Homer's *Odyssey*, the stories of the Brothers Grimm, and legends of King Arthur, Guinevere, and the Knights of the Round Table.

There are many sources of stories that are useful in the context of performance and leadership; I provide a few references in the appendices. However, you may enjoy just a couple that I particularly like and have used repeatedly. I am indebted to Sue Knight (whose book (2000) marked a milestone on the applications of NLP at work) for bringing my attention to the first and to David Hemery (the inspirational Olympic gold-medal hurdler) for the second. Both stories have been heavily adapted, more out of carelessness than design, as stories often are, in the telling.

The real secret of using these stories is never to translate the story or to start discussion about its meaning. Telling the punchline of a joke a second time is always counterproductive. Explaining the meaning of the story, embroidering the punchline, is just as bad. It interferes with the imagined world of the coachee and the significance of the story and its specific meaning for them. Let the coachee take the story and do what they will with it in the moments, weeks, sometimes years, that follow.

Up a Mountain, Down a Mountain

Many years ago, a salesman (or -woman) was traveling alone from one village at the top of a mountain toward another village at the bottom. It was a warm and pleasant day. About halfway down he saw a small sign on the path that stated "Prophet Center" and, it being such a nice day, and intrigued by the word he understood to be "Profit", he wandered down a side path heavily shaded by trees. Soon, the way became lighter and there were hedgerows and flowers.

Having walked a while, the salesman entered a clearing with a huge evergreen oak at its center and surrounded by tall bushes and forest. He stood for a while in the sun while his eyes adjusted to the light, and looked around. Eventually he noticed an old man sitting on a mat beneath the tree. Taking his sack off his back, he walked over to where the old man was seated cross-legged and eyes closed. The salesman coughed politely and the old man opened his eyes.

"Excuse me, sir," said the salesman, "good day to you. I hope you do not mind my disturbing you but I saw the sign and thought I would investigate."

"Not at all," said the old man.

To make conversation the salesman spoke again: "I have been trying to sell my wares in these parts and am on my way down the path to the next village. Can you tell me what the people are like there?"

"Yes," said the old man, "but why don't you tell me how you found the villagers at the top?"

"Well," said the salesman, "I have been most depressed by my sales there. I did not sell anything in all the morning. I thought them a bit distant and insular. I tried to interest them in my excellent products but they could not be roused to see the advantage of them."

"Ah", said the old man, "I am afraid you may find the people at the bottom of the mountain very alike."

With that, the salesman slouched off with a wave of his hand and proceeded down the mountain.

Later that day, a salesman happened to be walking up the mountain from the village at the bottom. He was on his way to the village at the top. He too misunderstood the little sign stating "Prophet Center" and decided to investigate.

The salesman wandered down the side path heavily shaded by trees. It was cool, so he adjusted his sack and slowed his walking to take advantage of this welcome shade. Soon, the way became lighter and there were beautifully pungent hedgerows and flowers of a myriad colors. He walked a while. The ground became spongy with the needles from pine trees; here and there were long orange caterpillars with black legs slowly munching fallen leaves; birds could be heard and seen. He stopped to take in the view and enjoy the sweet air.

Starting on his way again, the salesman was enthralled by a wonderful smell of magnolia, and he entered a clearing with a huge evergreen oak at its center. Tall bushes and forest surrounded the clearing. The magnolia that he could smell so strongly was nowhere to be seen. He could see an old man sitting on a beautiful hand-made mat and close by him a small fountain played into a little pool where carp were feeding quietly. The old man's eyes were closed. The salesman found some shade and settled down into a squat to wait for the old man to notice.

Soon enough, the old man opened his eyes.

"Excuse me, sir," said the salesman. "I am sorry if I disturbed you but I saw the sign and thought to find out what the Prophet Center is."

The old man smiled and his eyes twinkled warmly.

To make conversation the salesman spoke again: "I have been selling my goods in the region and am on my way up the path to the next village. Can you tell me what the people are like there?"

"Yes," said the old man, "but why don't you tell me how you found the villagers at the bottom?"

"Well," said the salesman enthusiastically, "I went for a few hours and have been there for three days. The people are so warm and hospitable. I have been well fed and looked after and have received gifts of food for my journey, which I would be happy indeed to share with you. I sold some products but received much more than money for my time. I have found friends there."

"Well," said the old man, "I am happy to tell you that I think you may find the people of the village at the top very alike."

A Runner's Dream

(This is the true story (Merrill and Sites, 2003) of Glenn Cunningham.)

Glenn Cunningham grew up on a Kansas farm in the early 1900s. As a child, he loved to run and he had a crazy idea: to break the world record for the mile! His brother also liked to run and they used to compete against one another on the farm.

Glenn attended the local, one-room school. He was used to chores and so, one cold morning, aged eight, he went to the schoolhouse with his brother to light the Franklin furnace and warm the room before classes began. The boys used kerosene. Hot coals caused a huge explosion—both boys' clothes were set on fire. Burning, Glenn pulled his brother to the door and then collapsed, unconscious. Neighbors rushed to the scene. Glenn's brother was dead.

Glenn was taken to hospital. He had deep burns from his waist down and he was not expected to wake again.

While seemingly unconscious in hospital, Glenn twice heard medical staff during the weeks that followed. On one occasion he heard a doctor say that Glenn would not live, and, the second time, better news: that Glenn would survive but would never walk due to the loss of soft tissues in his legs. On each occasion he told himself that the pronouncements were wrong—he would fight for life.

Ten years later, and still badly crippled at eighteen, Glenn was unable to stand or walk. Then, one extraordinary day, seemingly like any other, he attended a high school track event. While watching the running, he was suddenly inspired to overcome his disabilities and run again. Back on the farm, Glenn had his father help him. His father harnessed the horses to a walking plow and carried him to it. He then tied Glenn's hands to the handles. Glenn leaned into the plow and urged the horses forward. His crippled body was literally dragged across the wheat fields. His commitment and determination continued. Two years later, Glenn could finally stand without assistance and he could shuffle using a crutch or cane. He had achieved a miracle but his perseverance continued without a pause.

Five years later, in May of 1934, and at the age of twenty-five, Glenn Cunningham broke the world record for the mile at Princeton, NJ, in 4 minutes and 6.8 seconds. His world title was not broken again for over three years.

You may wish to know more, so I add this footnote:

In 1938, Glenn Cunningham ran a mile in just 4 minutes and 4.4 seconds. It took another five years for this record to be beaten at an authenticated race, when Arne Andersson of Sweden ran the mile in 4 minutes and 2.6 seconds. His compatriot, Gunder Hagg, then held the title for almost nine years when, in May 1954, Dr Roger Bannister took the world record for the first mile run in under four minutes—a stunning achievement.

Glenn's track career lasted twelve years and he competed in two Olympics, winning a silver medal for America at Berlin in 1936. Glenn once said, "To me it was a challenge. Once a person accepts something like that as a handicap, you're licked before you start."

Chapter Eight
Coaching Pitfalls and How to Avoid Them

It will be useful to look at some of the pitfalls of coaching and see where one can fall into a trap. Most of the illustrations we have seen so far show examples that worked (and sometimes I have mentioned in the text something I thought less than perfectly judged at the time). In this section we will go straight to failed interventions and hope to learn something from those as well. Some of the examples are taken from my own experience, others from experiencing and observing in coaching sessions.

Coaches can become so focused on performance, leadership, and success that their humility begins to be corrupted. A good coach experiences miracles on a regular basis. It's a small step from considering the wonderful privilege of this to that of imaging one has special powers. Also, if coaches are unaware of making mistakes, they are certainly poor coaches. Those who notice and learn are those who will deserve the mantle of coach. We can hope that complacent consultants will stay at home and not undermine the excellent work of fine coaches.

One could dedicate a whole book to the "away-froms" of coaching. I have observed a number, particularly among trainees. I have even fallen into some myself. Typically, this is because I have ignored my own advice!

Psychological projection

In discussing empathy, I attempted to show that this projection of the coach's emotional world into the coaching dynamic is normally inappropriate. This is one example of how the world of the coach can find its way into the coaching dynamic and corrupt the pure development of the coachee's own experience and their own solutions.

The expression of undesired traits and emotions by any individual constitutes projection (see for example Pervin and John, 2001; Carver and Scheier, 2000) and is a more serious manifestation. Projection finds expression by subconscious distortion of these psychological traits and emotions in order to prevent them from welling up into consciousness. An example is that of expressed homophobia, where it arises as a projective response to same-gender attraction. In psychological terms, the id is expressed in such a way that the ego and superego do not recognize it. In this way, the energy around the issue is diminished through an expression, even though it is inappropriate. In another example, I know of a coachee who was obsessed by people molesting children and harassed more than one colleague because of it. This appears, by all accounts, to be a distorted expression of his own unrealized attraction toward his young daughters. By converting this unwanted energy against his colleagues, he was probably finding release from dealing with his own issue. These are extremes, but milder forms of projection do crop up frequently. Countertransference is a form of projection from coach to coachee.

Countertransference and inspiration

To be precise, countertransference is the process of projecting feelings that the therapist or coach has about their coachee (Kennedy and Charles, 1992). Where these feelings arise, they may manifest in the coaching dynamic by distorting the quality of that dynamic. For example, if the coach begins to feel protective about the coachee or angry about what seems to be happening to them, this will undoubtedly change the dynamic in complex ways that affect both the therapeutic space and, often, the language (including the body language) of the coach.

Another frequent example is that the coach does not like the solution of the coachee and can think of a "better" one. The coach thus either suggests this other solution or continues questioning the coachee to provide them with more options. This illustrates how a coach transfers their own agenda into the world of the coachee, and with negative effect.

Similarly, the coach may feel attracted to the coachee and this may be a pattern, for example, of attraction to those in needy situations. The experience of countertransference reduces the quality of attention and can give rise to inappropriate strategies and poor interventions. The coach can help check for countertransference by performing a check after each session:

- Do I feel differently about the coachee?
- Am I unusually friendly or detached from this coachee?
- Do I feel frustrated by their issues?
- Do I feel excited by their enthusiasm or plans?
- Am I being unusually flexible?

Questions like these, asked and answered honestly and constructively, can yield some clues to our underlying feelings for the individual. Where countertransference is suspected, I suggest talking through with an associate coach. Remember, too, that coaching discipline expects you to maintain the best-quality attention to your coachee. When you are experiencing your own feelings within the coaching dynamic, your attention is necessarily reduced and your effectiveness similarly compromised. Feelings that arise within a session are best worked with *outside* the coaching dynamic. The support and help of an understanding coach is always useful.

Perhaps I have not stressed enough the importance of countertransference. Please do not overlook the fact that countertransference and inspiration (on the part of the coach) are both experienced by the genius and by the fool. Rarely does the coach have evidence that makes them a genius. Be wary of your insight. Encourage it to flow and do follow your instinct, *but* look to the coachee for confirmation by asking open questions (those that do not lead them into your "enlightened" view of their world). The arrogant, self-important coach will fall into a trap very easily. Their insight propels them to make statements like, "I sense that you're angry with your boss. Your reactions to his slow development of your career are due to this unexpressed anger." Coachees sometimes play their game, entering the coach's world briefly to keep the coach puffed up but achieving nothing lasting or empowering for themselves.

The habits of countertransference are very common in practicing "coaches" and it is incumbent on HR professionals to filter these people out and to recommend further training and development if within their own organization. The selection of coaches becomes easier where the coach is also a counselor or psychotherapy-trained. It is for this reason that Hogg Robinson Skillbase, for example, select their coaches on this basis. Julian Russell also promotes the desire that coaches have counseling training.

Separateness

The coach is in an unusual relationship for the duration of the session, giving attention and support on a strictly one-way basis. It demands discipline and other psychological skills to achieve this one-way street consistently.

The more the coach is amenable to moving sessions, providing ad hoc, interim support via email and telephone contact, the more the risk that the coachee will feel that their relationship with the coach is special. The flexibility may be seen as a particular favor and interpreted by the coachee as indicating a unique relationship. Again, we see how important it is to set the expectations of the coachee at the beginning of the relationship. High flexibility is not necessarily a bad thing. It might, however, be construed as dangerous and unprofessional if the coachee is not expecting that degree of flexibility. They may assume it to be due to your very special interest in them, accommodating them on a unique basis, a sign of friendship.

The whole issue of providing a caring and supportive arena for coaching is one that requires discipline, since the coach's principal aim must be to keep their very best attention with the coachee. Feelings may come but should be briefly noted (mentally) and left to one side for later attention. This is not the same as being remote, distant, or uncomfortable about the dynamic with the coachee. A coach who is immune to their own feelings is likely to be of very limited use in the therapeutic environment where emotion plays a part (Kennedy and Charles, 1992, pp. 25–26). Necessarily, it is where emotion is involved that the greatest potential for motivated growth and success comes. It is better, therefore, to face the challenge of being close to the coachee and to be familiar and "comfortable" with the consequences that the coaching dynamic can give to coaches who are working at this level of change. The coach whose own head is full of voices is strongly advised to go back to their own self-development before re-entering the coaching dynamic.

Our coachees bring with them echoes of our own experiences, issues, and emotions. Any of these can trigger emotional response and may even provide us with insight. However, the coach's "insight" may be misplaced. This is another good reason for always checking with the coachee with an open question about what they may or not be experiencing rather than dumping your perception into the dynamic. The language and intervention strategies illustrated in this book largely support this approach to coaching intervention.

Interpretation

When we find models that confirm our view of the world, then we tend to keep using them. However, models are simply different realities that we choose to adopt. It does not make them the truth. For example, the word "wavelength" comes from physics and suggests that light travels in waves with specific heights (amplitude) and peak-to-peak distance (wave-length). Thus, blue light has a shorter and thus more energetic wavelength than red light. The study of atomic behavior led to a new reality: that light travels in small pulses, quanta, each having a specific energy. Neither model suggests the truth but both have been enormously useful in stimulating new and inventive thought and solving problems. Both models have thrown up working formulae that are used routinely today all over the world, and beyond it, in space.

Models of human behavior are similar. The penis envy described by Freud is no longer thought of as useful. Therapeutic psychology has gone through several eras of dramatic change from those days. At this time, the Myers–Briggs Type Indicator has been revived and is used widely to attempt to stimulate inter- and intrapersonal learning in teams. This puts people into sixteen categories (or types) from just four dimensions. Neurolinguistic programming (NLP) has also made an enormous leap in the last few years. The toolkit of the NLP practitioner contains a number of measures that can help people learn about themselves and their relating to others. These include the meta-programs that categorize people, within a given context, as away-from, toward, associated, dissociated, and so on. There is no fundamental basis that links the two models, but both approaches are practical and work "some of the time". This confirms to us that the models are not describing truth (or absolute truth): they are just contrived realities that attempt to represent what is happening. The danger is that the coach, and specially the one-model coach, will have so much investment in their working reality (the model) that they come to specific understandings (assumptions) about the coachee's world and act upon them. It takes discipline not to do this. The mantle of coach belongs only to those who have this discipline. Let me give a couple of examples of what I mean.

In the first example the coachee has crossed their arms and kept them there for some minutes.

COACH: You seem to be holding back.

COACHEE: How do you mean?

COACH: Your arms are crossed in front of you.

COACHEE: I'm cold.

In the second example, the coachee's eyes begin to water.

COACH: So, you're upset because your boss has left.

COACHEE: I couldn't be happier, I've always wanted that job and now it will be mine.

In both examples the coach has made an interpretation, run to a conclusion or judgment about the etiology of the change in their coachee and taken them on a deviating tangent, away from their issues, experience, and learning. How much better might it to have said the following?

COACH: I notice that your arms are crossed. Does that signify anything useful to you?

COACH: What's happening with you now?

Even if you feel sure you are right, it is invariably better to go to the coachee for information than to seek specific confirmation about your diagnosis. In describing the need to be open to the limitations of the model used, I do not wish to give the impression that it is inadvisable to become expert in one approach. On the contrary, becoming expert in one approach is a great foundation for experimenting and extending the boundaries of that approach. This is likely to be a better philosophy of approach than a mixed bag of models chosen by the coach based on personal preference. The coach may learn a great deal by working within one discipline, having to use tools that are a personal challenge to them and learning from feedback whether they were used effectively or not.

Transference

Transference occurs when the coachee has feelings about their coach. The first indication of this in the coach is likely to be discomfort when the dynamic changes from a professional relationship to one that is threatened by expectation and judgments on the part of the coachee. These expectations and judgments may be numerous—examples include:

- the coach dislikes me
- the coach is attracted to me
- the coach wishes to be my friend
- the coach wants to look after me
- the coach is just like my mother/father (good or bad)
- I know the coach's reaction will be negative if I mention that
- I feel truly loved

A good coach will appear to be providing the most exquisite attention to their coachee; they will be listening, reflecting, and wholly supportive of performance strategies and personal growth. All of this occurs in a special relationship where this care is provided in a unique (coaching) context. However, this is only for the duration of the session and professional contact within expected guidelines. In spite of the fact that the coach has set out the expectations for the coachee, the latter may experience the most loving environment of their lives. This may be sad, but sometimes a reality. Is it surprising, then, that the coachee can enter into a state of transference or psychological projection onto their coach? When this occurs, the emotional intelligence of the coach, together with their experience and discipline, can rescue the situation before it escalates and becomes destructive.

The coach will need to tackle any issue of suspected transference as it arises before returning to any previous work. This has to be the strategy whether the underpinning feelings seem to be positive or negative in nature. In either case, these feelings distort the coachee's view of reality and are an unhealthy experience of coaching. It is also an unhealthy context for the coachee to make independent progress with their issues.

If the coachee feels that the coach is somehow "with them" or "against them" they are not dealing with the issue and most likely following a pattern of behavior. The underlying pattern may be cropping up elsewhere in their work relationships to a lesser or greater extent. The coach must attend to that before constructive work is recommenced. As an example, the coachee says, "OK, I will read the lists each morning for you." The coach might think to say, "You don't seem to be committed to doing this for yourself. Shall we find something you can commit to or should we work to find a more compelling reason for you to read these lists each morning at breakfast?" This would skip the issue: the coachee has made a clear statement suggesting transference, that the relationship with their coach is somehow special and that the coach has a private investment in the coachee beyond the session. Tackled directly the coach may say something like:

COACH: I'm here until 3 p.m. to assist you to achieve your own targets. After that, your commitments are for you. Why do you think I might want you to read these lists *for me* each morning at breakfast?

COACHEE: You seem very positive and supportive about these lists and suggested I might find a space each day to read them through. I think I'm more likely to read them each day because I know that I shall satisfy your expectations prior to the next session than if I undertake to do the reading for myself.

The coach can again let the issue slide and say, "Zero to ten, how certain are you that you will read the lists each morning at break-fast?" It's not a bad question, but one that deals more directly with the underlying issue may be better:

COACH: Let us forget about the lists for now. I'm going to suggest to you that being motivated by an expectation that you think I have is not the best strategy for success. Your expectation is based on an assumption. Do you agree?

COACHEE: Yes.

If a coachee accepts this view, the coach can leave a pause in which the coachee may further integrate their acceptance. The coach may then ask more questions, possibly to look for evidence of a pattern at work.

COACH: Can you give me any other examples at work where you feel motivated because you think, rather than know, someone will be pleased with you?

Coachee attraction

Certainly there are cases where the coachee forms an unhealthy attachment to their coach and the transference becomes physical as well as emotional. In one such case, our coach was working with the CEO and senior team of a successful SME. She felt that the attention of the CEO was inappropriate. She was unsure about the evidence and found it hard to confront him in case it cost us the contract. We had known the client some time before the assign-ment and hence he was already familiar with the coach. With hindsight this may have been an error on our part but he was, apparently, keen to have her as his coach.

What our coach observed was that the CEO developed an early habit of taking over the session for nontarget issues, inviting her to sit with him to look over plans and so on. It was some time before he actually asked her out on what she thought was a prospective date and the problem had to be confronted. This was done in two stages. The first was to have a senior consultant review our progress with the CEO and to ask him specifically about the use of a coach with existing familiarity with some of the coachees, including himself.

There was no overt indication of the issue (which met the wishes of our female coach). We had guessed that he might discuss this directly with our coach subsequently and in fact this was what happened. She had rehearsed what she wanted to say, which went along these lines:

COACH: I feel I'm failing as your coach because I haven't kept you adequately directed to your targets. Specifically, I've encouraged chatting about other issues and I feel uncomfortable enough to want to do things more professionally, if you will agree.

CEO: Don't feel bad. We get on very well and I'm entirely happy with our sessions.

COACH: I'm not meeting my needs to maintain a professional standard in these sessions. I feel it would be proper to let one of my senior colleagues take over if I'm having difficulty separating our professional role from the friendly association that I think we have both enjoyed for some time. I don't wish to damage that association and I'm sure that if I don't react to my instincts it'll damage that friendly association.

If the engagement had been a psychotherapeutic one, the issue might have been dealt with more directly at first base. This was not the best outcome, but we were able to maintain the coaching (with the same coach) without further problems. We have since reviewed our training in the context of intimacy issues. We now encourage earlier dialogue where there may be an issue and/or an immediate switching of the coach.

I had a similar experience with one of my female clients a few years back. She seemed to take increasing care about what she wore and was calling me once or twice between sessions. I could not be sure, but the natural increase in rapport seemed tinged by something more emotionally driven than was proper for the coaching sessions. Perhaps my flexibility and willingness to support her, photocopying articles between sessions and so forth, had attracted her in some way.

I do not necessarily discourage limited coachee contact between sessions, if I have time. I had no clear evidence but, because I had a slight discomfort about it, decided to make some changes before the next session. I decided to be less flexible about my boundaries in relation to her calls. By the date of our next meeting, I felt that the dynamic had improved and we finished our contract normally.

Other issues in the coaching dynamic

When a coach encounters resistance to a particular tool, it can be simply that the coachee is not attracted to a particular way of working. For example, inviting a coachee to use a highly visual tool like the SWISH may not be acceptable to them if they find creating mental images difficult or impossible. The wise coach moves on. Sometimes it is possible that the coachee is just tired or impatient with the coach. How do you tell the difference?

COACH: We've been working around your target for a while. Would you like to continue in the same area now or do you have a need for any other strategy at this time? If you want a break we can do that too.

COACHEE: I feel rushed. I want more time to integrate what's happening, maybe take some notes before moving on.

The coachee may have numerous reasons for needing a break apart from the obvious. It's the duty of the coach to check the dynamic and act appropriately.

I have already mentioned NLP eye cues (see Chapter Four) and recommend that no intervention be made based upon them:

coachees tend to find the whole idea of eye cues intrusive and manipulative. This does not negate their possible usefulness in coaching, but on balance I recommend not using them overtly.

Ethics

There is often a question mark for the inexperienced about the use of presupposition, inferred beliefs, perceptual positions, and walking the hierarchy of logical levels. This is a valid view. The resistance comes from a belief that there is something manipulative and devious in encouraging executives to "take on" new thoughts, beliefs and values. We should not let these issues pass without comment.

The whole arena of presupposition starts from the belief that individuals have a range of expression that they may not have fully explored. We are attempting to encourage them to check for wider expression from other contexts in their lives. Thus, when Robyn was asked to walk a hierarchy of logical levels with her presupposition that she had the identity of a board director (to which she had just been appointed), I hope that we were merely exploring the breadth of what is already part of her repertoire of beliefs. Clearly, she had a lack of confidence "as a director" in her new corporate board, but in other contexts she was already a competent "director." The coach is invariably doing just this, helping the coachee transfer competencies from one context of their experience to another.

A coachee is unlikely to embrace and be willing to "take on" presuppositions that are contradictions to who they really are. Indeed, coaching as explored in this book is underpinned by coachee permission at a pace dictated by the coachee. The coach is merely extending an invitation to explore elements of what is truly an authentic aspect of their nature.

The skills learned by coachees become fully effective only when integrated into their persona and where they fit the culture in which they live and work. Future pacing with coachees helps to check that their targets fit in with their world—an ecology test.

Another issue of ethics concerns respect for the coachee at all levels. From a humanistic standpoint, this means honoring all manifestations of our coachee's presence and coaching them in such a way that their material (their issues) are not clouded by the coach's language, patterns and behaviors.

Keen beginnings

If you have read the section "Mindsets for the coach" in Chapter Six, you will already be familiar with my thinking on a suitable mindset for entering the coaching dynamic. The novice coach can be overzealous, overenergetic and overpositive. I recall one novice whose brightly stated opening was approximately, "I trust that we're in a target-focused mood today!"

This was presumptuous. The coachee may have wished to use the coaching session to review their development plan or to seek learning about a technique that they had read about since the previous session. In their map of the world, these desires for the session may not have been targets and the introduction could unsettle them.

Bright and unusual beginnings do crop up with nervous or emotionally inadequate trainee coaches. These unnatural behaviors are invariably harmful to the establishment of a working rapport.

Another issue is that of dress and appearance. The coach does need to appear "professional" and their demeanor to be appropriate to the culture. Attention needs to be with the coachee and not the coach. I remember very well a demonstration of a particular brand of coaching where the facilitator was entirely dressed in black apart from a white collar. He also wore a jacket without lapels and with buttoned, turn-back cuffs. His appearance was bizarre in the context of the demonstration and it was clear from listening to delegates that this view was shared. He did not gain the confidence of his audience or that of his coachee subjects. One of my colleagues is a former SAS trainer who has worked undercover in many hot spots over the last twenty years. He talks of being "gray"—an adaptive skill of looking and behaving like those in the culture in order to disappear. Coaches do not need to disappear to this extent, but the SAS philosophy shows that the appearance and behavior of the coach can be critical to the relationship. The coach should not be trying to impress with the quality of their wardrobe and jewelry.

Pressing on

I have coached in sessions timetabled for two and half hours where my coachee has decided, upon invitation, to terminate the session in an hour or so. In one case, my coachee had moved briskly through some significant learning. He looked ready for more but soon appeared jaded. It was his work habit to press on when tired but this might not have been appropriate if he was to get the most enduring result from the session. We took a break and then reviewed what he had learned. Feeling satisfied with his progress and commitments, he was happy to stop the session and arrange for our next appointment. Coaches need to be flexible if they are not to lose willingness of their coachees to work with them.

Chapter Nine

Mentoring and E-Mentoring

We now look briefly at some of my thoughts on mentoring and my experience in the business of Internet-based mentoring. That experience also offers some helpful hints for those providing telephone-based mentoring.

Mentoring

My discussion on mentoring will be unusually short but that will reflect the definitions that I made at the start of this book. Let's see them again:

Coaching
The use of questioning, challenge, and silence to assist a coachee to a defined work-based target.

Mentoring
Mentoring ideally adopts all the skills of coaching. The best mentoring helps the mentee to find their own solutions using the three principal instruments. Most mentoring seems to be on culture-specific advice and suggestions. It contains information on organizational structures and procedures (e.g., politics, agendas and influencing strategies).

Julie Hay (1999) defines mentoring as a developmental alliance in which there is a relationship between equals in which one or more of those involved are enabled to increase awareness, identify alternatives, and initiate action to develop themselves.

In my map of coaching and mentoring, the best applied mentoring uses all the skills of coaching as set out in this book. In practice, mentoring is often the giving of instruction and advice and sometimes this is appropriate. I am minded, though, of the Chinese adage (Ei-Ichiro Ochiai, 1993):

Tell me, I will forget,
Show me, I may remember,
Involve me, I understand

In coaching, we are trying to engage the will of the coachee. Showing or guiding individuals, although practical and useful, is not usually of long-term use in developing the mental aptitudes needed by today's executives. That is not to say that there is no place for mentoring of that sort. One of my colleagues was engaged by a senior figure to instruct him on a one-to-one basis during more than twenty days of training because the executive did not wish to join a group program. His instruction was a mixture of telling, showing, and role play. I know another CEO who hired an undergraduate to give him one-to-one instruction on how to use a computer.

Mentors are often chosen from either existing senior staff or those who have retired. Typically, they will be two or more levels up in seniority so they can provide a wider view of the organization but still understand the cultural strengths and weaknesses at the level at which the mentee has to work. Because mentors with this background bring technical, cultural, and political know-how, the organization rarely makes sure that the mentor has real aptitude for passing on the knowledge effectively.

I hope readers are already aware that the art of gaining the motivation and will of individuals is one that has little to do with show-and-tell. It is one of the reasons why so many trainers make bad coaches. Professional "chalk and talk" may sometimes impress but it rarely makes a significant productive impact in the longer term, and little of what is presented over one day is remembered or applied the next. When chalk-and-talk trainers apply this philosophy to coaching, the result is just as poor.

In coaching, we are attempting to facilitate our charges toward new life skills—thinking strategies for personal change and performance that will endure throughout their careers. So how might mentoring gain the better of both approaches? I am partial to an approach that has its feet in coaching but a head that holds the experience of the traditional mentor. In other words, knowing what they know, can mentors offer lines of questioning that open up the thinking and perception of their charges so they discover what the mentor knows without being told explicitly? The answer is yes.

MENTOR: I think there may be another solution. If there is one, what do you think it might be?

MENTEE: I don't know.

MENTOR: And if you did know, what would it be?

MENTEE: I suppose it would be upgrading the interconnect software?

MENTOR: That's good. How about the area of switching? What could have impact there?

MENTEE: We could role-reverse the backup. It's brand-new and we have overcapacity, while the online equipment's now stretched to the limit due to the system failures last week.

MENTOR: Sounds good, too. What would be best and what contingencies could be put in place to secure what you choose to do?

These examples show a *degree* of leading but not *overt* leading—by the hand. The end result is that the mentee is learning how to think on their feet faster, as well as solving short-term problems.

The mentor can also tell compelling stories and give examples that will offer clues to possible solutions, allowing the mentee to find their preferred approach. One great gift the mentor can bring is one of choice. Where technical solutions are possible, the mentor, with their experience, should normally be able to provide several options for progress. This is a greater gift than offering what the mentor thinks is the "best" solution. Mentors need to know that the effectiveness of a solution is only as good as the individual carrying it out. The mentor's favored approach may not be the best one when carried out by the mentee. The best solution is probably the one that the mentee is most compelled to follow.

MENTOR: Yes, Bob had a problem rather like yours when he was plant manager. I thought we should replace the boiler system and there was some discussion too about improving insulation. Bob had another idea and took energy from the stack and routed it back to the boiler. He saved us hundreds of thousands in capital and twice that in lost productivity had we closed down. Is there another way to look at your problem?

E-Mentoring

In 1998, I had the idea of establishing an Internet-based mentoring service. With some colleagues, we set up a business and I came up with a name, Ask Max. We quickly found our first customer in the European supermarket chain Sainsbury's. The ethos we established came from the one described above. We endeavor to provide a coaching feel to the service by asking questions and being softer on challenge than in face-to-face work.

E-mentoring is a valuable adjunct to traumatic and strategic change programs in organizations and acts as an HR support for rolling out new programs. Executives anywhere in the world are able to get something off their chest at any time rather than let it ferment and prejudice the quality of their work. Amanda Harrington quotes (1999) several academic studies that all suggest that there is an increased willingness to enter in coaching when it is *not* delivered face-to-face. Of course there are cultural variations, as we have found, but, where email is very established, e-mentoring is a sensible option to consider.

E-mentoring also helps the mentee to set out their thinking in a coherent way. When people are upset about something, emotions can prevent that happening efficiently. In having to set out an email that a mentor can understand, the mentee is forced to structure their issue and describe it in clear terms. This activity can be a real gift to the mentee. Within 24 hours, sometimes much faster, they get their first response.

We realized that we could not keep asking questions because the time to solve an issue might then extend for days. I came up with a mentoring strategy that became part of our terms of service.

When we offer advice, we always try to offer at least three ways to progress. My thinking was this: with luck the mentee will find some strong appeal or rejection in one of the solutions, or, better, be stimulated to find a new or related solution due to the stimulation they had received. It seemed to work. Feedback from our work is often very flattering (see appendices) and numerous issues and targets have been overcome, thanks to Ask Max coaches.

There is no reason why any organization could not set up its own email mentoring service, although some degree of confidence in the confidentiality may be lost if it is run by internal mentors. Ask Max is set up so that each of our (external) mentors has his or her domain address, thus Max AA, Max AB, and so on. We are especially happy that Max can be appreciated as both male and female—we did not want to cloud issues with those about gender. Although it may sound tawdry, I also like the strapline, "MAXimize your potential with ASK MAX!"

In setting up an internal system (whether run by external consultants or not) having genderless names is worth considering, or, alternatively, a system whereby the mentee may choose the gender of their mentor.

Issues

As expected, a large proportion of issues at Ask Max concern relationships and communication. Others are about development and training choices. Then there are many about advancement and mental preparation (as well as specific technical help) with presenting. As a rule of thumb, we find that in stressed organizations more than 40 percent of issues have to do with the job, role, or pay. Relationship issues amount to over 25 percent of new issues. Where stresses are lower, the relationship issues increase as a proportion of the total.

How often do people use the service?

The rate of use depends upon the culture and the IT skill sets within it. It is also dependent on the level of confidence in the usefulness and confidentiality of the service and the way in which it is offered internally.

I have found that, over a quarter of a year, perhaps only 30 percent of the staff may use the service. Of those who do use it in that quarter, about three-quarters use it only once. Most of the others bring two or three issues in the same period and rarely more than four. The average actual quarterly responses made by Max are three, with the bulk of mentees receiving only one to four responses even where multiple issues are involved.

Feedback into HR

One of the great benefits of Ask Max has been the general information that has been available for HR. We tailor our feedback sheets for each organization and gather information on issues, perceived support weaknesses, and perceived training and development limitations. In this way, we are able to impact significantly on the policy for HR in the subsequent budget period. An example feedback sheet is provided in the Appendices.

Glossary of Terms
(in the context of performance coaching)

acknowledgment: While we may be familiar with acknowledgment coming from others, there is also a context for self-acknowledgment where this is useful in underpinning self-worth and action.

affirmations: Positive statement about self, typically used habitually to improve feelings of self-worth and to engender confident action.

ambivalent: Holding two or more contradictory emotions (feelings) at the same time

anchor: A mental representation that triggers a change of mental state or mindset. These occur naturally in everybody but can be "installed" using NLP techniques to provide a positive mindset.

anchored state: A mental state that is initiated by using an anchor.

archetype: A (fictional) character that holds particular meaning.

Ask Max: E-mentoring service available via McLeod's company.

authenticity: True to self. Authenticity (congruence) is exhibited where behaviors flow naturally from a state of true identity, beliefs, and values.

away-from motivation: Reactive motivations resulting from a desire to move away from "negatively perceived" experience (cf. **toward motivation**).

body-centered phrases: Expressions pertaining to an individual's physical experience of being.

body language: Habitual and observable physical manifestations that may link to particular mental states for a given person in a given context.

broken-record technique: A repeated phrase or sentence used to answer questions and thereby minimize the potential for the questioner to develop and extend their dominance.

catharsis: A leap in personal perception.

challenge: One of the three principle instruments of coaching. Challenge is used to help shift perception (in the context of an excellent working relationship).

chunking: See **follower's question** and **leader's question**.

clean language: Developed by Dr David Grove, clean language comprises questions that reduce the potential of the coach to dump their own limitations and perspectives onto their coachees.

client: The person or organization that contracts to pay for coaching.

closed question: A question that may be answered simply by the word yes or no (cf. **open question**).

coach: Facilitator of executive change.

coachee: An executive who is willing to make personal changes in perception and efficacy using a coaching relationship to facilitate that change

co-coaching: An arrangement like that of co-counseling, where two coaches come together and coach one another on an equal footing and without payment.

congruence: An NLP term meaning authenticity.

conscious perception: Exploring and developing understanding by widening and being open to new thinking, ideas, and perceptions.

contradiction: A situation where the coachee holds two or more opposing ideas or beliefs that limit their efficacy.

context-free (questioning/ coaching): A language of coaching that does not require detail (contextual information). Helpful where the coachee desires to limit information.

contrived second position:	Where a coachee imagines that they are another individual not related to the current issue but having a similar situation (context) (cf. **first position; second position; third position**).
contrived future scenario:	Imagining a possible future scenario that is likely to happen and may mimic past experiences. Applied usefully where a coachee has learned new ways of dealing with difficult situations.
counterprojection:	Where the coach perceives insights into the coachee that are merely representations of their own emotional experience or state.
displacement activity:	Formerly considered as a means of habitually diverting unwanted anger, typically manifested by behavioral changes. Now includes the same mechanism used to divert attention from any unwanted emotion.
distracting questions:	Designed to help a coachee get out of a particular mental state and return, ultimately, to the coaching dynamic.
dynamic:	The whole, and holistic, interaction between coach and coachee.
dynamic preference:	The extent to which an individual wants more or fewer actions/targets/projects running concurrently.
EI:	Emotional intelligence, normally represented as "**EQ**" (q.v.).
EQ:	Emotional quotient. The equivalent to IQ (intelligence quotient), in emotional terms.
ecology:	Wider-context, or more systematic (or holistic), appreciation of an issue or goal.
ecology check:	Means whereby the coachee finds out whether their target has wider implications (to self, relationships, and family life) that make it acceptable or unacceptable.
ego:	Cognitive and mediating aspect of the mind, including perception, problem solving, and memory.

emotional association:	Emotional connectedness with an issue.
emotional dissociation:	Emotional detachment from an issue.
empathetic projection:	Where a coach presents their own feelings and/or solutions to a coachee owing to a perception that their own emotional history has been similar.
empowering belief:	A belief that engenders motivated action.
experience:	A holistic attention to self that may include physical, emotional, and wider sensory perceptions.
external reference:	Where a coachee habitually seeks external approval before action, in a given context.
eye cues:	An NLP device making statistically supported connections between eye movement and mental processing.
facilitate:	To assist people to learn and act with their own resources in a holistic way and in the broad context of their life experience.
feedback:	Written or verbal communication as a result of interaction or communication with a colleague or colleagues.
fifty-one percent rule:	McLeod's device for assisting coachees to understand a more responsible and effective way of dealing with interpersonal issues.
first position:	Where a coachee is recalling and attempting to relive a situation as themselves (cf. **contrived second position; second position; third position**).
flexibility:	Mental agility in being open to new ideas, thinking and experiences.
follower's question:	For example, "What stops you?" (Cf. **leader's question**).
frames of reference:	Factors that contribute to an individual's reality. Coachees need to test and reassess in many areas to improve performance.

free association: A device whereby the therapist encourages wider perceptions by seeking instinctive replies to words, sounds, or images.

future desired state: The target, or goal but experienced holistically, in the present

future pacing: A check to make sure that a new approach or action is likely to be successful in a future scenario. This is facilitated by role play or by the coachee's mental agility.

Gestalt: With roots in Zen and the psychology of perception, Gestalt seeks to explore reality within a special, therapeutic relationship. People learn how to fulfill their needs by stepping away from their own limitations and limiting perceptions. They also gain higher levels of understanding about interconnectedness and consequence.

GROW: The coaching model made famous by John Whitmore, it is an acronym: **g**oal-setting, **r**eality-checking, **o**ptions and **w**hat/when/whom.

hierarchy of logical levels: A motivation model of change having purpose and values at its top and environment at its base.

holistic: A broad view embracing the widest possible sensing, feeling, thinking about a given situation.

id: The instinctive, unconscious mind.

induced state: A mental state that the coachee decides to enter.

inner conflict: A situation where two or more ideas or beliefs compete.

inner dialogue: Internal voice.

inner game: Gallwey's model of coaching based upon awareness, choices and trust.

internal reference: Where a coachee habitually experiences internal approval before action, in a given context.

interrogative: In the form of a question.

intervention: Any change made by the coach that stimulates response in the coachee. This can be physical

	movement, a cough, smiling, silence, question, or challenge.
kinesthetic:	Of feeling, including touch, taste, and smell.
Kócs:	Hungarian town from which the word "coach" is derived, and the inspiration for the word in the context of facilitated change (see Appendix One).
LAB profile:	Language-and-behavior model widely promoted by Shelle Rose Charvet.
leader's question:	For example, "What does that do for you?" (Cf. **follower's question**).
left brain:	Where logical processing is thought to originate predominantly (cf. **right brain**).
limiting belief:	A belief that inhibits motivated action.
mentor:	Typically, a colleague who will provide advice.
metaphor:	A story that echoes something real in the conscious, often visually represented as a static or moving image.
metaphoric representation:	An imaginary representation of a situation or thing.
meta-program:	NLP term for mental filter.
mindset:	Mental state taken from an authentic range of personal experiences and understandings in order to focus the mind with the best attitude for a given challenge.
model (v.):	To emulate the **mindset** (q.v.) and behavioral characteristics of someone else in order to see if it helps one's own performance. NLP term.
modeling:	The act of establishing the **mindset** (q.v.) and behaviors of an achiever in a particular context, in order to apply it to self or others.
motivation traits:	The four NLP meta-programs that are particularly linked to motivation: *proactive*, *toward*, *internal*, and *procedures*.

neutrality:	Applied to the coach, a state of being that does not express, through any means, a reaction to a coachee's expressed emotion. This is in order to help them stay with their own material without external reference for it.
NLP:	Neurolinguistic programming. A set of tools, some borrowed, that assist personal growth and, in the right hands, lasting change.
nonverbal communication/ expression:	An expression by physical manifestation, often minor and subliminal.
observer:	The observer (or observer perspective) is that from which a coachee takes on a mental attitude of an imagined third party in order to get distance and logical information (primarily) in reliving an issue, in order to acquire new insight and learning.
open question:	A question that may not be answered simply by yes or no (cf. **closed question**).
outcome:	Target. Typically meaning "desired" outcome.
PDP:	Personal development plan.
PDR:	Personal development review.
Pattern breaker:	An NLP device, typically physical, to try to break a habitual and unwanted chain of thinking or mental events that have led to particular behaviors.
perception:	A reality as understood by the individual. Individuals need to test their perceptions in order to change and become more effective.
phobia:	Fear.
perceptual position:	In a situation, typically replayed and experienced in the mind of the coachee, there may be two or more perceptual positions. These invariably include *first position* (self) in that scenario, *third position* (observer) and *Second Position* (another person involved in that situation) (cf. **contrived second position; first position; second position; third position**).

personality profiling instrument: Models that assist HR professionals and recruiters to assign jobs but better used as models for exploring similarity and differences within teams in order to improve mutual understanding and contribute to effective communication, influence, and performance.

positive intention: A mental trick where the coachee tries to imagine what possible positive intention an individual might have had in doing something (that they had thought was negatively motivated against them).

positive listings: Lists of positive achievements in numerous contexts that help an individual to acknowledge their successes and raise self-worth and motivation to perform.

Power of Silence in Coaching: Workshop developed by McLeod and Breibart, which provides delegates with a powerful understanding of the value of silence in coaching.

presupposition: An idea or belief that assumes something to be true.

principle instruments: *Questioning*, *challenge* and *silence*, the three fundamentals of coaching.

projection: Imagining that another person has your own emotional state and/or needs.

psychological flow: A high-attention state characterized by focused activity and inattentiveness to the world around the task itself. About 20% of people routinely enter this state, many of them without acknowledging that they have done so.

questioning: One of the three **principle instruments** (q.v.) of coaching.

rapport: NLP term meaning the establishment of good relating.

reality: A set of perceptions that adequately meet the needs of the individual for understanding their experience of the world around them.

reframe: A mental trick used by coaches to encourage a new perception on a particular issue, characteristic, or behavior.

reflective language: The coach's use of the coachee's language, exquisitely, to help maintain them in their issue.

representation systems: NLP term, normally represented by "VAKog": the three main ways in which NLP attempts to describe how individuals mentally represent information. These are *visual*, *auditory*, and *kinesthetic* (including *olfactory* and *gustatory*: smell and taste).

resourceful state: A mental state that is useful in order to manage a particular situation.

right brain: Where creative thought, play, and emotions are thought to originate predominantly (cf. **left brain**).

second position: Where a coachee is recalling and attempting to relive a situation as another person (in that situation) in order to gain insights (cf. **contrived second position; first position; third position**).

sensory acuity: NLP term. Ability to attend to sensing in a more holistic way, not merely by hearing and looking.

separateness: Pertaining to the coach, a state of emotional detachment (cf. **neutrality**).

servant leadership: A way of being that sees oneself as a facilitator of others rather than as a director.

silence: One of the three **principle instruments** (q.v.) of coaching and the most successful for facilitating catharsis.

soma: Body.

stakeholder: A tertiary person (e.g. line manager) who has a legitimate interest in the coaching assignment.

state: Pertaining to psychology, a mental and emotional way of being.

state management: Means of controlling or opening up to a particular psychological way of being.

STEPPPA: Acronym. McLeod's coaching model, discussed in detail in Chapter Five.

submodalities: Variants of an experience.

superego: The aspect of the mind or self in terms of ethics and moral codes and conduct.

SWISH pattern: An NLP method for changing a negative pattern of "being" into a (visually represented and desired) new experience.

symbolic modeling: A way of facilitating motivated coachee solutions by encouraging metaphoric development.

third position: Where a coachee is recalling a situation in which they are a remote, outside observer in order to gain insights (cf. **contrived second position; first position; second position**).

timeline: An NLP tool whereby the coachee connects their present situation to a specific target in the future.

tool: A model or mental device for encouraging change.

totem: An animal or object of significant representative value.

toward motivation: Target-oriented motivations resulting from a desire to move toward "positively perceived" experience (cf. **away-from motivation**).

trance: State of self-absorption indicated, typically, by fixed focus of attention and slowed speech.

transference: Where the coachee perceives insights into the coach that are merely representations of their own emotional experience or state.

trigger: Something that initiates a chain of mental (and typically behavioral) changes, usually on a habitual basis.

truth: The Holy Grail of coaching. It is doubtful whether the coachee moves toward or away from it. Anyway, of no consequence, since the aim of coaching is to help a coachee to find a reality and mindsets that work for them most phenomenally in the context of work targets.

value imprinting: McLeod's method for facilitating value alignment in teams.

virtual timeline: Timeline that is conducted in the coachee's imagination rather than by physically moving or walking.

visualization: Imagining using images, typically to find positive and motivating metaphors to encourage successful action.

well-formed
outcome: NLP term. A target for which there is a motivated path to a specified timescale; one that is obtainable and realistic; one for which the consequences have been fully explored in a holistic context.

Appendix One

A Brief History of Coaching

By Steve Breibart

From small beginnings only a few short years ago, coaching has today become a key part of the personal- and professional-development toolkit. Although coaching as we know it today may be a new phenomenon, the story of coaching reaches back a very long way.

The word "coach" derives from the small town of Kócs in Hungary. Here, it is said, were invented the first wagons and, wherever that technology spread around the world, the name of this small town spread with it.

The term "coach" was next applied to tutors, who, like the wagons before them, metaphorically "carried" their pupils through examinations. More recently, we have become used to the term in the context of sport, where a coach is a combination of tutor, mentor, trainer, and probably several other things besides.

Coaching is now generally understood to be a process where the hidden resources and tacit knowledge of an individual are brought to the surface—this in the service of achievement of a particular target through the facilitation and guidance of a coach.

Coaching draws on a number of sources, some of which go back to ancient times. Perhaps the earliest influence is that of mentoring. According to Homer, when Odysseus set forth for the Trojan wars, he asked his friend Mentor to watch over his son, Telemachus. In the absence of Odysseus, and with the guiding hand of Athene upon him, Mentor acted as teacher, friend, and surrogate father to Telemachus.

However, the sometimes directive nature of mentoring was recognized as limiting the opportunity for individuals to release their own potential, by allowing them to rely on the advice and guidance of their mentor.

A further key influence on coaching came with the ideas of Carl Rogers, laid out in his 1951 book, *Client-Centered Therapy*. Rogers here laid the foundation of modern counseling, based on his notion of the "actualizing tendency." This he defined as the built-in motivation present in every life form to develop its potential to the fullest extent possible. Anyone involved in coaching will recognize this (at least as it applies to humans) as a key presupposition for any successful coach.

Rogerian counseling usually takes the form of a conversation in which the counselor constantly reflects back the client's words to check that the meaning has been understood. This will often cause the client to question their own statements, leading perhaps to some new enlightenment.

In coaching, asking questions and challenging the coachee becomes the responsibility of the coach. The notion of asking questions instead of giving direct orders is, of course, not new, and examples can be found reaching back to the work of Plato. More recently, in 1936, Dale Carnegie suggested precisely this in his seminal work *How to Win Friends and Influence People*.

Closer to our own times, coaching was perhaps best known in the terms that it was employed by the sports fraternity. It has been suggested that the first person to use the word "coaching" in the sense that we use it today was Werner Erhard, founder of what has become the Landmark Forum. But it was a former sports champion who really set the modern world of coaching alight.

In 1974 Timothy Gallwey's book *The Inner Game of Tennis* was published. *The Inner Game* was not based on giving orders, nor even on making suggestions: rather Gallwey's technique was to ask questions that would make his students reflect on and learn from their own experiences. Practical application of these ideas soon indicated that the best coach was often one without experience of the sport being coached. An understanding of the coaching process was recognized as being more important than knowledge of the subject content—there being a risk that knowledge provided by a coach might get in the way of a coachee's discovery of their own hidden resources.

It wasn't long before Gallwey's ideas were transferred to the business world and subsequently taken to Europe, by John Whitmore, author of *Coaching for Performance*.

During the early nineties, an accountant and financial planner from San Francisco was helping clients in ways far beyond his nominal brief. Recognizing the enormous potential of his coaching practice and wanting to help others become successful coaches, Thomas Leonard founded Coach University in 1992. Coach U (as it is known) training and coaching services are largely based on telephone contact, which has allowed Coach U to achieve global reach very quickly. Leonard went on to found the International Coach Federation in 1994 and in 1996 sold Coach U to his friend and colleague Sandy Vilas. Four years later in 2000, taking advantage of the prevalence of Internet access, he founded CoachVille, a coaching school and a vast repository of resources for coaches, available through a website.

Now, there are many coaching schools all over the world, all of which owe at least something to these founding fathers of the modern profession. Perhaps more importantly, coaching has been recognized as being valuable to almost anyone with responsibility for other people, be they managers, parents, teachers, health workers, or whatever. Indeed, coaching skills offer everyone the opportunity to help reveal enormous untapped potential.

In the spirit of passing on coaching skills to "professionals who coach" as well as "coaching professionals" and guided by the vision of our now honorary president, Sir John Whitmore, Angus McLeod and I gave birth to the Coaching Foundation in 1998. This not-for-profit organization provides continuing professional development for all who have an interest in developing their coaching skills. The foundation draws on as wide a range of influences as possible. We believe that coaches have something to learn from almost every field of human endeavor.

Appendix Two

Mindsets for the Coachee

As with coach mindsets, it is useful to find empowering beliefs that create a healthy attitude in the coachee for working. They also need to understand that the purpose of coaching is to deal with issues, define motivated targets, and be happy to engage with the process.

Empowering beliefs for the coachee

Empowering beliefs are those that are designed to lead to motivated action. They contribute to the mindset of the coachee. Here are some examples:

- The pace of learning is up to me.
- Challenges bring me opportunities for new understanding.
- My coach is here to facilitate my learning.
- I permit myself to be open to challenge and learning.
- I permit my coach to challenge me and facilitate learning.
- I allow myself to go with the flow.
- I am open to change.

This last is really a statement of identity. As we have seen, identity is a prime influencing level for influencing change.

Values

Values, like empowering beliefs, also contribute to the coachee mindset. Some appropriate ones are:

- I value risk taking.
- I value challenge and learning.
- I value openness and flexibility.

These are best put into one's own words and affirmed to create a healthy mindset for the session.

Interpersonal Issues with the coach

Before the session begins is may be useful to check out any resistance to working with the coach. Any outstanding issue may limit the quality of the coachee's work. One strategy may be to mentally set aside the issue with the coach. A preferred strategy is to deal with it directly:

"I feel uncomfortable with this situation. I don't know whether this has to do with coaching or you, but I'd like to get beyond this before we start on any other issue."

Ignoring the situation is not really an option for quality learning. Where the coach is external there may be a possibility of change. However, attend first to the issues that you have. Are these likely to be reproduced with other coaches or with colleagues? If so, then persevering and changing your outcome to deal with these issues with the existing coach may be a desirable outcome for both you and your organization.

The primary aspects of being an excellent coachee have to do with responsibility. Moreover, practice makes perfect. The more we engage as coachees in scheduled coaching sessions, the quicker and easier we install a healthy mindset for good work.

Appendix Three

Mentee Feedback to Ask Max

"Speaking to somebody that I either don't know or doesn't know me is great."

"Thank you for your useful service."

"Your comments were spot on—I gained valuable experience. My assignment went very well and I scored another merit! Once again, your advice has proved itself again."

"This opportunity has allowed me to refocus on my current role and the weaknesses that I have identified and relate them to the role I am now in to some of my successes in my previous roles."

"… meant that I actually did something about the issue, I was avoiding it."

"It allowed me an external view of the issues and helped me put a plan of action together to cope with the situation. Though the issue is still not resolved I feel 100 percent better about it and feel that it will be resolved in the future."

"The great benefits of the process are in its simplicity and impartiality (no hidden agendas), i.e. simply having someone that is not related to the company asking you questions, challenging your thinking, and providing advice and guidance."

"Have used the email service and have found it excellent."

"The responses have been of an extremely useful nature."

"The advice you gave has been invaluable."

"Thanks again for some great advice. I shall put all of your recent emails into a plan of action."

"Thanks for your reply—it is definitely one of the most useful emails I have ever been sent."

Appendix Four

Code of Conduct and Methods for E-Mentors

Coaching and mentoring

The Ask Max code of conduct for e-mentoring is based upon coaching "best practice" as defined in this document. There is one major difference. We *may* offer three or more different advice strategies, *but* only after the mentee has been assisted to properly define and reframe their issue.

We acknowledge that the method of e-communication is limited if we only use questioning to help the mentee define and reframe their issue. Having gone through a process of ensuring the mentee has completely defined and explored their issue using all resources available to them (other people, source materials, agencies, personal experiences in other contexts, etc.) it *may* be that the mentee has not moved forward. Then, it may seem appropriate to offer "advice strategies."

Ask Max will only offer advice after the definition and reframing stages and the advice provided shall *always* offer a minimum of *three* differing strategies/options. In this way, we hope the mentee will find a solution nearer to their own preferred motivational strategies or, better still, will be encouraged to come up with a derivative or new solution, all their own.

Definition of terms
Coaching: Coaching presupposes that every one of us has a greater potential than we use on a day-to-day basis. The coach is responsible for facilitating the development of excellent performance from

their mentee. The coach does this, helping the mentee to discover and exploit inner resources.

Coach: The person responsible for guiding the process and helping the mentee achieve their targets.

Mentor: Mentors may use personal experience to offer 3+ solution options to mentees.

E-mentor: Net use to provide coaching and mentoring strategies as above.

Mentee: The person wanting to achieve a particular target(s).

Sponsor: The person who pays for the coaching intervention (sometimes but not always, the mentee).

Stakeholder: Any other person who has a legitimate interest in the coaching assignment—for example, the mentee's line manager.

What is the purpose of this code of conduct?
- To define the responsibility of e-mentors and their accountability to the mentee and sponsor.

- To set the mentee's and sponsor's expectations appropriately.

- To provide a consistent approach from all e-mentors abiding by the Code.

- To establish a consistently high standard for professional e-mentoring.

E-mentoring assignments are driven by the needs of the mentee and as such are all different in approach and content. However, effective e-mentoring assignments utilize best techniques and highest ethical standards. The ground rules, laid out below, provide our framework for all assignments.

- E-mentor's should never work beyond the bounds of their capability, experience and expertise to the point where they do not feel confident in providing the mentee with proper support. When appropriate, e-mentors should seek advice from Ask Max master mentors who may pool resources and offer suggestions.

- The confidentiality of the mentee remains paramount at all times. *At no time* will an e-mentor disclose any part of the relationship to any person whosoever, without the explicit agreement of the mentee. Any notes or other records of e-mentoring sessions shall remain at all time the property of the mentee. They may, for convenience, be retained by the e-mentor but may be requested by the mentee at any time. Master mentors have access to all e-mentor communications.

- E-mentor's have a responsibility to highlight any ethical issues (such as conflicts of interest) that may arise during an assignment at the earliest opportunity.

- E-mentors must not attempt to do the mentees' job for them—the mentees have the ability and the potential, the e-mentors' job is to help them realize it.

- E-mentors may be challenging but never rude.

- E-mentors should not take on the mentees' problems. E-mentors need to stay objective: disinterested but not uninterested.

Agreeing a contract

In our e-mentoring assignments, the basis of the relationship with the sponsor and stakeholders will be detailed separately. Where we are offering the possibility of telephone and/or personal face-to-face support, the guidelines and methodologies for this are provided to e-mentors on a sponsor-specific basis.

- The e-mentor will always agree clear, measurable outcomes with the mentee.

- It is the e-mentor's responsibility to ensure that the mentee is clear about their responsibilities in the relationship and what is expected of them between e-mentoring communications.

The e-mentoring process
- Where an e-mentoring session strays into other areas (e.g. counseling), the e-mentor should make clear that this has happened and only continue if they have appropriate skills and experience. If the area entered falls outside of the agreed objectives or boundaries of the e-mentoring assignment, the e-mentor should point this out and only continue with the agreement of the client. If the diversion becomes a major one and the mentee wishes to continue, the e-mentor should return to the contracting process before continuing.

- In general, e-mentors will facilitate the learning process for the mentee. It may, however, be appropriate for the e-mentor to provide advice or lead the mentee from time to time. The e-mentor should always make clear to the mentee that this is what they are doing.

Completing the assignment
E-mentors will check for feedback that the defined target(s) have been met or that an alternate and satisfactory outcome has been achieved. E-mentors may offer mentees the possibility of completion (for that issue). There are separate feedback mechanisms for mentees concerning quality of the service provided my e-mentors.

Termination
- The mentee retains the right to stop the assignment at any time if they feel it is not helping them.

- The e-mentor has a responsibility to complete the assignment as contracted and has a responsibility to ensure that they can work effectively with the mentee. If this is not the case, then an Ask Max master mentor should be contacted immediately.

- If the e-mentor has, for some reason, to terminate an e-mentoring relationship unexpectedly, they must contact an Ask Max master mentor immediately.

If, while working for *ASK MAX* on an e-mentoring assignment, an associate is found to have contravened the terms of this code, then Ask Max will offer the associate no further work.

This code of conduct was developed by the founder members of Ask Max. We are constantly working to make this code more useful and effective and would value any suggestions that you may wish to contribute. Please forward your suggestions to:

Ask Max E-mentoring at:
sales@angusmcleod.com

E-Mentor Questionnaire: An Example

There are a maximum of sixteen quick questions and answers that will help us to tailor the mentoring service to your needs and those of the company. In just two minutes you can make a valuable contribution. Return anonymously by mail if you wish.

1. How many issues/questions did you seek support from your mentor?

None	❏	Please go to Q 2
Once	❏	Please go to Q 3
Twice	❏	Please go to Q 3
Other number	❏	Please go to Q 3

2. If you answered none, please write why not. Please use the back of the page if necessary.

Now, please go to Q8

3. If you answered once or more, How useful was the support received?

No use	❏
Some use	❏
Useful	❏
Very useful	❏
Other comment	_____
	_____

4. How was the speed of service compared to your expectations?

   Slow   ❏
   Reasonable   ❏
   Fast   ❏

5. What *specific* difference did the mentoring make to you, if any?

6. Would you recommend the e-mentoring service to anyone else?

   Yes   ❏
   No   ❏
   Other comment   _____

                           _____

7. Was the issue raised one that you were unlikely to source anywhere else?

   Yes   ❏
   No   ❏
   Other comment   _____

                           _____

8. Would you have wanted telephone contact had it been available?

   Yes   ❏
   No   ❏
   Other comment   _____

                           _____

9. Would you have wanted face-to-face contact had it been available?

   Yes   ❏
   No   ❏
   Other comment   _____

                           _____

10. Whether you used the service or not, did you feel it confidential enough?

    No   ❑
    Minor doubt   ❑
    Yes, confidential   ❑
    Other comment   _____

    _____

11. Did you have a clear idea of what the mentoring service could offer you?

    Yes   ❑
    No   ❑
    Other comment   _____

    _____

12. What else do you think it should have offered help with?

    _____

13. Do you have any comment to make about your mentor not using a first name? Is the sex of the mentor an issue for you?

    Comment   _____

    _____

14. Would you mind providing your age range?

    16–20   ❑
    21–25   ❑
    26–35   ❑
    36–45   ❑
    46–55   ❑
    Over 56   ❑
    Other comment   _____

    _____

15. May we quote you, subject to management approval?

    Your name   _____

    Your position   _____

16 Would you like to have this kind of service available as a permanent feature?

    Your name   _____

    Your position   _____

Appendix Six

Web Resources

Training courses

UK Coaching Academy	www.the-coaching-academy.com
US Coaching Training Institute	www.thecoaches.com
US Comprehensive Coaching U	www.comprehensivecoachingu.com
US Thomas Leonard	www.graduateschoolofcoaching.com
US Coach U	www.coachu.com
UK Industrial Society School of Coaching	www.theworkfoundation.com
UK Newcastle College	www.ncl-coll.ac.uk
UK Oxford School of Coaching and Mentoring	www.oscm.co.uk
Sydney/Calif. 1-2-1 Suzanne Skiffington	www.1to1coachingschool.com
UK Best Performance Ltd.	www.bestperformance.net

Supporting information noted in the text

Clean language and symbolic modeling
David Grove	www.davidgrove.com
The Developing Company (Lawley/Tompkins)	www.cleanlanguage.co.uk

Coaching e-forums (free)
The Coaching Foundation	subscribe-coachingfoundation@yahoogroups.com
Coach Universe	www.coachuniverse.com
Coen de Groot (Bristol, UK)	www.eurocoachlist.com
European Coaching & Mentoring Council	www.mentoringcentre.org
Coaching Academy (Regions)	www.coachlists.com
Coach Forum (UK)	www.coachforum.co.uk

Emotional intelligence
Jill Dann, Consultation Ltd., UK	www.emotionalfitness-uk.com
Buckholdt Associates	www.emotionalintelligence.co.uk
Reuven Bar-On: NY and Toronto	www.mhs.com

Glenn Cunningham

Merrill, M. W.   www.allprodad.com/characterestore.asp
Sites, J.   www.madisoncofc.org

Horse whispering applied to people

Pat Parelli (Colorado)   www.parelli.com
Andrew MacFarlane (UK)   www.leadchange.com

Inner game

Timothy Gallwey   www.theinnergame.com

Left-Right Brain

Left-Right Brain   www.mtsu.edu/~devstud/advisor/LRBrain.html

Motivation

Robin Stuart Kotze   www.managementlearning.com/art/perscmot
Solutions Coaching   www.solutionsology@cwcom.net

Commercial coaching resources

Angus McLeod   www.angusmcleod.com
Cheryl Richardson (MA, USA)   www.cherylrichardson.com
Diana Robinson (NY)   www.choicecoach.com
Coachville   www.coachville.com
Coach University   www.coachu.com
Coen de Groot   www.coendegroot.com
Ibility   www.ibility.se
International Coaching   www.coachfederation.org.uk
  Federation UK
International Coaching
  Federation US   www.coachfederation.org
Leadership Insight   www.leadership-insight.com
Performance Consultants   www.performanceconsultants.co.uk
  (Whitmore + Hemery)
Performance Partners   www.ppiglobal.com
  International
Skillbase (Hogg Robinson)   www.entegria.co.uk/services-resourcing.htm
Teleclass   www.teleclass.com
Vievolve Ltd.   www.vievolve.com
  (Lynne Kerry & Ian Ross)

Bibliography

Bailey, R., LAB Profile Self-Study Kit, Georgian Bay NLP Centre, North Richmond Hills, TX.

Bandler, R., and Grinder, J., 1975, *The Structure of Magic*, Science and Behavior Books, Palo Alto, CA.

Bandler, R., and MacDonald, W., 1988, *An Insider's Guide to Sub-Modalities*, Meta Publications Inc., Capitola, CA.

Barber, P., 2002, *Researching Personally & Transpersonally*, Gestalt in Action, University of Surrey, Guildford, UK.

Barber, P., January 2003, private communication.

Bar-On, R., May 2000, *Emonet Digest*, Vol. 403.

Bateson, G., 1973, *Steps to an Ecology of Mind*, Paladin Press, Boulder, CO.

Buzan, T., 2000, *How to Mind Map*, Thorsons, London.

Cameron-Bandler, L., 1985, *The Emprint Method: A Guide to Reproducing Competences*, Grinder/Delozier Press, Santa Cruz, CA.

Carnegie, D., 1994, *How To Win Friends and Influence People*, Hutchinson (Random House), London.

Carver, C. S., and Scheier, M. F., 2000, *Perspectives on Personality*, 4th edition, Allyn & Bacon, Needham Heights, MA.

Chomsky, N., 1957, Syntactic Structures, in *The Architecture of Language*, 2000, Mouton de Gruyter, and N. Chomsky (eds), Oxford University Press, Oxford, UK.

Dann, J., January 2003, private communication.

De Shazer, S., 1985, *Keys to Solution in Brief Therapy*, W. W. Norton, New York.

Ei-Ichiro Ochiai (tr.), 1993, *Journal of Chemical Education*, 44, American Chemical Society, Washington, DC.

Erdmann, E., Hubel, D. H., and Stover, D., 2000, *Beyond a Wall Divided: Human Values in the Brain–Mind Science of Roger Sperry*, Authors Choice Press.

Evison, R., and Horobin, R., 1990, *How to Change Yourself & Your World: A Manual of Co-counselling Theory and Practice*, Co-Counselling Phoenix, Phoenix, AR.

Farrelly, F., and Brandsma, J., 1974, *Provocative Therapy*, Meta Publications, Capitola, CA.

Forman, G., January 2003, *Desert Island Discs*, (radio programme), BBC Radio 4, London.

Frossell, S., 1998, Well-Formed Outcomes, *Rapport 41*, 34–35, ANLP.

Gallwey, T., 1986, *The Inner Game of Tennis*, Pan Macmillan, London.

Gallwey, T., 1999, ICF plenary lecture.

Gallwey, W. T., 2002, *The Inner Game of Work*, Texere Publishing, New York and London.

Gawain, S., 1982, *Creative Visualization*, Bantam, New York.

Goleman, D., 1996, *Emotional Intelligence*, Bloomsbury Publishing, London.

Greenleaf, R. K. and Spears, L., 1998, Power of Servant Leadership, in *Focus on Leadership: Servant-Leadership for the 21st Century*, 2001, Berrett-Koehler, K. Blanchard, L. C. Spears, M. Lawrence, and L. Spears (eds), John Wiley, New York.

Hall, L. M., and Belnap, B., 1999, *The Sourcebook of Magic*, Crown House Publishing, Carmarthen, UK.

Harrington, A., 1999, *E-mentoring: The advantages and disadvantages of using e-mail to support distant mentoring*, M.Sc. thesis, Hertfordshire Technical Education College, UK.

Harris, T. A., 1995, *I'm OK, You're OK*, Arrow, London.

Hay, J., 1999, *Transformational Mentoring*, Sherwood Publishing, Watford.

Kelly, J., December 2002, private communication.

Kennedy, E., and Charles, S. C., 1992, *On Becoming a Counsellor*, 2nd edition, Gill & Macmillan, Dublin.

Knight, S., 2000, *NLP at Work: The Difference that Makes the Difference*, 2nd edition, Nicholas Brealey, London.

Lamont, G., 2002, *The Spirited Business*, Hodder & Stoughton, London.

Lawley, J., and Tompkins, P., 2000, *Metaphors in Mind*, Developing Company Press, London.

Leeper, R. W., 1948, A Motivational Theory of Emotions to replace emotion as a disorganized response, *Psychology Review 55*, 5–21.

Lorenz, K. Z., 1966, *On Aggression*, Methuen, London.

Luke 4: 23 and Matthew 7: 1–3 (King James edition).

McLeod, A. I., 1997, Fundamentals for the Coach, *Rapport 37*, 15–16, ANLP.

McLeod, A. I., 1998, Fundamentals for the Coachee, *Rapport 40*, 37, ANLP.

McLeod, A. I., 2000, *Me, Myself, My Team,* Crown House Publishing, New York and Carmarthen, UK.

McLeod, A. I., 2001, Bringing out the Best in People, *Rapport 55,* ANLP.

McLeod, A. I., 2002a, The Power of Silence, *Effective Consulting 1,* 8, 31–32, Pentre Publications, Welshpool, UK.

McLeod, A. I., 2002b, Transforming Beliefs in Coaching, *Rapport 56,* 35, ANLP.

McLeod, A. I., 2002c, Emotional Intelligence in Coaching, *Rapport 58,* 53, ANLP.

McLeod. A. I., 2002d, Provocative Coaching, *Rapport 58,* 17, ANLP.

McLeod, A. I., 2002e, Mantras and Magic—State Management in Coaching, *Rapport 56,* 59, ANLP.

McLeod, A. I., 2002f, Mindsets for the Coach—Coaching with Attitude, *Effective Consulting 1,* 8, 29–30, Pentre Publications, Welshpool, UK.

Merrill, M. W., 2003, and Sites, J., 2003: Web-based information (see appendices).

O'Connell, A., 2003, private communication.

Patterson, K., 2000, An EQ Opportunity for NLPers, *Rapport 47,* 47.

Pervin, L. A., and John, O. P., 2001, *Personality Theory and Research*, 8th edition, John Wiley & Sons, New York.

Roberts, M., 1997, *The Man Who Listens to Horses*, Arrow, London.

Rogers, C., 1967, *On Becoming a Person*, Constable, London.

Rogers, C., 1983, *Freedom to Learn for the Eighties*, Charles Merril, Columbus, OH.

Rogers, C. R., 1951, *Client-Centered Therapy: Its Current Practice, Implications and Theory*, Houghton Mifflin College, Boston.

Rogers, C. R., 1997, *On Becoming a Person: A Therapist's View of Psychotherapy*, Constable & Robinson, London.

Rogers, C. R., and Freiberg, H. J., 1994, *Freedom to Learn*, Prentice Hall, Englewood Cliffs, NJ.

Rose Charvet, S., 1997, *Words that Change Minds*, 2nd edition, Kendall/Hunt Publishing, Dubuque, IA.

Shervington, M., 2002, Integral Coaching, *Rapport 57,* 46–47, ANLP.

Tompkins, P., December 2002, private communication.

Whitmore, J., 2002, *Coaching for Performance*, 2nd edition, Nicholas Brealey, London.

Further reading

Alpha leadership

Deering, A., Dilts, R., and Russell, J., 2002, *Alpha Leadership: Tools for Business Leaders Who Want More from Life*, John Wiley & Sons, Chichester, UK.

Coaching

Flaherty, J., 1999, *Coaching: Evoking Excellence in Others*, Butterworth-Heinemann, Oxford, UK.

Kinlaw, D. C., 1997, *Coaching*, Gower, Brookfield.

MacLennan, N., 1995, *Coaching & Mentoring*, Gower, Brookfield.

Transactional analysis

Berne, E., 1961, *Transactional Analysis in Psychotherapy*, Souvenir Press.

Gestalt

Perls, F., 1969, *Gestalt Therapy Verbatim*, Real People Press.

Person Centered Therapy

Rogers, C., 1983, *Freedom to Learn for the Eighties*, Charles Merril, Columbus, OH.

Stress

Williamson, A., 1998, *Still—In the Storm*, Crown House Publishing, Carmarthen, UK.

Storytelling

Canfield, J., and Miller, J., 1998, *Heart at Work: Stories and Strategies for Building Self-esteem and Reawakening the Soul at Work*, McGraw-Hill Education, New York.

Corvellec, H., 1997, *Stories of Achievements: Narrative Features of Organizational Performance*, Transaction Publishers, Piscataway, NJ.

De Selincourt, A., 1956, *Odysseus The Wanderer*, Criterion Books, New York.

Lundin, S. C., Paul, H., and Strand. P., 2002, *Fish Tales: Real-life Stories to Help You Workplace & Your Life*, Hyperion, New York.

Parkin, M, 1998, *Tales for Trainers: Using Stories and Metaphors to Facilitate Learning*, Kogan Page, London.

About the author

Angus McLeod was an academic before moving into industry, where he held a number of roles, first in technical management, including quality, then in marketing and sales. He then moved into general management and consultancy. He has held numerous commercial directorships and continues to sit on five or more company boards, mostly in the training-and-development sector. His business experience includes a buy-in MBO for an international financial institution. His consultancy experience in the last ten years has developed into leadership, team development, and coaching.

McLeod is widely published in the USA and UK, where his business focus has been primarily directed. He wrote *Me, Myself, My Team* (2000), which focuses on the development of the personal qualities of those who work in teams and the application of that learning for team management and development.

McLeod co-founded the Coaching Foundation Ltd., a not-for-profit organization helping to develop best practice in coaching and exposing its members to a wide range of new thinking in coaching. He also co-founded another not-for-profit organization, the Learning eXchange, which offers budget-priced programs using business and novel, creative learning initiatives in the context of personal development. He runs personal-development courses, including the Question of Balance and the Write-One writing and holiday courses, now available in Greece.

He was the motivator for Ask Max, the Internet-based e-mentoring service, which is available via his company, Into Changes. He is a director of Best Performance Ltd., which produces CD-ROM-based learning packages for business (and personal development) under the 3D brand as well as offering novel and inspirational training courses as part of a holistic approach to change in organizations.

McLeod has bachelor and doctoral degrees in chemistry. He is trained in NLP and co-counseling and has a diploma in performance coaching. He is a full member of the Neuro Linguistic Psychotherapy Counselling Association.

(sales@angusmcleod.com, www.angusmcleod.com)

Linguistic tips

Tools

Main index

(entries in **bold** type indicate where a subject is dealt with in greater detail; *italic* entries signify the names of people used in case examples)

USA *orders to:*
Crown House Publishing
P.O. Box 2223, Williston, VT 05495-2223, USA
Tel: 877-925-1213, Fax: 802-864-7626
www.CHPUS.com

Canada *orders to:*
Login Brothers Canada, 324 Saulteaux Crescent
Winnipeg, MB, R3J 3T2
or 291 Traders Blvd. E., Mississauga, ON, L4Z 2E5
Tel: 800-665-1148, Fax: 800-665-0103
E-mail: info@www.lb.ca
www.lb.ca

UK & Rest of World *orders to:*
The Anglo American Book Company Ltd.
Crown Buildings, Bancyfelin, Carmarthen, Wales SA33 5ND
Tel: +44 (0)1267 211880/211886, Fax: +44 (0)1267 211882
E-mail: books@anglo-american.co.uk
www.anglo-american.co.uk

Australasia *orders to:*
Footprint Books Pty Ltd.
Unit 4/92A Mona Vale Road, Mona Vale NSW 2103, Australia
Tel: +61 (0) 2 9997 3973, Fax: +61 (0) 2 9997 3185
E-mail: info@footprint.com.au
www.footprint.com.au

Singapore *orders to:*
Publishers Marketing Services Pte Ltd.
10-C Jalan Ampas #07-01
Ho Seng Lee Flatted Warehouse, Singapore 329513
Tel: +65 6256 5166, Fax: +65 6253 0008
E-mail: info@pms.com.sg
www.pms.com.sg

Malaysia *orders to:*
Publishers Marketing Services Pte Ltd
509 Block E, Phileo Damansara, Jalan 16/11,
46350 Petaling Jaya, Selangor, Malaysia
Tel: 03 7553588, Fax: 03 7553017
E-mail: pmsmal@po.jaring.my

South Africa *orders to:*
Everybody's Books
Box 201321 Durban North 401, 1 Highdale Road,
25 Glen Park, Glen Anil 4051, KwaZulu NATAL, South Africa
Tel: +27 (0) 31 569 2229, Fax: +27 (0) 31 569 2234
E-mail: ebbooks@iafrica.com